In this extraordinary book, Lacanian Psychoanalysis meets political theory in the streets of the city. The necessity of a radical political theory of the urban is explored with exquisite clarity and unwavering commitment to progressive change. If there is any hope for a different and politicized urbanity, it begins to shimmer between the covers of Dan Webb's book.

Erik Swyngedouw, *Professor of Geography, The University of Manchester*

Inner city gentrification is a violent form of exclusionary dispossession, visited upon the vunerable and precarious. Webb's wonderful book urges progressive urban scholars to respond in kind.

Nick Blomley, *Professor of Geography, Simon Fraser University*

Critical Urban Theory, Common Property, and "the Political"

Dan Webb explores an undervalued topic in the formal discipline of political theory (and political science, more broadly): the urban as a level of political analysis and political struggles in urban space. Because the city and urban space is so prominent in other critical disciplines, most notably, geography and sociology, a driving question of the book is: what kind of distinct contribution can political theory make to the already existing critical urban literature? The answer is to be found in what Webb calls the "properly political" approach to understanding political conflict as developed in the work of thinkers like Chantal Mouffe, Jodi Dean, and Slavoj Žižek. This "properly political" analysis is contrasted with and a curative to the predominant "ethical" or "post-political" understanding of the urban found in so much of the geographical and sociological critical urban theory literature. In order to illustrate this primary theoretical argument of the book, Webb suggests that "common property" is the most useful category for conceiving the city as a site of the "properly political." When the city and urban space are framed within this theoretical framework, critical urbanists are provided a powerful tool for understanding urban political struggles, in particular, anti-gentrification movements in the inner city.

Dr. Dan Webb has a PhD in Political Science from the University of Alberta and is an occasional member of the avant-garde academic circle known as the "Edmonton School." He is an independent scholar, author, and aspiring documentary film-maker based in Port Alberni, BC. When he's not reading iconoclastic leftist political theory, he's most likely surfing off the west coast of Vancouver Island or watching Lars von Trier movies with his wife, Lisa.

Routledge Innovations in Political Theory

58 **Hegel and the Metaphysical Frontiers of Political Theory**
Eric Lee Goodfield

59 **Time, Memory, and the Politics of Contingency**
Smita A. Rahman

60 **Michael A. Weinstein**
Action, Contemplation, Vitalism
Edited by Robert L. Oprisko and Diane Rubenstein

61 **Deep Cosmopolis**
Rethinking World Politics and Globalisation
Edited by Adam K. Webb

62 **Political Philosophy, Empathy and Political Justice**
Matt Edge

63 **The Politics of Economic Life**
Martin Beckstein

64 **The Temporality of Political Obligation**
Justin C. Mueller

65 **Epistemic Liberalism**
A Defence
Adam James Tebble

66 **Hegel, Marx, and 21st Century Social Movements**
Democracy, Dialectics, and Difference
Brian Lovato

67 **Ideologies of Experience**
Trauma, Failure, and the Abandonment of the Self
Matthew H. Bowker

68 **Post-Politics in Context**
Ali Rıza Taşkale

69 **Claus Offe and the Critical Theory of the Capitalist State**
Jens Borchert and Stephan Lessenich

70 **Equality Renewed**
Christine Sypnowich

71 **Rethinking Utopia: Place, Power, Affect**
David M. Bell

72 **Hugo Grotius and the Modern Theology of Freedom**
Jeremy Seth Geddert

73 **Critical Urban Theory, Common Property, and "the Political"**
Desire and Drive in the City
Dan Webb

Critical Urban Theory, Common Property, and "the Political"

Desire and Drive in the City

Dan Webb

Routledge
Taylor & Francis Group
LONDON AND NEW YORK

First published 2017 by Routledge

2 Park Square, Milton Park, Abingdon, Oxfordshire OX14 4RN
52 Vanderbilt Avenue, New York, NY 10017

Routledge is an imprint of the Taylor & Francis Group, an informa business

First issued in paperback 2019

Library of Congress Cataloging in Publication Data
A catalog record for this book has been requested

ISBN: 978-1-138-73597-2 (hbk)
ISBN: 978-0-367-37178-4 (pbk)

Typeset in Times New Roman
by Wearset Ltd, Boldon, Tyne and Wear

This book is dedicated to all those unemployed, underemployed, and precariously employed PhDs out there. The system of higher education is broken. As a group we can work together to change it, but as an individual don't be afraid to quit it. There are many ways to live a meaningful life outside of the university.

Contents

Introduction

Upon reflection, the word "urbane" is a peculiar one. It originates from the Latin *urbanus*, meaning "belonging to the city," but has come to signify the possession of refined, sophisticated, and cultured characteristics. The etymological connection to *urbanus* is telling because, of course, it is the city-dweller who is considered fine-mannered and courteous, while those who live in the country are uncouth, ignorant of culture, and lacking in social graces. There is no direct antonym for urbane in English, only a constellation of words that need to be invoked together in order to negate it completely. As a relic of the sixteenth century, the current definition of urbane as intimately tied to city life might appear puzzling. Sure, most high-culture amenities are found in cities, and urbanites tend to be more educated, but are not urban areas also where people do not know their neighbours, gang violence and drug addiction are rampant, and residents don't feel safe going out at night? Is it not in the country where people are more mannerly, hospitable, and honest, even if relatively simple and less worldly? If cities are so great at producing cultured and morally superior humans, why has it been such an object of scorn for so many of Western civilization's greatest minds: the Dickenses, Rousseaus, Emersons, and Heideggers of the world?

There are, of course, no answers to these questions because if there ever did exist a sixteenth-century consensus on the normative distinctions between city and country, it has long since collapsed. The only indisputable cultural truth about the social value of the city throughout history is that it has served as an object of fascination, invoking awe and disgust, promises of salvation and damnation, progress and corruption. If anything, in the contemporary context urbane should mean something more like "culturally uncertain" or "consisting of ambivalent social value." From a philosophical standpoint, this ambivalence may be a result of the city resembling something akin to a Kantian sublime object, although whether it belongs to the category of the mathematical or dynamic sublime, is unclear. Some cities are overwhelming to the senses due both to their tremendous size (mathematical) and by virtue of their prodigious diversity, energy, and utter complexity (the dynamic). Although coming to conceptual grips with the city has preoccupied philosophers, novelists, poets, and politicians for hundreds of years, attempting to define the city in its totality is a fool's errand – it is quite simply impossible, because of its sublimity. In fact,

I assert that theorizing the city poses the same problem that Theodor Adorno points to regarding the relationship between concepts and objects, whereby the truth of the latter will never be covered fully by the former. For Adorno, the task of the philosopher is to highlight that aspect of the object left out of its concept in order to grasp the truth of non-conceptuality. Politically speaking, to emphasize only one aspect of an object, while ignoring others, is always an act of power – power in the service of reproducing particular social discourses that define reality. In relation to urban matters, Adorno's insights are supported implicitly by Geoff Vigar et al. when they state:

> Invocations of the nature of contemporary cityness are … inevitably power-laden acts. They [urban planners] will pick out and highlight a small subset of the unknowable totality that constitutes an urban place in an effort to support particular normative notions of urban re-ordering, urban politics and urban redistribution over others.[1]

Maria Kaika provides an interesting example of how such a single aspect of an urban space is emphasized as representative of cityness in general, when she discusses how cities can be understood as "viewed" (eagle-eyed) and "lived" (urban praxis). An eagle-eyed view of the city is the perspective of the developer and "growth at any cost" politician. As "viewed," great cities are equated with dramatic skylines and vertical development. She claims that cities (like London) that have oriented much of their recent planning in the construction of new iconic buildings (the "Shard" and the "Gherkin"), demand that we approach the city as viewed. Kaika's point is that when cities are imagined falsely as totalities from the "viewed" perspective, we are simply to trust that these iconic buildings and skylines produce good cities.[2]

In the spirit of recognizing the impossibility of approaching cities as totalities, in this book I will examine the city from a particular or partial perspective, namely, through the lens of critical political theory. More specifically, I am interested in exploring ways in which all manner of urban political phenomena could be privileged as an object of inquiry by critical political theory, in order to uncover how certain urban discourses contribute to the reproduction of urban injustice. As it stands now, political theory in general is largely disassociated with specifically urban concerns for several reasons that I outline in the body of this book. As a goal, urbanizing critical political theory is not an entirely novel endeavour, but it is certainly quite rare. Political theorist Warren Magnusson has, for example, devoted much of his career to such an enterprise, although his approach is not oriented toward privileging the city as a site of politics, but more so as a way of breaking the hegemony of studying politics through a state-centric lens. Iris Marion Young is another important political theorist who has contributed to urbanizing the discipline. Her work in *Justice and the Politics of Difference* demonstrates how the city holds out the best hope for moving away from identarian politics and toward a "politics of difference." And in a localist-republican manner, Benjamin Barber asserts that democracy can be practised in its strongest form at the municipal level. Despite their influence in the field, these urban-oriented political theorists are very much the exception, and not the rule in political science.

While I am heavily indebted to these disciplinary trailblazers, my theorizing of the city is clearly distinct from their work in several ways. First, my research is committed to thinking about urban political struggles in the Schmittian/Mouffian tradition, wherein the "political" is defined as an antagonistic realm of exclusions and aspirations to hegemony. This is starkly contrasted with the elusive and ever-shifting conception of politics that characterizes much of urban critical political theory today. Second, I rely heavily on Lacanian psychoanalytic theories in order to understand political phenomena. In this respect, the work of Slavoj Žižek looms large in the text, projected onto the urban level of analysis in a way that, as far as I know, no one has attempted before now. I contend that in the same manner that Žižek has politicized Lacan by bringing his work out of the clinic, one can "urbanize" Lacanian categories like jouissance, desire, and drive, by incorporating them into a theory of the politicized city. Third, moving away from the abstract-theoretical realm, the new politicized conception of the city I develop in this book is encapsulated by the category of "common property." I argue that when cities, and more importantly neighbourhoods, are approached by residents and activists as common property, actual empirical struggles for control over urban space, or social justice in the city, is strengthened and made intelligible within a social system dominated by private property and market relations. More than anything, my approach to understanding the city, and my normative position regarding progressive urban activism, may strike the reader as highly counter-intuitive. This is because I aim to challenge most of the prevailing left-wing, progressive, or critical assumptions regarding the good life, as well as the values of democracy, inclusivity, and openness. If the city is to be conceptualized as a properly political site of antagonism and struggle, I believe that this requires embracing correspondingly antagonist tactics and exclusionary collective self-identification.

What is it about the city that makes it deserving of such a privileged place in the eyes of critical political theory? This is the point in the introduction of any good urbanist volume when the author lists the multitude of reasons why cities are so important today. It is difficult to find a piece of academic writing on the theme of cities or urban space published in the past 10 years, which does not begin with the observation that over half the world's population now lives in cities. This is, indeed, a historical event of world-changing magnitude and a development worthy of a paradigm shift in social science research. Therefore, with this demographic observation out of the way, we can move on to other reasons why cities are so very important and should be treated as the central site of political and other social-scientific research.

It has long been assumed in academic and policy-making circles that the nation-state is the site of the highest level of politics. This is because the nation-state is defined by the most authentic and determinate form of political power: sovereignty. No other collective actors share this mystical, yet binding, type of authority, and therefore the nation-state is considered the supreme political actor that may or may not devolve power to subsidiary bodies. This long-standing assumption of the pre-eminence of the nation-state is now eroding in the face of several phenomena, none greater than globalization which is largely seen as a process that limits and dilutes sovereignty via free trade agreements, globalized market forces, and transnational political institutions. This process is no better observed than in the context of genuinely global environmental problems like climate change. While virtually all nation-states acknowledge the threat of increasing global temperatures, they have been largely ineffectual in confronting it. Regardless of whether this failure has been due to the inability to agree to an international plan, or because states have simply not been able to meet emissions-reduction targets, nation-states simply have not been up to the task of tackling climate change.

The ineffectiveness of nation-states is mirrored in international institutions – the UN, EU, WTO – that many had hoped would develop into bodies capable of overcoming international anarchy and the problems associated with the parochialisms enabled by sovereignty. This brings us to the first claim regarding the importance of cities: increasingly they have been compelled to take on leadership roles in tackling global or national problems by enacting their own legislation relevant to important issues. In some ways this is nothing new. It was the cities of medieval Europe, and not the nations or kingdoms in which they were situated, that had to devise creative solutions to specifically urban problems, like waste disposal and access to potable water. More recently, Barber has argued that cities like New York are now initiating their own programs to fight manifold issues including climate change, gun control, and health problems (e.g., Bloomberg's bold attempt to ban over-sized soda containers in order to deal with New York's obesity epidemic).[3] Finally, in rapidly ascendant China, the Communist Party has established urbanization as the central policy intended to reduce poverty and inequality. In the Chinese economy, most well-paying jobs are found in cities and by encouraging rural Chinese to move to them, the government hopes that poverty will be decreased in absolute terms. This urbanization strategy, by all accounts, has succeeded in achieving these policy goals, while allowing China to become the industrial superpower it is today.

Such a shift in legislative initiatives across the world is not only symptomatic of the diminishing power of nation-states, but also the rising power of some cities. This is illustrated by former New York mayor Michael Bloomberg who hinted at the state-like powers of his mega-city when he declared: "I have my own army in the NYPD ... my own State Department."[4] The sheer size of cities and their tax-bases, along with an imperative to be innovative in the face of ever-dwindling federal and provincial (or state) funding to cities, combined with the offloading of responsibilities from more prominent levels of government, creates greater autonomy for cities. As cities become more autonomous and owe less to the largesse of higher levels of government, it should be no surprise if cities in the future increasingly demand more *formal* independence. This sort of discourse is already emerging, at least in North America.[5] Six years ago, in an interview with the *Globe and Mail*, Canadian television-producer Chris Haddock explored the idea that Vancouver should consider assuming the role of a city-state, bypassing its relationship with Victoria, and dealing directly with Ottawa as an "individual economic and cultural entity."[6] Alan Broadbent has made similar overtures in respect to Canada's three biggest cities – Vancouver, Montreal, and Toronto – all of which, he suggests, could thrive as independent provinces (at the very least, he argues, they should be given special taxation/revenue-producing powers).[7] And Barber explores the idea of the world being run by a council of mayors, arguing that at the municipal level mayors can pass legislation politically unfeasible at higher levels and that such a council would govern effectively because mayors tend to be less ideological and more pragmatic than their national counterparts.[8] While not all cities have the capacity for self-rule like Vancouver and New York might, in a world of 28 mega-cities with metropolitan populations over 10 million, 423 cities with between one and 10 million residents, and another 372 with between 500,000 and one million residents, there is no reason to believe that cities could not effectively assume responsibility for some state-like powers.[9]

If the spirits of critics of the nation-state system are buoyed by the paradigm-changing potential cities possess for governance, there is also reason to fear for our collective urbanized future. Cities are facing great challenges to their flourishing and sustainability. Mike Davis, for example, has shown that a significant portion of the globe's over 3.5 billion urban residents live in vast slums on the outskirts of the world's largest cities.[10] As of 2010, the UN estimated that 33 percent of urban residents in the developing world live in such squalid conditions, and although the UN met its Millennium Development Goal by helping 225 million residents move out of slums well before its 2020 deadline, the overall global slum population nonetheless increased from 776.7 million in 2000 to 827.6 million in 2010.[11] Many of these slum dwellers lack access to clean water and satisfactory sanitary facilities.[12] The growing problem of slums is indicative of the changing character of global inequality, long associated most starkly with the urban–rural divide. A new mounting concern in urban areas is their *internal* socio-economic inequality. Connectedly, anyone who follows the news pertaining to global unrest, reflected in the seemingly endless string of protests directed at national governments over the past 15 years, cannot ignore its strikingly urban character. Whether it is Bangkok, Istanbul, New York, Caracas, or Kiev, the protests have been organized in and facilitated by urban spaces, even if the aims of the protestors are often national in scope.[13] Viewing these conflicts through an urban lens helps explain subsequent national developments that may otherwise appear inexplicable.

Take the 2011 street protests in Cairo as an example. The narrative created to explain them, at least for Western observers, was that the protesters were made up mostly of young, well-educated, and relatively secular individuals and groups seeking an end to government corruption and the establishment of a more democratic political system. This was greatly encouraging for pro-democracy reformers in the Middle East, and portrayed an unfamiliar image of the Arab world for many Westerners accustomed only to associating countries in this region with terrorism and religious fundamentalism. It must have been confusing for many Western onlookers, therefore, when the Muslim Brotherhood candidate Mohamed Morsi was elected as president, after Hosni Mubarak was finally deposed. The image of the progressive protesters we all witnessed on television simply did not conform to the perceived conservative religiosity of Morsi and the Brotherhood. While this is only speculative on my part, two plausible explanations (among others) for the dissonance between fact and representation of the Egyptian protests occur to me immediately. First, and most intuitively, the major Western media simply misrepresented who the protestors were. Instead of a democratic aspirational middle-class revolution, the revolt against Mubarak was much more popularly widespread and included a much greater conservative, anti-democratic element than the media portrayed. However, what if the intelligibility problem of interpreting the ostensible inconsistencies of this event is due to an inappropriate territorial framing of the situation? When the casual Western spectator tries to make sense of the events leading up to Morsi's election, they understand them as an *Egyptian* phenomenon, instead of a protest for and by the residents of *Cairo*. When watching CNN coverage of the Cairo protests, it is easy to forget that Egypt is a huge, primarily rural,[14] and overall religiously conservative country. Much like cities the world over, the collective population of Cairo is much more progressive, secular, and attuned to Western political ideals than is the general Egyptian population. In a way, it seems intuitive that we would know this. Most people are consciously aware that a cultural and political divide exists between the urban and rural areas in their own countries, so why do they assume it is different elsewhere? But perhaps they don't assume such a difference. What if, instead, the intelligibility problem is that we consume media reports about foreign events through an implicitly nation-state-centric lens?

Whatever might account for the difficulties of interpreting political conflicts, it should be no surprise that academia has shown an ever-increasing concern with all questions dealing with the city and urban space. This is most pronounced in the social sciences and humanities, where the topic of "the city" appears to be becoming the early twenty-first-century equivalent to the 1990s' "globalization" as a buzzword signifying the "sexiness" of a topic that will make it into the title of thousands of MA and PhD theses, conference papers, and scholarly articles. Various (non-scientific) database keyword searches of "urban theory" and "the city" support this claim, by showing a marked increase of the terms in scholarly publications.[15]

Indeed, there is a certain "hipness" to urban studies, as a generation of scholars have begun to appreciate the perceived authenticity and excitement of living in the inner city. In this regard, the last few generations have come to perceive a contrast between the vitality of urban life and the stale, culturally arid environs of their parents' suburbs. As a latter-day Jane Jacobs, Richard Florida has detected this growing appreciation for the cultural amenities and opportunities on offer in the city, not only amongst academics, but also to a much broader "creative class" of artists, designers, computer programmers, and so on. Arguably the singularly most influential theorist on planners and urban policy-makers over the past 10 years, Florida has made urbanism mainstream with a series of best-selling books that both describe changing urban tastes among the well-educated and upwardly mobile, and how cities can satisfy them. Florida's ideas have become almost hegemonic within most planning and policy circles, as cities become more and more committed to doing whatever it takes to attract the creative class. Density, diversity, tolerance, and culture: these are the new characteristics and values that drive contemporary urbanism.

This cultural shift toward the desirability of urban living is a double-edged sword. On the progressive edge of the sword, because the influential force that is the creative class (along with the current generation of city planners) has recognized both the cultural and logistical merits of urban living, cities are able to finally implement, with little resistance, plans for densifying downtowns, encouraging greater reliance on public transit and other alternative forms of transportation to the private car, pedestrianize streets, and zone for mixed-use neighbourhoods. In short, municipal politicians are finally able to create the kind of liveable cities that Jane Jacobs envisioned over 50 years ago in *The Death and Life of Great American Cities*. The progressive potential of this urban moment should not be underestimated. The wholesale redesign of major metropolitan areas will have a profound impact on, not just ecological sustainability and infrastructural innovation, but also the very nature of human sociability and subjectivity. As David Harvey declares, "The question of what kind of city we want cannot be divorced from that of what kind of social ties, relationship to nature, lifestyles, technologies and aesthetic values we desire."[16] In other words, determining what kind of cities we build is simultaneously the determination of *who* we want to be. But this future is far from written and the question of *how* these changes will impact our collective development as a species, will be in part determined through political struggle.

The inevitability of political conflict over the future of our cities is due to the other edge of the urban sword: the capitalist appropriation of the desire for urban living and revitalization. While Jacobs's and other progressive urbanists' visions for liveable neighbourhoods is driven by a spirit of the public good and the ideal of citizens creating their cities by voluntary, democratic practices, the reality of inner-city revitalization is that it has become guided largely by rent-seeking capital and in the interest of economic growth. In 1976, Harvey Molotch famously identified this problem when he theorized cities as "growth machines."[17] He shows how all places can be understood as commodities that exist at the intersection of use- and exchange-value. A place has use-value to the extent it is inhabited by human beings who use it, whether as a place to sleep, eat, work, or play. But such places also have financial value to the extent they are exchangeable in the market and/or they produce rents. While use-value contributes to the determination of exchange-value, from the perspective of capitalism the exchange-value of any particular commodity is more or less divorced from its use-value. In an elaboration of the growth machine thesis, Logan and Molotch claim that in terms of conceptualizing cities, exchange-value has become the primary determinant of planning policies. This, they argue, is illustrated by the hegemony of "growth" as the primary policy goal of municipal governments. Logan and Molotch demonstrate that whatever differences exist between rival politicians or municipal political parties, the one principle they all agree on is that achieving economic growth is the priority for their cities, and that they can act to help harmonize the interests of local "growth coalitions."[18] Growth is, of course, an abstract concept in the sense that it does not specify how growth should be realized, but just that it should happen. This translates into policies designed to attract investment and generate economic activity, divorced from the impact they will have on quality of life, disrupting residents lives or, indeed, destroying neighbourhoods.

While Logan and Molotch's analysis has become canonical in urban critical political economy as an interdisciplinary field of research, other influential scholars have pushed their position further down a critical theory trajectory. This includes radical geographer David Harvey who is celebrated for, among other achievements, demonstrating the crucial role cities play as sponges for surplus capital during times of economic crisis. Citing Binyamin Appelbaum, Harvey argues "It is a longstanding pattern … that Americans recover from recessions by building more homes and filling them with things."[19] Likewise, Nicholas Blomley suggests that we have witnessed a shift over the past 30 years from a focus on liveability in cities to "place marketing, positioning … [cities] as platforms in an emergent economy of flows" (i.e., competing for tourists, investment opportunities, amenities for the rich and famous, etc.).[20] And finally, echoing Logan and Molotch, Sharon Zukin observes that cities are caught in a conflict between place and market and that currently the market is winning: "abstract market forces that detach people from social institutions have overpowered specific forces of attachment identified with place" (this is a "creative destruction" that Schumpeter didn't predict).[21] Whatever the methodological or ideological differences, all critical urbanists are united by the insight that cities are intense sites of capitalist investment and are therefore characterized by political struggles between various social groups over resources, access to space, and the overall direction in which the city will develop. A critique of the relationship between market forces and social justice is the necessary hard core of any discourse claiming to belong to the field of critical urban studies.

There is no particular process that highlights more starkly the dialectic between use and exchange-value in the city – manifested in the struggle between marginalized and privileged – more so than gentrification. Gentrification, defined for now as the displacement of poor and marginalized city residents as a result of more affluent segments of the population moving into the former's communities, degrades the current use of specific urban spaces in order to improve their financial value (their "highest use," as it is known euphemistically). The starting premise for anyone opposed to gentrification is that no matter how blighted or run-down an inner-city neighbourhood happens to be, it possesses use-value for its residents, and when that space is appropriated for the use of wealthier people, exchange-value has clearly been prioritized over use-value. When city officials and developers try to legitimize revitalization schemes that result in gentrification they employ arguments to cover-over their privileging of exchange-value, but it is difficult to deny that, in the process, functioning communities are destroyed. There has been no lack of critical attention given to the problem of gentrification in scholarly circles. A whole generation of theorists have emerged over the past 40 years that orient their research toward this process, most importantly, Neil Smith, David Ley, Loretta Lees, Tom Slater, Elvin Wyly, Peter Marcuse, and Sharon Zukin. As people continue to move to cities, and the cultural (and developers') taste for denser, more central neighbourhoods increase, the scope and intensity of gentrification correspondingly will likely escalate. In an environment of deregulating real-estate markets, cutbacks in social housing funding, and a reduction in rental units, the fundamental issue of access to housing for significantly large portions of urban populations promises to emerge as one of the most acute sources of urban political conflict.

Considering all of the different ways in which cities are related to the most dramatic of current political events and processes, one might justifiably assume that the academic discipline most associated with the formal study of politics – political science – would consider the city as a central political unit. But this is not the case. Instead it is sociology and geography that have treated the city in a privileged manner, while political science devotes most of its energy to describing and analyzing the populations, discourses, and actions of *nation-states*. Suffice to say for now that political science studies the nation-state because it is considered to possess the highest type of formal collective political power: sovereignty. The city is treated as an afterthought in political science, confined largely to the tiny and theoretically uninspired subfield of "urban politics."

But it was not always this way, as the sub-disciplinary tradition of political *theory* makes abundantly clear. Chapter 1 of this book explores how the canon of Western political theory begins with the study of *cities*, specifically the city-states of Ancient Greece. The Ancient Greeks, such as Plato and Aristotle, understood their cities to be ideal sites of political community for much the same reasons that many today idealize "local" politics: because their relatively small sizes facilitated quasi-democratic practices, self-sufficiency, and the implementation of a particular understanding of the good life. The Greek emphasis on the importance of small-scale politics aimed, in large part, to avoid subsuming the good life by the impersonal, alienating, and inefficient effects of imperial or (modern) nationalist power structures continues through the medieval and modern periods, represented in the thought of Machiavelli, Rousseau, Bakunin, and Marx. While not as clearly emphasizing the city per se,[22] as the Ancients did, they all formulate logical and moral arguments that implicitly support an urban-centric vision of the good life.

But, of course, as the European nation-state came to establish its hegemony as the highest form of political power, political theory naturally came to privilege it as the premier site of political community. Overlapping chronologically with the above-mentioned canonical thinkers, theorists like Bodin, Hobbes, Montesquieu, and especially Hegel argued morally and pragmatically for the sovereign power of the state. Whether the theoretical justification for the primacy of the state was divine right of kings, religious unification, or the historical unfolding of Spirit/Reason, cities were relegated to subsidiary positions vis-à-vis the state at best, and threats to the state's perfect rational harmony/order, at worst. If thinkers like Sassen, Barber, and Magnusson are to be believed, such an emphasis on sovereignty has done a disservice to political science because it limits its scholars' ability to think and imagine politics beyond the nation-state, which is an increasingly less powerful site of policy-making. In this respect, the category of the city may be slowly coming to challenge the priority and power of the nation-state, much like international relations theorists in the 1980s and 1990s had to face the reality that economic globalization had upset the discipline's founding assumption that nation-states are the only important actors in international politics. But if the city is emerging as an alternative site of politics in a direct challenge to the nation-state, then political scientists are not catching up to this reality as quickly as IR scholars did in respect to globalization. The city is still as underappreciated in political science as it was 20 years ago.

From a critical political theory perspective, this should be of some concern. Why? Because, despite the fact that the city serves as a hallmark of modernity as much as the state does, it is no longer treated as the site of the good life – where humans come together to perform great acts, or produce great works of art, like in the Ancient Greek tradition. Nor is it privileged as a site of progressive political organization, despite the fact that *almost all* significant progressive organizing happens in cities! While the eyes of critical political theorists are fixated on national or global politics, inner-city activists are organizing workers and immigrants, resisting gentrification, and providing services for the most needy; encampments are popping up and within them people are experimenting with alternative ways of living, while alliances of widely disparate citizens are claiming ownership of central city squares and stubbornly refusing to move when confronted by riot police; less militant urbanites are experimenting with car and bicycle sharing programs, planting community gardens, and demanding better public transit infrastructure. All of this happens in cities, and it is time that political theorists acknowledge it and took it seriously.

This overriding focus on the state is not the case, however, across all the social sciences. Indeed, as mentioned above, in the late twentieth century a renewed emphasis on the political nature of the city emerged in critical social science research, especially in the disciplines of human geography and sociology. It should be no surprise that these disciplines led the charge in urbanizing the study of politics, as their institutional identities were never defined by a preoccupation with sovereignty, but instead the founding objects of study are the built environment (in the case of human geography) and human interaction (in the case of sociology). Indeed, for sociology, the city had long been approached as the site of the *social* (as in the work of Max Weber) versus the state as the site of the political. These two disciplines have made the lion's share of contributions to the interdisciplinary field of "critical urban studies," that I define loosely as concerned with issues of social justice in the city from a left-wing or progressive perspective. The sheer amount of work that now composes the body of critical urban studies is impressive. What is even more impressive is how some of its most important contributors are widely known and influential well outside of their own disciplinary communities. Harvey stands out in this regard, but other notable figures include Manuel Castells and Saskia Sassen. But, again, for an interdisciplinary field, critical urban studies is conspicuously lacking representation by political theorists proper, with the few exceptions I mentioned earlier.

If such good work is being done elsewhere, one might ask, is there any particular need for political theory to enter the fray of critical urban analysis? What can political theory contribute to the field that does not simply reproduce what is being furnished in geography and sociology? As a major theme throughout the book, I assert that most of what is considered critical urban theory lacks a distinctly *political* character, and instead approaches political action in the city through an *ethical* or *post-political* framework. What this means will become abundantly clear in the coming chapters, but for now the answer to the question: "What can political theory contribute to critical political studies?" is "a properly *political* analysis."

Chapters 2 and 3 are devoted to working through some of the features that characterize a genuinely political theory capable of politicizing the critical urban studies approach to the city. The starting premise is that contemporary critical political theory is dominated by what Chantal Mouffe calls a "post-political" consensus. Drawing on the work of Carl Schmitt, she argues that the "political" is defined by any situation in which social antagonisms exists – adversarial distinctions between an "us" and a "them" – and that the contradictory interests that characterize each side are not resolvable through processes of dialogue and consensus-seeking. Conversely, the post-political is an approach that denies the existence of fundamental antagonisms in political matters and instead posits the possibility of reaching consensus via dialogue or other deliberative processes. Best represented by Rawlsian and Habermasian methodologies, Mouffe claims that the essential failing of post-politics is its inability to recognize that all social groups, even groups claiming legitimacy based in universal consensus, are formed by constitutive exclusions. There are always dissenters to ostensibly consensual political ideas and systems and, therefore, consensus-based politics only serve to exclude such dissenters from legitimately participating in political processes. This creates a situation in which the powerless and frustrated excluded are bound to react outside of formal institutions, often in a violent manner. When such a pushback on the part of the excluded produces a legitimacy crisis of existing political institutions, those who had believed in the existence of a broad social consensus can react with only "bewilderment in the face of its manifestations and to impotence in dealing with them."[23]

In Chapter 2, I explore the distinction between the political and post-political in rigorous detail. I argue that most of contemporary critical political theory – ranging from cosmopolitanism all the way to hard post-structuralism – can be understood as post-political (with some notable exceptions). However, influenced by thinkers like Jodi Dean, I have reframed the debate by using the lexicon of the political and the *ethical* (as a stand in for the post-political), largely because post-political theorists do not recognize themselves as such (that is, they believe that they are very much "political" in their work). Instead, being post-political is a disavowed position for most critical scholars. Their regular use of the words ethics and ethical in the place of politics is symptomatic of this disavowed position. Overall, I refer to this "ethical turn" in critical political theory as characterized by a post-political desire to live outside of power relations, by rejecting the existence of fundamental antagonisms and the need for exclusions in political struggle. Instead, the ethical critical theorist tends to promote a fetishized normative emphasis on inclusivity, openness, and dialogue in the course of their theorizing. These ethical imperatives of openness and inclusivity are intimately associated with contemporary critical models of subjectivity, in which human beings are understood teleologically as desiring freedom. Freedom is here interpreted as aspirational and procedural: aspiring to be free requires the ability to experiment, to be mobile, and to experience the "new." In short, the normative conception of the subject that sustains the ethical turn is closely associated with the fluidity of "becoming" as opposed to the fixity of "being."

In Chapter 3, I explain precisely why it matters that critical political theory reject an ethical approach to thinking about politics, and instead adopt a properly political position. If political theory is to be considered "critical," it is so by virtue of being opposed absolutely or relatively to the predominant ideas and power structures that govern contemporary society. The ideas and institutions that a critical political theorist contests includes most importantly capitalist social relations, but often also the state (especially to the extent that the contemporary "neoliberal" state form exists primarily to bolster capitalist social relations), racism, sexism, colonialism, and other forms of oppression. All of these principled positions are constitutive of most strains of contemporary critical theory, with of course varying levels of emphasis (in particular anti-capitalism and anti-statism are nowhere near as popular as they were in, say, the 1960s and 1970s). Whatever the particular emphasis, because critical theory is dominated by ethical imperatives of inclusion and diversity, the prescriptive analyses devised to oppose oppressive power structures have, over time, come to crystallize in almost a singularly monolithic category: "democracy." The calls for greater democracy are now ubiquitous in both the scholarly and activist Left. As Dean claims (when she characterizes the ethic of contemporary critical theory), the answer to our lack of democracy is always that we just need more democracy! Democracy, however, is a slippery concept and, indeed, virtually no one on the Left nor the Right, rejects the need for more democracy. As an ethical *qua* political category, I argue, democracy has become an empty container for the Left's desire for living outside of power relations; it is symptomatic of the desire for democracy to be identical to its own concept, which is impossible, as Wendy Brown contends. This means that democracy is conceptualized as a politics absent antagonism and exclusions; one in which *all* live without experiencing the disciplining effects of power nor exerting power over others. Formally speaking, this is precisely the same desire and promise of neoliberal capitalism. The challenge for critical political theory is, then, to find a way to clearly disassociate a progressive-leftist normative vision of the good life from that of its adversary. This does not necessarily require giving up on democracy, but it does suggest the need for disidentifying democracy with the ethical values of openness and inclusivity. Therefore, consistent with Brown's analysis, Chapter 3 concludes by asserting that in order for critical political theory to make democracy meaningful as an emancipatory discourse, it must embrace an "anti-democratic" element that is always present in democracy, namely, exclusion and antagonism.

Chapter 4 begins with a demonstration of how the ethical turn in political theory has impacted the field of critical urban studies. In contrast to earlier (e.g., Harvey, Smith) and some contemporary (e.g., Slater, Swyngedouw, DeFillipis) manifestations of critical urbanism, I show that post-political imperatives for spatial openness and inclusivity have assumed an almost hegemonic centrality in discourses about the city as a site of political struggle and the good life. I contend that this predominant approach to understanding the city, which I call the "open" city, is best exemplified by the tradition in critical human geography associated with theories of the "postmodern" city, represented in the work of theorists such as Michael Dear, Ash Amin and Nigel Thrift, and Edward Soja. Similar to my critique of the enabling relationship between contemporary critical political theory and neoliberal capitalism, I maintain that normative conceptions of the postmodern city, along with other nominally critical urban approaches, forward an understanding of the city that is also shared by neoliberal urbanists. That is to say, even though such critical urban theorists criticize mainstream capitalist urban processes for creating inequalities, destroying communities, and privileging exchange-value over use-value, their recommendations for addressing these problems are informed by virtually the very same normative principles espoused by pro-free market developers and politicians: encouraging openness, circulation, and inclusivity. The result is that when critics highlight the lack of democracy or social justice in urban space, the very same values that underlie the causes of such unjust outcomes are employed by critical urbanists in the name of challenging them. This should not be considered a "homeopathic" remedy to urban problems because the identity of cause and cure are *disavowed* by these critical urbanists. The reality is that there are few curative properties in such critical discourses; indeed, the prescriptions are more likely to *enable* unjust processes, than they are to rectify them.

In Chapter 5 I draw on the insights gleaned from the previous chapters to explore a particular urban phenomenon, namely, gentrification. My central claim is that the values associated with the predominant approach to critical urban studies – the approach that promotes normative conceptions of the open city – complement gentrification as an empirical process. In order to make this argument, I employ the insights of Paul Virilio that constitute his theories of dromology and dromocracy. Dromocracy, according to Virilio, is a distinctly modern type of informal governance that uses cultural imperatives to move and to speed up one's life (on the micro-level), in addition to speeding up processes of social change and development (on the macro-level), to discipline populations. Dromocracy is another manifestation of the social values associated with the ethical turn in critical political theory. Theorists of the open city unknowingly subscribe to such normative dromocratic imperatives when they argue for removing barriers to circulation in the city, attacking the logic of gated neighbourhoods in favour of mixed-income communities, and asserting that the city is for *all* of its residents. While these may be noble goals in the abstract, in many ways they are simultaneously *depoliticizing*. Rent-seeking urban capital, "fixed capital" notwithstanding, thrives on such an ethic of openness and inclusivity to the extent it strives to justify opening up neighbourhoods to redevelopment.

If the entire city should be open to all, then surely this logic applies to all distinct areas of the city, rich or poor. But the truth is, creating a nominally inclusive city rarely works both ways; it is extremely uncommon that the poor move into or otherwise appropriate the spaces of the wealthy, especially in terms of housing. In fact, it is almost always the reverse that occurs (the rich displace the poor). In order to combat such dromocratic thinking, I contend, critical urban studies needs to reconsider its approach to conceptualizing the city, informed by the properly political insights worked out in Chapters 2 and 3.

I have opted to call the next chapter a "Philosophical Excursus" because it is quite abstract-theoretical in nature and, therefore, may appear incongruent as a segue bridging Chapters 5 and 6. The aim of this excursus is to establish the theoretical foundation for a politicized understanding of the city via Žižek's Lacanian ontology of desire and drive. I am convinced that any critical political theory, let alone its urban variants, requires a strong understanding of the relationship between political action and human psychology (both individual and social). This is because purely rationalist political theory, most notably liberalism, simply never can account fully for political phenomena (because people act irrationally all the time). The point of employing psychoanalysis is that it can fill in the explanatory gaps that rationalist approaches to politics invariably produce. By considering the unconscious affective motivations of political actors, or the libidinal investments they make in certain political ideas or structures, psychoanalysis reveals a dimension of politics arguably more fundamentally constitutive than rational deliberation or self-interest maximization. Consistent with Žižek's theory that the cultural imperatives of capitalism have changed from one based in prohibiting desire (Fordism) to one in which we are commanded to enjoy (post-Fordism), I argue that the open city of critical urban studies is the urban manifestation of this imperative – what I call the "city of desire." But desire, according to Lacanian theory, is always a desire for full enjoyment (jouissance), which is ontologically impossible to achieve. In order to deal with this ontological frustration, "drive" acts to organize desire in a manageable manner by seeking enjoyment in the very failure to achieve full enjoyment. Drive allows subjects the ability to find pleasure in the partial enjoyments associated with repetitive, compulsive, or addictive behaviour. In social terms, Žižek suggests that in the face of capitalist imperatives to enjoy, a leftist position might be formulated around rejecting desire, at least in the manner it serves as a motivating force for the reproduction of capitalism, and instead demand the *right not to enjoy*. Drawing from this insight, I assert that perhaps a way to begin challenging the open/dromocratic city of desire, is to conceive of urban spaces as sites of routine and fixity, in other words, a *city of drive*.

Chapter 6 returns to a more traditional, less abstract, political economy strain of critical urban studies by exploring the category of common property. At this point in the book the task has been set: to find a way to politicize critical theories of the city. This requires searching for analytic and normative categories that can counteract most, if not all, of the principles informing the open/dromocratic city. I claim that common property can achieve this politicization because the category itself is defined by exclusionary politics (whereby an identifiable community claims exclusive collective use rights to discrete spaces), is established through routinized behaviour (or traditions of use), and is anti-utopian because common property is currently operative in many legal jurisdictions governed by common law (examples of common property legal categories include adverse possession, treaty rights, and housing cooperatives).[24] Contrary to thinking the city as a single "commons," common property breaks the city up into identifiable areas/neighbourhoods and therefore challenges the idea that the city is for all. It establishes a legally recognized category that poor and otherwise marginalized urban populations can make use of, in a manner similar to how the rich use discourses of *private* property to pursue their interests (although the rich invoke common property quite effectively also). Finally, on a discursive level common property is a valuable tool in the battle over how the nature of anti-gentrification struggles are perceived. By framing such conflicts in the discourse of common property, gentrification can be re-conceptualized as not primarily a process of *dislocation* (which is a private-property/market-oriented understanding) but as one of *dispossession*. I suggest that the potential for accruing greater public support to the cause of anti-gentrification activists is strengthened significantly when the greater public understands affected communities as having their property *stolen*, rather than non-owners simply being forced to *move*.

In Chapter 7, I conclude the book by exploring a series of case studies chosen to illustrate the arguments I have been making throughout. The manner in which I employ these case studies may be unexpected. I do not conduct my own original field research, but instead employ the method of immanent critique to explore case studies included in the work of some of the most prominent critical urban theorists writing today. In particular, my intent is to demonstrate how these case studies illustrate my central claim regarding the ethical or post-political nature of contemporary critical urban studies. In all the cases I have chosen, the authors examine instances of urban struggles over common property and attribute to the associated activists a set of political principles that supposedly motivate their actions. What becomes quite clear, I argue, is that these political principles tend not to be political at all, at least in the way I defined the political in this book. This is interesting, not because the authors hold post-political values, *but because the empirical events as reported by the scholars in question actually testify against them*. The featured protagonists are, indeed, acting in a properly political manner. However, when the authors ascribe political values to these actors, *these values do not correspond to the empirical description of the relevant events*. For example, in all these cases when an activist group behaves in an *exclusionary* manner (creating an "us and them"), as the narratives makes clear they do, the theorists nonetheless describe the group as promoting *inclusion*. By the method of immanent critique, I demonstrate how some of the most thoughtful of theorists disavow their very own accounts of the events that should lead to properly political conclusions. I contend that the inconsistency or mismatch between empirical description and normative ascription is a result of certain post-political values having achieved hegemonic standing in critical urban studies. As such it has become *unintelligible* that valorized actors would not subscribe to them. This is not an attempt on my part to discredit the work of these scholars (whom I admire and have learned a great deal from), but rather to draw out from their field research lessons that can help critical urban theorists foster more distinctly political analyses of urban struggles for social justice.

Notes

1 Geoff Vigar, Stephen Graham, and Patsy Healey, "In Search of the City in Spatial Strategies: Past Legacies, Future Imaginings," *Urban Studies* 42(8) (2005): 1393.
2 Maria Kaika, "Whither Urban Studies," Discussion at the University of Manchester, last updated November 16, 2012, accessed November 17, 2013, http://progressivegeographies.com/2012/12/01/10340/.
3 Benjamin R. Barber, *If Mayors Ruled the World: Dysfunctional Nations, Rising Cities* (New Haven: Yale University Press, 2013), 6.
4 Quoted in ibid., 6.
5 Incidentally, in the European context and at the time of writing, the region of Veneto (which is the metropolitan area of Venice) has just completed a referendum on seceding from Italy. A total of 2.36 million eligible voters cast ballots, with 89 percent in favour of secession. See: Hannah Roberts, "Venice Votes to Split from Italy as 89% of the City's Residents Opt to Form a New Independent State," last updated March 22, 2014, accessed April 4, 2014, www.dailymail.co.uk/news/article-2586531/Venice-votes-split-Italy-89-citys-residents-opt-form-new-independent-state.html.
6 Ian Bailey (interview with Chris Haddock), "Da Vinci Creator Floats Idea of Vancouver as a City State," *Globe and Mail*, last updated November 21, 2010, accessed March 21, 2014, www.theglobeandmail.com/news/british-columbia/da-vinci-creator-floats-idea-of-vancouver-as-a-city-state/article1314958/.
7 Alan Broadbent, *Urban Nation: Why We Need to Give Power Back to the Cities to Make Canada Strong* (Toronto: HarperCollins, 2009).
8 See: Barber, *If Mayors Ruled the World.*
9 *Demographia*, "World Urban Areas," 9th annual edition, published March 2013, http://demographia.com/db-worldua.pdf
10 Mike Davis, *Planet of Slums* (New York: Verso, 2006).
11 United Nations, "UN Millennium Development Goals," 2011 Report, "UN Habitat State of the World's Cities," accessed March 10, 2014, http://unhabitat.org/.
12 Davis, *Planet of Slums*, 142–143.
13 At the time of writing the Kiev situation appears to be expanding significantly into a nation-wide civil war (the primarily Ukrainian-speaking west versus the primarily Russian-speaking east), if not an internal conflict, as Russia has occupied Crimea.
14 According to statistics drawn from the World Bank for 2012, 56.3 percent of the Egyptian population lives in rural areas. See: www.tradingeconomics.com/egypt/rural-population-percent-of-total-population-wb-data.html.
15 A brief Ngram tracking search on Google Books shows that in 1938 there are no references to "urban theory," but starting in 1939 its usage rises steadily until 1967, where it plateaus, until taking off again in 1991, rising steadily to 2008 (latest year available). Another search, on the "Web of Science" database (tracking only social science and humanities indices), shows a drastic increase in the use of the term "the City." The 40 years between 1960 and 2000 return only 9,177 entries, while the nine years between 2001 and 2010 return 11,664 hits. The final search covering the four years of 2010–2014, returned 8,836 entries.
16 David Harvey, "The Right to the City," *New Left Review* 53 (September–October 2008): 23.
17 Harvey Molotch, "The City as a Growth Machine: Towards a Political Economy of Place," in *City Reader*, 5th edition, ed. Richard T. Legates and Frederic Stout (New York: Routledge, 2011).

18 John Logan and Harvey Molotch, *Urban Fortunes: The Political Economy of Place* (Los Angeles: University of California Press, 1987), 62–65.
19 David Harvey, *Rebel Cities: From the Right to the City to the Urban Revolution* (New York: Verso, 2012), 50.
20 Nicholas Blomley, *Unsettling the City: Urban Land and the Politics of Property* (New York: Routledge, 2004), 29–30.
21 Sharon Zukin, *Landscapes of Power: From Detroit to Disney World* (Los Angeles: University of California Press, 1991), 4.
22 Rousseau, in particular, was openly hostile to large cities (like Paris). Nonetheless, the logic of his argument supports the devolution of national political power to smaller units like municipalities. See my analysis of Rousseau in Chapter 1 for more details.
23 Chantal Mouffe, "Politics and the Limits of Liberalism," in *Hegemony, Radical Democracy, and the Political*, ed. James Martin (New York: Routledge, 2013), 120.
24 For a discussion specific to communal ownership of housing, see James DeFillipis, *Unmaking Goliath: Community Control in the Face of Global Capital* (New York: Routledge, 2003), chapter 4.

1 Validating the City in Political Theory

> Instead of the spectre of communism, it is the spectre of the urban, the shadow of the city that now haunts Europe.[1]

> Radical politics must begin from historical givens and conceive radical change not as the negation of the given but rather as making something good from the many elements of the given. The city, as a vastly populated area with large-scale industry and places of mass assembly, is for us a historical given, and radical politics must begin from the existence of modern urban life.[2]

The city, as an object of critical scholarly inquiry in the social sciences, has been largely confined to two disciplines: human geography and sociology. A quick glance at the *Blackwell City Reader* (an authoritative anthology of critical writings on the city) attests to this fact: out of the 55 authors included in the anthology, a plurality (16) are trained as or associated with sociology departments, followed closely (14) by geography. That sociologists and (human) geographers possess a strong interest in the city is not surprising considering their disciplines' founding preoccupations. For sociologists, cities are the most intense site of human interaction and a hallmark of modernity, while for human geographers, cities are constructed landscapes that contain distinct spatial processes, and mark all sorts of social boundaries (gender, class, race) expressed in the built environment. While these disciplines possess innate characteristics that draw their practitioners to the study of cities, there has been an especially pronounced eruption in creative and innovative critical work on the city in sociology and geography since the "spatial turn" of the 1980s and 1990s.

However, an observation that some might find surprising is the lack of interest in the city on the part of political scientists, and especially political *theorists*. In terms of the *Blackwell City Reader* tally, only four of the 55 authors are (or were) practising political scientists, and *only one* is a bona fide political theorist (the late Iris Marion Young). On the other hand, perhaps this should not be considered surprising; after all, is it not the state that serves as the natural and primary object of study for political scientists, due to its ability to exercise sovereign power?[3] And connectedly, is the city not a subsidiary body to the state and therefore lacks formal authority of any significance? The standard political science account is that the city is the site of the *social*, not the properly *political*.[4]

The formal discipline of political science emerged and grew alongside the development of the modern state system, and it would seem natural that in the balkanized halls of the modern academy at least one discipline would come to devote its energy almost exclusively to the study of statecraft. Why not political science?

Indeed, political science has generally been occupied primarily with the study of the state – "national philosophism," as Derrida calls it[5] – but this concession does not hold for the entire discipline. Of all the subfields in political science, political theory has always fit the least comfortably with the others, due in large part to its philosophical origins and tradition, which spans over two millennia, and contains very little material that might be considered properly "social scientific" in character. In fact, most work in political theory (formal theory aside) possesses a flavour much more akin to that of the humanities than the social sciences. For example, it is much more likely for a political theorist to explore the depth of the human soul, than to quantify human behaviour via statistical models. In addition, this tradition began long before the rise of the modern state system, which is another way of saying that political theory existed long before the advent of modern political science. While Plato and Aristotle had a name for something approximating the state (the "nation," in translation), their primary interests were in the politics of the city. The rest of this chapter outlines a brief history of political theory's relationship to the category of the city, beginning with the Ancient Greeks and ending with the contemporary moment. It is not an exhaustive account, but instead highlights the central contributions particular theorists have made in producing the Western canon of political thought. Such an endeavour helps establish the theoretical context for reasserting the city as an essential category for thinking about politics from a critical political theory perspective.

The Ancient Greek *Polis*

Many political scientists will argue that the city in Ancient Greece should be considered simply a precursor or analogue to the state. Ultimately, the argument goes, the difference between modern states and cities like ancient Athens is primarily a matter of scale, after all, we commonly refer to these latter political units as city-*states*. From this perspective, the formal structure of the city and the state appear identical, as do their respective roles in creating rules regarding citizenship, commerce, foreign policy, and maintaining monopolies on the legitimate use of violence. But this obscures some of the strong normative dimensions peculiar to city life so strongly articulated by the likes of Plato and Aristotle. A brief glance at the works of the Ancients shows clearly that when the city marks the limit of legitimate political authority, the political experience of its citizens is qualitatively different, and the Greeks would say enriched, than those in larger political units that possesses multiple cities or nations, spread across a wide territorial expanse.

In this respect, when contrasting cities and states, the first consideration is, quite simply, the size of the *polis*. The political system of ancient Athens is routinely valorized (if not romanticized) because all citizens had the right and duty to directly participate in governing, suggesting that the dream of contemporary radical democrats – "direct" democracy – is feasible and functional if the political unit in question is confined to a reasonably small population. This sort of claim must, of course, always include the qualifier that the majority of the inhabitants of ancient Athens were not legally citizens and, therefore, its (direct) democracy was highly exclusive and required slaves and other oppressed and marginalized groups to function. This criticism will be dealt with in good time, but for now I am simply interested in highlighting some of the most important ideas about the city that inaugurate the canon of Western political thought, and the first is that physical or geographical size mediates the possibilities for types of rule.

While Plato was no fan of democracy, he does provide several comments regarding the importance of small-scale political organization, and certainly he never questions if the city should serve as the primary site of political power. He argues that the most important characteristics of the city are that it remain "unified" and "self-sufficient." In a conversation with Adeimantus, Socrates illustrates this position:

> And what, I said, will be the best limit for our rulers to fix when they are considering the size of the State and the amount of territory which they are to include, and beyond which they will not go?
>
> What limit would you propose?
>
> I would allow the State to increase so far as is consistent with unity; that, I think, is the proper limit.
>
> Very good, he said.
>
> Here then, I said, is another order which will have to be conveyed to our guardians: Let our city be accounted neither large nor small, but one and self-sufficing.[6]

By "unity," Plato is referring to his famous definition of justice in the city – that all inhabitants accept their roles, and perform them well, without envy or resentment toward their fellows.[7] Self-sufficiency, on the other hand, appears to mean that the city possesses all that is required for its inhabitants to live without concern for their security and wellbeing. For Plato, the self-sufficient city is a city without luxuries or unnecessary accoutrements. It therefore requires a severely disciplined society, devoted to the preservation of the city over all other concerns. Flowing from this condition, Plato argues that the city is also to be planned in an intensely rational manner, and should contain no spontaneous elements. This is another way of saying that every aspect of the city should be designed intentionally so as to ensure its unity and that it is not deficient in any necessity. For example, in Book II of *The Republic* he identifies the various types of workers necessary for creating a self-sufficient city, from servants to "neatherders."[8] Betraying his Pythagorean mysticism, in *The Laws* Plato actually provides a specific number that he believes represents the ideal population for a city: 5,040,[9] roughly the size of Humboldt, Saskatchewan.[10]

Despite major differences in relation to his thoughts on the city, Plato's most famous student – Aristotle – also expresses a great concern with the normative importance of the size of the city. In concert with his teacher, Aristotle asserts an explicit relationship between self-sufficiency and justice in the city by constructing an analogy between the just/self-sufficient man and the corresponding city. This perspective is intimately associated with the good life of the individual, in that

> [h]e who has the power to take part in the deliberative or judicial administration of any state is said by us to be a citizen of that state; and, speaking generally, a state is a body of citizens sufficing for the purposes of life.[11]

In the Aristotelian city, citizens live the good life only when they are not dependent on others, and when they have control over their own political affairs. At first glance, and contra Plato, Aristotle believes there is no direct relationship between the number of inhabitants of a city and its greatness, because the greatness of a city is a qualitative consideration, not a quantitative one. What matters, primarily, is the number of *good* inhabitants in the city.[12] Nonetheless, he prefers cities with smaller populations because, in them, citizens have a greater ability to know each other and thereby grow fond of each other. Ultimately, for Aristotle, not only are small cities preferable to large ones, but the desire for the latter betrays an inherently tyrannical predisposition, as he states: "those who value most highly the life of a tyrant deem that city the happiest which rules over the greatest number."[13]

Perhaps the most important Aristotelian insight regarding the city is, however, connected to one of his central categories of the good life: friendship. For Aristotle, friendship stands at the apex of the hierarchy of virtuous human relationships, particularly those friendships in which two individuals desire good for each other.[14] A city in which numerous friendships have grown and flourished is sure to be a good city, but not just as a result of the existence of virtuous relationships. On Aristotle's account, not everyone has the ability to foster genuine friendships of equals, but only virtuous individuals, and it is these individuals who will also rule and choose rulers in the city. Therefore,

> if the citizens of a state are to judge and to distribute offices according to merit, then they must know each other's characters; where they do not possess this knowledge, both the election to offices and the decision of lawsuits will go wrong. When the population is very large they are manifestly settled at haphazard, which clearly ought not to be.[15]

It is the possibility of face-to-face solidarity in the reasonably sized city that allows for virtuous rule in the Aristotelian mould, a condition of existence largely absent in all contemporary representative democracies (at least at the national level of government).

Finally, the Ancient Greek perspective on the city was intimately associated with a teleological understanding of human nature. As Aristotle formulated, humans are by nature political animals, and as such require the *polis* to achieve their potential in this respect. For the Greeks, the good life was inextricably linked to the existence of a public sphere in which men could act in accordance with their political nature. Hannah Arendt elucidates this in her classic distinction between the private and the public: "The realm of the *polis* … was the sphere of freedom,"[16] that is, the place where political life happens and the necessity of the private is transcended. She continues: "The law of the city state was … quite literally a wall, without which there might have been an agglomeration of houses, a town (*asty*), but not a city, a political community."[17] In other words, the community as defined and governed by law was embodied in the *physical* space of the city, and provided the conditions of possibility for human flourishing. The lessons political theorists can take away from this brief gloss of the Ancients is that size matters when it comes to conceptualizing formal political communities, but contra the physiological witticism, bigger is not necessarily better. The good life, to the extent it is based on a teleological conception of what it means to be human, requires an *urban* setting as the primary container of politics.

It is with this peculiar normative position regarding political life that the tradition of Western political theory begins. While the city qua ancient *polis* would never regain such a pre-eminent position in the canon of political theory as it did with the Greeks, the value of small-scale, or localized politics, consistently reappears in the thought of, more or less, every age. It is implicit in the localism of some of the iconodules of the Byzantine era,[18] the localized patriotism of the Italian city-state of the fifteenth and sixteenth centuries (supported by Machiavelli's opposition to the logic of sovereignty),[19] the anti-monarchist and anti-enclosure proto-anarchism of sixteenth- and seventeenth-century England,[20] and very much explicit in the radical democratic thought of eighteenth-century Romanticism. In terms of the latter, Jean-Jacques Rousseau is undeniably the most influential and representative romantic thinker of the normative importance of small-scale political units for the practice of democracy, and as such it is worth examining his ideas in greater detail.

Rousseau's Defence of Freedom in the City

Because, for Rousseau, all individuals possess both a particular will and constitute part of the general will, there always is a tension at the level of individual will. While the general will never changes, each particular will conflicts with every other particular will, and thereby they all negate each other. What is left can only represent the collective good, that which reflects the individual's interest as citizen and not as private, self-interested actor. It follows that the greater the population in any given polity, the greater shall be the tensions between particular wills. Thus, mathematically speaking, the individual's share of sovereign power decreases as the population increases, and Rousseau concludes that "the larger the State, the less the liberty."[21] All this means is that the greater the population of any state, the less legislating capacity the individual possesses qua citizen or voter. This accounts for Rousseau's fondness for his hometown of Geneva, and the other autonomous Swiss cities of his day. It also points to a necessary correlation between large states and heightened levels of repressive government. Unlike his theory of the general will, there is nothing ambiguous about the logic of his position concerning the desirable relative size of states. Very much akin to the Greeks, Rousseau outlines a series of practical problems that naturally accompany large states, as well as virtues that can only be realized in small ones. To summarize, in comparison to small polities, for Rousseau, large states are:

1 more costly, wasteful, and difficult to govern by virtue of increased administrative responsibilities (due to the distance between municipalities and redundant administrative levels);
2 less able to maintain orderliness;
3 less able to foster admiration for their rulers and mutual affection between their citizens;
4 less able to avoid soulless, bureaucratic rule;
5 less able to defend their borders; and
6 less able to care for the happiness of their people.

These insights appear just as intuitive today as they must have in Rousseau's time, and it may be that present-day Switzerland, to some extent, attests to their enduring truth.[22]

Despite these proclamations, critics of Rousseau have not focused much on his defence of localism, but instead they tend to target the general will which is intended by Rousseau to legitimate a sort of radical democracy. The most common argument against the general will is that it possesses an inherently authoritarian quality and is therefore incompatible with liberal individualism because the good is defined collectively without taking into account individual rights.[23] This position is largely sound, but tends to ignore the problematic relationship between the general will and the size of the population in a state's corresponding polity that Rousseau makes very explicit. It seems that any hope for defending a relationship between the general will and democracy, if one were so disposed, relies on the recognition that scale, in terms of population, matters for proper political organization. Part of the problem with modern and contemporary critiques of Rousseau is that those rendering judgment against him tend to treat large-scale nation-states, constituted by heterogeneous, multicultural populations as the default frame of reference when they attempt to imagine the general will in practice. There is little doubt that if the contemporary nation-state serves as the assumed site of politics, then the general will is rendered *unintelligible* in radical democratic terms. But things change when one re-coordinates this frame of reference *precisely* as Rousseau insisted we should. If freedom decreases as population increases, a democratic expression of the general will can only be imagined in a relatively small community (and even this insight may not be able to save the Rousseauian general will, but it does render it more intelligible). It is therefore disingenuous for a serious reader of Rousseau to judge the general will as a concept within the exclusive context of, say, a great national event like the

French Revolution, and yet this is precisely what the secondary literature does. It may be that this discursive erasure (or cognitive dissonance) of localism in some readings of Rousseau is symptomatic of a failing on the part of political science in general, after all political science is defined by a fetishization, or "reification" of the nation-state as the natural container of politics.[24] In an interesting way, then, a comprehensive defence of Rousseau's political theory may only be feasible when his work is read through an urban lens, as opposed to a state-centric one.

Up to this point in the canonical chronology, the insights rendered by Plato, Aristotle, and Rousseau regarding the importance of limited, relatively small-scale political community, stand simply as attempts to outline general principles of political governance – principles that are, presumably, meant to be transhistorical in nature. The Greeks did not think in terms of linear and developmental historical progress, at least in any way approximating how many of the moderns did. Therefore, their political philosophy was understood as revealing a set of historically transcendent principles of human nature and political rule. Rousseau, on the other hand, thought very much in terms of historical progress, despite the fact that he maligned most of it as a march toward incivility. His thought on the ideal size of political community, however, has very little to do with the specific social relations of his age but it can be thought of instead as a rearticulation of Ancient Greek ideas: human beings flourish qua human beings in small political units, even if for Rousseau the goal of such political organization was democracy and equality, while for the Greeks it was order and the human flourishing of only a select portion of the population. Their contributions are important for connecting the human good to city life, but not for thinking about the city as a site of political life serving as the condition of possibility for greater human progress. While this is not a widely shared opinion, I argue that it is not until Karl Marx came on the philosophical scene that political theory recognized the *historical* importance of the city and urban political organization for setting the groundwork for realizing the final *telos* of humankind: complete freedom.

Karl Marx and the Revolutionary Potential of the City

Karl Marx is not generally regarded as a theorist of the city, and the city was never of sustained concern to him, both theoretically and practically.[25] He did not write explicitly about how the city plays a strategic role in revolutionary politics, indeed, he and Engels were severe critics of the radical municipalism of their time,[26] because they believed it distracted the revolutionary forces away from what should have been considered their primary target: overthrowing the state and ultimately establishing global communism. But Marx was very much aware of the importance of *urbanization* as a historical stage in the development of capitalism – symptomatic of the radical new age of modernity – and as a prefiguration of the society that would replace it. For the Ancient Greeks and Rousseau, that at the time of their writing the vast majority of human beings in the world lived in rural areas in no way affected their political analyses (although Rousseau showed utter contempt for certain urban milieus, especially Parisian social circles). For Marx, however, it is strongly implied that the distinctly modern, revolutionary working class could only be realized when the majority of people had come to live in, if not always properly *urban* areas, places with significantly large populations and high levels of *density*; a social reality that capitalism facilitates itself, as a dialectical materialist reading of history attests. As Merrifield states: "What Marx condones here is anything that hastens the agglomeration of population, the centralization of industry, capital, and property."[27]

In the *Communist Manifesto*, Marx invokes the phrase the "idiocy of the rural," a powerful, controversial, and oft misunderstood concept. The idiocy of the rural should not be understood as simply an arrogant and chauvinistic expression of distaste for the "backwardness" of peasants on the part of Marx (although he may very well have possessed such an attitude). It should, instead, be approached as an analysis of the limitations to progressive political organizing under pre-capitalist relations of production. Under feudalism labour was primarily situated in the countryside, as the main source of wealth was agricultural in character. Most peasants, by far the largest category of workers, lived far away from the cities, in sparsely populated communities, and laboured in relative isolation from their co-workers. The onset of capitalism began to change all this, as the site of power and wealth accumulation shifted from the aristocratic land barons, to the emergent bourgeoisie of the cities ("bourgeoisie" means literally "city-dwellers"). New technologies that allowed for the mass production of consumer goods and other industrial commodities required a vast pool of human labour to be concentrated at the new primary site of production: the factory. Whether factories were situated in or near existing cities, or the establishment of factories led to the creation of cities to support them, rural labourers flooded into these urban areas in search of work.

This process had profound effects on the labourers in question. As Marx observed, for the first time workers were in a position to *organize* themselves in a sophisticated way – to educate themselves using the resources of the city, and to create bonds of solidarity due to the intense concentration of workers at the site of production. In other words, on Marx's account, workers possessed an unprecedented capacity to understand themselves as a *class*, and not just any class, but the *universal* class. When used to describe the "rural," then, the word "idiocy" should be considered in its etymological context – the private and particular, or "idiosyncratic" – peasants were considered "idiotic" because they lived isolated lives and therefore lacked the conditions of possibility to understand the greater historical, universal movement that the workers constitute as a united force. That is to say, agrarian workers were limited in their ability to organize themselves as a (modern) revolutionary agent because of their material conditions of existence.[28] It is, then, the process of urbanization that for Marx constitutes the conditions of possibility for overcoming this idiocy, and it is a lesson that political theorists should pay considerable attention to in today's rapidly urbanizing world.

However, it should be noted that, despite his claim of the *actuality* of an urbanized proletariat in the polemical rhetoric of the *Communist Manifesto*, the overwhelming majority of workers in Europe of the 1840s were still agricultural labourers.[29] This is why, for anyone who considers themself a "critical" political theorist, Marx's insights are more relevant in the present socio-historical juncture than they were in his own time. In a world in which the majority live in cities, it seems not only an appropriate, but crucially important moment to return to Marx's thoughts regarding the connection between progressive politics and urbanization. This does not require that one identify as a "Marxist" or dogmatic leftist of any stripe to recognize the importance of the city for contemporary progressive struggles. In fact, it seems that one could demonstrate quite easily that virtually every contemporary mass movement is, at its core, an *urban movement*. Was the outpouring in Tahrir Square in 2011 a reflection of "Egypt's" desire for an end to corruption and the introduction of democracy? Or is it better understood as representing the desires of young, middle-class inhabitants of *Cairo*? The same question can be asked of the 2013 protests in Istanbul and Ankara. Are the Occupy movements that gripped North America and elsewhere truly reflective of a significant segment of the entire population? Or, considering that most of the localized occupations were based in cities, should they also be thought of as peculiarly urban political actions? Answering these questions is beyond the scope of this book, but whether these events were middle-class or genuinely populist in character, they do point toward a certain political logic that I think can go a long way toward understanding processes of urbanization as they relate to contemporary political action. More specifically, they support the Marxist insight that *cities* facilitate the capacity for millions of people to organize and articulate themselves as "the people."

It is frustrating, then, that in many ways Marx's thought marks the end of any serious critical consideration of the importance or viability of the urban as a focal point of political action in the tradition of Western political thought. Afterwards, it is the nation-state that assumes unquestioned hegemony in the study of political theory, whether from a Marxist or liberal perspective. Over the past 50 years, the study of the urban and the local has been relegated to correlate disciplines (sociology and geography), although political science does eventually provide limited space for scholarship on municipal government within the discipline (the anemic pseudo-sub-discipline of "urban politics"). What accounts for this shift toward the nation-state in political theory, and what are its consequences? Can we simply chalk the shift up to disciplinary divides in academia, in which the state is the proper object of analysis for political science (and, therefore, political theory)? Or is there something deeper, something ontological – perhaps a disavowal of the way that power actually operates – that explains political science's state-centricity?

The City's Particular to the State's Universal

It is quite commonplace to understand the development of state-centric political thinking as originating coevally with the birth of the nation-state system, inaugurated by the Treaty of Westphalia of 1648. According to this narrative, the modern state is defined primarily by what is considered a distinctly modern form of political power: sovereignty. At this time, sovereignty, as defined by kings, statesmen, and legal experts, became the ultimate and exclusively legitimate institutional form of political power, severely challenging all other claimants to such authority. To quote Warren Magnusson:

> As new forms of political organization took shape in the modern era, it became apparent that sovereignty would be one of the organizing principles of the new world order. In each country there would be a central authority beyond which there could be no appeal, and the rulers would extend mutual recognition to one another. The claims of universal religion, clan loyalty, tribal identity, and regional solidarity were to give way to the power of the state.[30]

Centring political power on sovereignty was considered the most rational organization of politics because all states would be treated equally, and irrational forces that might encourage conflict with other states on the basis of religious, ethnic, or other localized affiliations would not affect the logic of rule.

As internal law goes, the establishment of the Westphalian state system was certainly something new in a formal sense. But in another manner, it simply marked a watershed moment in a long, historical struggle between two forces: the particular and the universal. In Western philosophy, traditionally the "universal" – those properties shared by all specific instances of an object – is considered primary and valorized. In contrast, the particular – that which defies universalization – is treated with scorn and derision; the particular is feared because it disrupts the rational harmony of the universal. In the tradition of Western political thought this privileging of the universal over the particular manifests itself in its treatment of power and authority. Political theorists from Plato to Rawls have been preoccupied with the question of where the source of political authority lies. Many of these thinkers have answered the question in quite disparate ways (divine right, natural inequality, natural law, social contract, the individual, historical destiny, and so on). However, where they tend to converge when answering this question is in their rejection that multiple, particular sources of authority may have equally valid claims vis-à-vis the universal. A universal authority must exist and this authority will not stand for competitors that challenge its claim to power. If there is a theoretical category that epitomizes this position in the discipline of political science, it is undoubtedly "sovereignty."

One can argue that, as operative in the modern state, the logic of sovereignty is simply another manifestation of a universalizing power used to overwhelm and dominate the particular or local. Here, Deleuze and Guattari's notion of the interaction between "*Urstaat*" and "war machine" is instructive. The *Urstaat* represents what they consider to be the transhistorical logic of the state in any form; that is to say, the state is always at its "fundamental moment" an apparatus of "civil capture" or "machinic enslavement,"[31] meaning that it is an entity that always strives to exert its authority over populations. The *Urstaat* knows only power and control, and taps into humans' ability to desire their own subjection; it produces in the subject "arboreal" reasoning – authoritarian thinking that understands power hierarchically, with a centre around which subsidiary powers lie.[32] However, as with all post-structuralist thought, where power exists, so too does resistance. Deleuze and Guattari's category of resistance to the *Urstaat* is the "war machine" – a purely conceptual energy that is defined by absolute "exteriority" to the state. The war machine resists capture and, in contrast to the arboreal nature of the state, is structured "rhyzomatically" in that it creates "lines of flight" from the state. It is informed by a "nomadic science" that does not think in simple terms of linear progress, and it creates corresponding "nomadic subjects" who flee the logic of the *Urstaat*.[33] What Deleuze and Guattari present here is simply a convoluted version of Nietzsche's narrative of the recurring battle between Rome and Jerusalem, and their normative position is similarly a rearticulation of the desire for a revaluation of values. However, the logic of their argument also proves productive within the framework of the tension between the particular and the universal and, more specifically, between their politically spatialized analogues: the city and the state, respectively.

By thinking in terms of a timeless conflict between the universal and the particular in a sort of Nietzschean genealogical manner, the reified character of the state as the natural container of politics can be challenged – "de-reified," as it were. Instead of privileging state sovereignty, the notion of a natural or inherently proper site of politics is upset altogether, and whatever site of authority comes to be considered legitimate in any given moment is perceived simply as the outcome of political struggle (i.e., the "winner" of such a struggle legitimizes itself through its superior force). At the very least, if it is indeed possible to associate the struggle between state and city with Deleuze's *Urstaat*/war machine model (or Nietzsche's Rome/Jerusalem conflict), certainly it would be a mistake to assume that the era of the city has been relegated to the dustbin of history. What is clear from the perspective of the state and sovereignty is that local forms of power, especially if they are fuelled by strong bonds of situated and solidaristic identity are, and always have been, taken very seriously by the state as a severe threat to its legitimacy.

The category of legitimacy is key here. A central principle of modern liberal democracy is that the state remains legitimate only to the extent it maintains legitimacy in the eyes of its people. While in theory, this premise does not extend to most other types of regimes (for example, absolute monarchy) in practical terms all governments require a strong basis of social support, even if it is only the support of a powerful minority population, to remain viable and ward off popular challenges to their rule. In the context of the historical struggle between particular and universal, the issue of legitimacy can be recast in terms of questions of "loyalty." Any political community, whether organized on a geographic, religious, or ethnic basis, requires the loyalty of its constituents to greater or lesser extents. The stronger the bonds of loyalty to a particular community, the more that community can press its interests against those of its rivals. In terms of the rise of the nation-state, Magnusson summarizes this well:

> Since nation-building requires intense loyalties, the state is accorded a monopoly on the symbols of patriotism, which it invokes against internal and external challenges. This monopoly of patriotic symbolism is the

ideological counterpart of the monopolies of political authority and legitimate violence that are implicit in the principles of state sovereignty.[34]

At the level of elite solidarity, one might point to Benedict Anderson's insight regarding the development of a common national vernacular, as required for the growth of the print industry, as an instance of a type of meta-symbol of national identity – a language that displaces or demotes regional dialects to the position of the vulgar local. In Anderson's mind, of course, this was a necessary condition for the development of a shared political identity amongst disparate communities full of people who were otherwise strangers, but it can also be cited as another example of the logic of universalization at work, this time at the intersection of language and politics.[35]

While the logic of nation-building qua the construction of identities (via both concrete and abstract symbolization) for the purpose of fostering loyalty is not peculiar to the age of the nation-state (see for example my and Peter Brown's work on the iconoclast conflicts of ninth-century Byzantium), it can be argued that the success of modern nationalism was, in part, a result of its sustained physical and discursive attack on the legitimacy of cities as sites of political authority. Perhaps no one expresses the violent, physical aspect of the historical imperial assault on the city better than Umberto Eco in his historical-fiction novel *Baudolino*. The backdrop of the eponymous character's fantastic adventure is Frederick II's attempt to consolidate the Holy Roman Empire across Europe, but especially in Italy. The greatest obstacle to his aspirations is clearly the fierce independence of the Italian cities, along with a correspondingly intense urban loyalty of their inhabitants. A common trope of Eco's account of this urban intransigence is the accession of cities to imperial dictates, but only in order to buy time while they improve their defences:

> Meanwhile, the Poet kept him informed of the exploits of Frederick. The Italian communes were not keeping faith with all the oaths they had sworn at the Diet of Roncaglia. According to the pacts, the unruly cities were to demolish their walls and destroy their war machines; but instead the citizens pretended to fill in the moats, and the moats were still there.[36]

The reaction of Frederick to such examples of betrayal is always one of wrath; a single-minded desire to eliminate all resistance by completely destroying the cities themselves. It's difficult for the reader to keep track of the number of cities razed as a result of their disobedience, but they include Terdona, Spoleto, Crema, Milan, Lodi, Iconium, and Pndapetzim (not to mention, later, Istanbul). At one point, citizens whose cities had been destroyed, and were loyal to the "anti-Imperial League," took it upon themselves to build a new city called Allesandria. They did so in order to spite the emperor and to stall his progress east. When Baudolino suggests that Frederick could simply order his troops to bypass the new city on their way east, "No, no," they answered, "you don't know the emperor…. A city that rises without his consent is an offense to be cleansed in blood; he'll be forced to lay siege to it."[37]

This logic of urban loyalty can be expressed in properly scholarly terms. During the periods of Late Antiquity and the Middle Ages, the sovereign explicitly demanded the fealty of the cities based on various, but always absolute, principles of political legitimacy: divine right of kings, might makes right, ecumenical or papal decree, or as Barber suggests, "natural law":

> Despite their importance in the early modern period, the so-called state-of-nature philosophers who rationalized the emergence of new nation-states in the early modern period ignored cities as political precursors to the state. Instead, they looked back to family and tribe and beyond.... Theirs was at best an abstraction necessary to making an argument for obeying kings and other sovereigns.[38]

As such, the Aristotelian notion that humans, as *zoon politikon*, are only intelligible qua humans when they live together in cities, is bypassed by the primacy of the question "who should rule?" In a natural law context, the father is shown to be the original authority and, therefore, the monarch is the social analogue. Cities are conceived, then, as having no particularly privileged role in the organization of politics, except that they are smaller and subsidiary to the greater kingdom, nation, or empire. This justification for the subsidiarity of cities changes, however, in the discourse of modern political theory. The democratic sentiment that slowly came to characterize political thinking in the modern age reoriented the problem of the city, from one of illegitimacy to accusations of ungovernability.

The political philosophy of G.W.F. Hegel most starkly illustrates the transition from thinking the city as illegitimate vis-à-vis the state, to the city as ungovernable. As Michael Shapiro points out, Hegel did not write much on the city because he was primarily a "metaphysical" nationalist, only interested in the abstract space of the state.[39] For Hegel, it is clear that the state is the only site in which the universality of citizenship can be realized, primarily because it is understood in terms of sovereignty, law, and rights, and not immediate, emotional, or other such idiosyncratic considerations. Conversely, Shapiro speculates, the city was most likely seen by Hegel as "disorderly" and a threat to the unity of the state.[40] Thus, it would seem, for Hegel the city represents a sort of particular space that must be overcome or tamed by the universal state. As part of civil society, that distinctive area of ethical life that stands between family and state,[41] the city represents an excess or disruption in the dialectic; it is considered irrational and deviant, in a certain way. Therefore, it is to the rational, universal, law-based institution of the nation-state that political loyalty and identity of the citizen is to be attached. Any other such attachment, based on localism, to one's town, city, or region is treated as so much parochialism – irrational and archaic in the context of the historical unfolding of *Geist*.

The city is, then, in constant tension with the nation-state – always pushing against its authority and, perhaps contra the wishes of Hegel, it never fully accedes to the state's hegemony. This was one of the core insights of the canonical sociologist of modernity, Max Weber. Cities, on Weber's account, are a hallmark of modernity, and their autonomy from the state places them in a unique position vis-à-vis political and social life. Magnusson illustrates this concisely: "As Weber recognized, this civic space of economy, society, culture, personal religion, and politics was never captured completely by the power of the emergent modern state."[42] In fact, Magnusson demonstrates how Weber identified that the freedom exerted by cities (and the relative freedom of thought and action enjoyed by their inhabitants) was always in tension with relatively weak states, and that this tension was a central factor in the rise of Western modernity:

> characteristically modern ways of thinking and being originated in places that the great states could not control … characterized, in large degree, by … "non-legitimate domination": political authority of a sort that was at odds with prevailing norms of legitimacy.[43]

Thus, for Weber, cities are historically speaking viewed as a third power, contrasted with church and state, in relation to the emergence of modern European politics. Cities formed the crucial economic bases of the modern society, producing the wealth needed to sustain both the nation-state and the church, while simultaneously being considered threats to their authority.[44] As such, historically speaking, city walls literally had to come down as the nation-state emerged in Europe because they were symbols of urban independence.[45] In the absence of walls, political constructions so crucial to Arendt's normative vision of the Ancient *polis*, modern nationalism literally and discursively evacuated or flattened the political geography of Europe of some of the greatest sources of the politically particular, at least for most of the last three centuries.

Twentieth-Century Critical Urban Theory

From a Weberian perspective, therefore, it appears that Hegel was right to be worried about the disruptive nature of the city, as it has never been fully tamed; in fact, it constantly "challenges and disrupts the order of the state or the state system."[46] To quote Alan Broadbent, "Nations come and go, but cities last forever."[47] This is a foundational premise that I will build from throughout this book: states cannot fully control and determine the course of cities. Cities, while not completely organic and spontaneous in their organization, nonetheless should be understood as actors that constantly exert a certain autonomy from the state; they disrupt national narratives while often being simultaneously mistaken for the very same narratives. In historico-philosophical terms, the city acts as a sort of remainder of difference or non-identity in the process of the development of the state, a "bone in the throat," to speak in Hegelian terms.

However, despite the potentially disruptive power of the city, modernity was defined by nation building, and that is where political-theoretical interest lay throughout the eighteenth and nineteenth centuries. In the early to mid-twentieth century, the state remained the chief object of concern for political theory for thinkers on both the Left and Right. While the modern exclusive association of citizenship with the nation-state was just as much in force as in the previous decades, the focus on the state was reinforced by the occurrence of several distinct historical developments. In brief, the most important of these developments were the sheer power that nation-states came to wield in the twentieth century (exemplified by the military might of the two Cold War superpowers), the very successful projects of social democratic nation-building in Western Europe and North America, the ever-enlarging scale of economic production and trade, and the various national liberation movements that sprung up in the colonized countries of the global south. In terms of critical political theory, the various Marxist traditions (Leninism, Trotskyism, Maoism) emphasized the importance of capturing the state in order to overthrow the capitalist system. Later, in the 1960s and early 1970s, structural Marxism sought to demystify the state–capital nexus highlighted by the work of Althusser, while the debate between Poulantzas and Miliband on the nature of state autonomy is still, to this day, required reading for all political economy and comparative politics graduate students. With the notable exceptions of figures like Walter Benjamin, Henri Lefebvre, and Herbert Marcuse, up to around 1970 thinkers on the Left largely ignored the progressive potential of the city as a site of resistance to capitalism and the state, despite the fact that the world was becoming increasingly urbanized and the problems associated with the contemporary inner-city (widespread violence, poverty, and substance abuse) had by then become prevalent in (at least North American) urban landscapes.[48]

But it is not uncommon for theory to lag behind empirical reality. The politics of the 1970s was defined in large part by an explosion in left-wing militancy, much of which was centred in poor and racialized urban core neighbourhoods. The paradigmatic case of such militancy was the actions of the Black Panthers Party, whose goal was to protect and empower poor neighbourhoods while simultaneously promoting a socialist political project. This sort of activism inspired an advancement of critical theorizing from both within the black revolutionary movement, as well as the academy. Perhaps the best-known figures that represent these two branches of critical theory are respectively, Angela Davis and her academic supervisor, Herbert Marcuse.

This particular tradition of radical urban activism and theory lives on today in militant, often anarchist, inner-city anti-poverty and anti-racist organizing, but it represents only one strain of a larger anti-statist ethos that came to characterize much of the critical Left in the late twentieth century. Over the past 30 years or so, critical theorists from all academic disciplines have increasingly turned against conceptualizing the state as the privileged site of politics. More specifically, this anti-statist tendency has branched out on two separate (but oft-connected) trajectories: one focused on the global level of analysis, and the other on the urban. In terms of the former, on an analytic level a new generation of theorists has identified globalization as a process that challenges the sovereign power of the state. From a normative perspective, the global contains the potential for a cosmopolitan world free of petty nationalisms, as well as unprecedented collective problem-solving, resource sharing, and prospects for universal citizenship. Conversely, the new critical *urbanists* have identified many of the same benefits of organizing politically on a local level in cities that I discussed above.[49] For such theorists, the lives of citizens in nation-states are lived in a more abstract sense than they are in cities, and yet the state wields immense power over them. As Magnusson argues, the dominant perspective for political scientists regarding the city/state relationship is perceived as we are *here*, and the power that governs us is *there*, and for some reason we accept this as normal and legitimate.[50] Indeed, it is in cities where people live out their everyday lives in a more immediate manner, interacting with their fellow urbanites, using their cities' physical and social infrastructure. Put plainly, cities are perceived as tangible, non-abstract places where people share similar immediate concerns and are forced to live with each other, despite their differences; the state is where individuals currently and historically become citizens in a *concrete* sense.[51] This is in contrast to the state or nation, which is largely "imagined" in Benedict Anderson's word; the state is really quite mysterious, if not mystical, when its discourses are interrogated. Consonant with Marx's critique in *On the Jewish Question*, it is where individuals become citizens in an *abstract* sense. In addition, critical urbanists perceive the city as an incredibly dynamic place, where anything can and does happen. "It's in the city," as Merrifield puts it quite eloquently "where things melt into air most of all; it's there, especially, where all that is holy becomes profane."[52] This harkens back obviously to Marx's, but also Weber's and Hegel's respective insights into cities: they are pregnant with the potential for creativity, innovation, unruliness, the unexpected, and politics. But contra Hegel, in the new critical urban literature the disruption that cities can instigate in relation to national or universal narratives, is something to be celebrated, not feared.

Contemporary Urban Political Thought

As I mentioned earlier, the focus on the city as a site of progressive or emancipatory politics emerged primarily in the disciplines of geography and sociology. Influenced by scholars like Henri Lefebvre, critical geographers including Andy Merrifield, Edward Soja, and the scholars of the "Edmonton School," revolutionized Marxist urban studies and inspired a whole generation of critical theorists bent on shifting the discipline in an urban direction. The same can be said for sociologists like Manuel Castells, John Logan, and Harvey Molotch. While critical geographers and sociologists have come to be influential in the discipline of political theory, this fact has not radically shifted its emphasis toward cities. If anything, critical political theorists have become more interested in the global level of analysis than the urban. However, it would be a mistake to claim that there are no recently or currently active critical political theorists who have explored what it would mean to privilege (or at least not treat as subsidiary) the urban over the state as a site of politics. Most noteworthy, at least for the work I am interested in, Warren Magnusson has devoted the past 20 years of his career to using the urban as a fulcrum for deconstructing political science's fetishization of state sovereignty, and as a tool for reimagining progressive politics. Similarly, Susan Fainstein, Iris Marion Young, and Michael J. Shapiro, although their work is not as germane to my project as Magnusson's, deserve to be acknowledged for their contributions to urban political theory. More recently, it appears that a new generation of, not exclusively "critical" political theorists, is creating a space for political theory to take the city seriously. By way of anecdote, at the 2013 Canadian Political Science Association meeting in Victoria, BC, I attended a panel that represented itself in just this way (I believe the word "trailblazers" was invoked). The name of the panel was "The Just and Diverse City," and the panellists included Margaret Kohn (University of Toronto), Loren King (Wilfrid Laurier), and Patrick Turmel (Université laval), and was chaired by Daniel Weinstock (Université de Montréal). All three presenters came at the problem of urban justice and diversity from different theoretical traditions: critical theory, normative political theory, and left-liberalism, respectively. There was a general consensus that for far too long political theory had not paid enough attention to the category of the city, and the present task was to work through exactly what distinct type of contribution political theory could make to urban scholarship. While this question was not answered in any definitive way at this panel, it was fascinating to witness the beginning of the discussion, at least in the context of the Canadian political theory scene.

While it is encouraging, then, to observe some movement in the right direction within the formal study of political theory, there exists a major obstacle to be overcome and that is the way in which the term "political" is understood and employed; that is to say, in much of this literature what could be distinctly "political" about political theory's contribution is either underdeveloped or absent. This, as I outline in the next two chapters, is largely a function of a major shift in the character of critical political and social theory writ large that has occurred over the last 40 years; a shift that substitutes what I call "ethical" theory for properly political analysis. Despite all of the very important innovations in critical urban studies, in my view this body of literature suffers due to a paucity of properly political theory. So, on the one hand, critical scholars have indeed been correct in returning to the city as an analytical and normative object of study, while simultaneously depoliticizing it as a category for thinking the political. The first task on the road to "urbanizing" critical political theory is, then, ensuring that our analyses are informed by genuinely "political" principles.

Notes

1 Stuart Elden, *Understanding Henri Lefebvre: Theory and the Possible* (London: Continuum, 2004), 143.
2 Iris Marion Young, "The Ideal of Community and the Politics of Difference," in *Feminism/Postmodernism*, ed. Linda J. Nicholson (New York: Routledge, 1990), 317.
3 For an extended discussion of political science's almost exclusive association with sovereignty and the nation state, see: Warren Magnusson, *The Politics of Urbanism: Seeing Like a City* (New York: Routledge, 2011).
4 Warren Magnusson, "Politicizing the Global City," in *Democracy, Citizenship, and the Global City*, ed. Engin Isin (New York: Routledge, 2002), 291–292.
5 Michael Shapiro, *The Time of the City: Politics, Philosophy and Genre* (London: Routledge, 2010), 49.
6 Plato, *Republic*, Book IV, ed. Max Bollinger (London: The Big Nest, 2012), 314–315.
7 Ibid., 314.

8 In Book II of the *Republic* Plato outlines Socrates's notion of self-sufficiency, when he writes that the following workers are required for the self-sufficient city: husbandmen, builders, weavers, shoemakers, carpenters, smiths, and many artisans, neatherds, shepherds, and other herdsman, merchants (for trading with other cities), retailers, and hired servants of the state (ibid., 36). This of course is a description of the minimalist city, i.e., the city without luxuries or Glaucon's "city of pigs."

9 Plato, *Laws*, Book V, trans. Benjamin Jowett, digireads.com (2009), 76.

10 This number refers only to citizens. The ideal population is closer to 50,000 when one accounts for slaves, women, and children. See: Rajendra K. Sharma, *Demography and Population Problems* (New Delhi: Atlantic Books, 2000), 26–27.

11 Aristotle, *Politics*, trans. Benjamin Jowett (Kitchener: Batoche Books, 1999), 53.

12 Ibid., 159.

13 Ibid., 154.

14 Aristotle, *Nichomachean Ethics*, Book VIII, Chapter 3, trans. W.D. Ross (University of Adelaide, 2014), http://ebooks.adelaide.edu.au/a/aristotle/nicomachean/contents.html.

15 Aristotle, *Politics*, 159.

16 Hannah Arendt, *The Human Condition*, 2nd edition (Chicago: University of Chicago Press, 1998), 30.

17 Ibid., 63–64.

18 Peter Brown, "The Rise and Function of the Holy Man in Late Antiquity," *The Journal of Roman Studies* 61 (1971).

19 Warren Magnusson, *The Search for Political Space* (Toronto: University of Toronto Press, 1996), 13.

20 George Woodcock, *Anarchism: A History of Libertarian Ideas and Movements* (Toronto: University of Toronto Press, 2004).

21 Jean-Jacques Rousseau, *On the Social Contract* (New York: Dover, 2003), 39.

22 Ibid., Book II, Chapter 9.

23 See, for example, Isaiah Berlin's criticism of what he refers to as the "unchecked sovereignty" that the general will logically leads to, as well as his thoughts on the type of nationalism that Rousseau inspires: Isaiah Berlin, *Two Concepts of Liberty: An Inaugural Lecture Delivered Before the University of Oxford on 31 October 1958* (London: Clarendon, 1959); and Karl Popper, *The Open Society and Its Enemies* (London: Routledge, 2002).

24 Magnusson, *Search for Political Space*, 51.

25

> But for all its [*Das Kapital*'s] unprecedented historical vision, colossal scope and intellectual content, which makes mincemeat of traditional disciplinary boundaries, Marx never saw the need to reflect on the city itself, never really hooked up the development of industrialization (and production) with the development of urbanization (and production of the city).
>
> (Andy Merrifield, *Metromarxism: A Marxist Tale of the City* [New York: Routledge, 2002], 29)

For a more detailed argument concerning Marx's relationship to the city, see the introduction of: Merrifield, *Metromarxism*.

26 Magnusson, *Search for Political Space*, 171.

27 Merrifield, *Metromarxism*, 23.

28 Of course, near the end of his life Marx famously rethought his position on revolution to include the possibility of peasant revolutions. See: Karl Marx, "First Draft of Letter to Vera Zasulich," *MECW*, Volume 24, 346, June 1989, www.marxists.org/archive/marx/works/1881/03/zasulich1.htm.

29 See: Bertell Ollman, "Marx's Use of 'Class'," *The American Journal of Sociology* 3(5) (March 1968). Ollman demonstrates that Marx could only sustain the claim that the proletariat constituted a majority of the population of Europe if he included peasant workers as proletarians.

30 Magnusson, *Search for Political Space*, 12.
31 Gilles Deleuze and Félix Guattari, *A Thousand Plateaus: Capitalism and Schizophrenia*, ed. and trans. Brian Massumi (Minneapolis: University of Minnesota Press, 2004), 460.
32 Ibid., 360.
33 Ibid., 359.
34 Magnusson, *Search for Political Space*, 57.
35 See: Benedict Anderson, *Imagined Communities: Reflections on the Origin and Spread of Nationalism*, new edition (New York: Verso, 2006).
36 Umberto Eco, *Baudolino*, trans. William Weaver (New York: Harcourt, 2000), 86.
37 Ibid., 156.
38 Barber, *If Mayors Ruled the World*, 60.
39 Shapiro, *Time of the City*, 24.
40 Ibid., 26.
41 Bryan S. Turner, "Cosmopolitan Virtue: Loyalty and the City," in *Democracy, Citizenship, and the Global City*, ed. Engin Isin (New York: Routledge, 2000), 130.
42 Magnusson, *Search for Political Space*, 16.
43 Magnusson, *Politics of Urbanism*, 61.
44 Ibid., 282–283.
45 Shapiro, *Time of the City*, 49.
46 Magnusson, *Search for Political Space*, 17. See also: Ash Amin and Nigel Thrift, "The 'Emancipatory' City?" in *The Emancipatory City: Paradoxes and Possibilities*, ed. Loretta Lees (London: SAGE Publications, 2004), 232.
47 Broadbent, *Urban Nation*, 119.
48 I explore Marcuse's thought in greater detail in Chapter 5.
49 One exemplary figure associated with this trend in urbanism is political scientist Richard Dagger, who believes that the city is the most appropriate site of citizenship, but that the contemporary city has become too *large* for this to be meaningful. In this respect, he taps into the insights of Rousseau and Plato, respectively. See: Richard Dagger, "Metropolis, Memory and Citizenship," in *Democracy, Citizenship, and the Global City*, ed. Engin Isin (New York: Routledge, 2002), 34.
50 Magnusson, *Search for Political Space*, 61.
51 Turner, "Cosmopolitan Virtue," 130.
52 Merrifield, *Metromarxism*, 22.

2 Post-Politics and the Ethical Turn in Political Theory

Critical theories of the city are always situated within broader traditions of social and political thought. As debates in these traditions shift our perspectives on social and political phenomena, so too will critical urbanism shift. With this in mind, Chapters 2 and 3 of this book do not deal with anything specific to the city or urban space. Instead they examine the state of critical political theory in order to demonstrate how, as a discipline, it has become increasingly "depoliticized" or "post-political" over the past 40 or so years. The significance of this "post-political turn" for critical urban studies will be explored in Chapters 4 through 7, but suffice it to say that to comprehend the predominant critical approach to understanding the city, one must first be familiar with this theoretical turn in political theory.

Traditionally, the issue of depoliticization has been framed as a debate between conventional leftist discourses like Marxism and those emergent in the latter half of the twentieth century considered more heterodox and associated with postmodernism and identity politics. Anyone already familiar with progressive political theory will be well-versed in the crux of this tired deliberation. The critique of the post-political that I outline in Chapters 2 and 3 seeks to avoid another one-sided rehash of this debate, wherein a caricature of postmodernism and identity politics is presented and denounced decidedly for destroying some imaginary unified left-wing political project. In my opinion, the terms of the controversy require a more nuanced recalibration. Instead of focusing on master categories for anchoring political organizing (class versus race, gender, sexuality), I argue that the discussion should centre on tensions between post-political principles and what I call "properly political" principles, such as inclusion versus exclusion, openness versus closure, and deliberation versus antagonism. In other words, before one can determine what counts as critical political theory, one must have a clear sense of what politics and the political are, which is something lacking in post-political discourse.

What exactly is meant by the "post-political" turn in political theory? Since the 1970s, the character of political theory has changed significantly, especially in the tradition of "critical" political theory, but also in relation to the various schools of liberalism. In terms of the latter, contemporary liberalism has increasingly moved away from representation as the core principle of democracy, and placed the striving toward rational consensus, contained in the form of "deliberative democracy," at the centre of its project.[1] In terms of critical theory, with the advent of various forms of postmodern philosophy and social theory, and the corresponding rise of so-called "identity politics," late twentieth-century or "contemporary" critical thought is commonly perceived as born of a decisive break with the Marxism that dominated left-wing academic thinking for the previous 50 years. Critics have denounced both deliberative democracy and identity politics as post-political. By way of example, liberalism has been taken to task by theorists like Chantal Mouffe for not acknowledging the reality of antagonism in politics, while classical Marxists have attacked the postmodern turn for its inability to establish a moral and political anchor for constructing a progressive political project.[2] As will become clear, I tend to agree with Mouffe's characterization of post-politics but reject, for the most part, the Marxist animosity toward postmodernism. By approaching political theory via a critique of post-politics, one realizes that the fundamental issue at stake is not with which collective one *identifies*, but instead how one relates normatively to *power*.

Taken together, and this is very important for my argument, I call critical theory's post-political shift in the character of critical theorizing the "ethical" turn in political theory. In this context, the term "ethical" and "post-political" are largely interchangeable (and will be used as such throughout this book). Very briefly, the difference between the "political" and the "ethical" is related to the question of power. While the political recognizes the impossibility of living outside of power relations, the ethical is informed by an imperative to negate power. Thus, when I refer to a "properly" political position it first and foremost means a willingness to engage in and employ power in one's collective interests; to recognize and name enemies; to avow political conflict and one's own desire to exert power in such a way that one determines the power relations of society. Conversely, conceiving politics in an ethical register means to assert a false social unity, informed by a fetishized normative relationship to inclusivity and consensus-based political processes. The category "ethics" is useful for thinking about the post-political because it is often used as, not precisely a stand-in for politics, but more like a signifier of politics suffering a subtle slippage of its meaning. That is to say, ethics is commonly invoked as a normative concept in the work of post-political theorists when they ostensibly are discussing politics. Because very few critical theorists recognize their work as post-political, by employing the term ethics in the place of politics, they reveal a symptom of a disavowed post-political position.

Dispersed throughout the rest of this book I will comment specifically on the post-political nature of some of the most prominent contemporary critical-theoretical positions in the humanities and social sciences. In an attempt to demonstrate that the political/post-political debate should not be framed reductively as modernism versus postmodernism, I show instead that the range of post-political theory spans a surprisingly wide swath of political thought. This includes Habermasianism, social democracy, communitarianism, post-structuralism, (post-)anarchism, and even some expressions of (neo-)Marxism.[3] The shared ethical framework of these critical approaches is a kind of moral cosmopolitanism, whether avowed in the case of Habermasianism or disavowed in radical leftist discourses like the various strands of postmodernism and post-structuralism. Such a position, informed by a fear of exerting power in the service of political ends, suggests either (avowedly or disavowedly) that the good life is one outside of coercion, representation, hierarchy, exclusion, and so on. However, if political theory is intended to facilitate political change consonant with these principles, the theoretical and practical outcomes of such a position are counter-productive to its own aims. This is because, from a critical political-economy standpoint, these principles of opposing power relations are *also the stated principles of neoliberal capitalism* (explored in greater detail in the next chapter). Thus, instead of challenging the ideological and structural relations of domination produced by global capital, ethical theory actually enables, in most cases, the smooth functioning of capitalist social relations. On a theoretical level, ethical discourses have an enabling effect largely because they confuse politics and ethics on a conceptual level; they fetishize the ethical and disavow the political (in particular, when it comes to theorizing "democracy" and its relationship to power). By unpacking this conceptual misrecognition of the ethical and the political realms of human behaviour, one can identify core components required for a *re-politicization* of political theory.

The Post-Political and the Ethical

Before I move on to explain how I am using the terms "post-political" and "properly political," I should make a quick clarification in order to avoid confusion for those readers coming from a critical urbanist tradition. In critical urban studies, arguably the most influential theorist of the "post-political hypothesis" is Jacques Rancière. His main thesis is that any given society will be defined by a structure, called the "police," that orders or partitions its constituent elements and claims that this ordering is always legitimate, fair, and just. The police is characterized by normal consensual (post-)politics and an ostensible suturing of the political. However, for Rancière, the police is always defined by an excluded part – a "part which has no part" – understood as marginalized social collectivities deemed has having no authority to speak or contribute to the functioning of the police. *Politics proper* occurs when this "part" disrupts consensus and demands to be included in the police.[4] This has been taken up by critical geographers like Erik Swyngedouw to argue that urban conflicts can be conceptualized as irruptions of politics proper, as in the cases of Occupy Wall Street or Tahrir Square.[5] Similarly, Mark Purcell sees the specifically urban manifestation of Rancière's theorization of the political as something useful for those pursuing social justice in cities, namely, as "against the neo-liberal city, a commodified and privatised city in which property rights and economic growth are the main logic of the urban spatial order."[6] I do not use Rancière's definition of the post-political in this book, although there is certainly some overlap between my understanding of the properly political and his. While his theory possesses some similarities with my own approach, I do not find it as convincing or useful as other formulations of the post-political. The primary issue I have with Rancière's theory is that his understanding of the "properly political" is not characteristic of social relations as such, but only emerges in rare moments of resistance by collective actors railing against exclusion.[7] This is reminiscent of the Event/Act construction popular in some French philosophical circles. From my perspective, the political is always present, if not always (or perhaps even usually) acknowledged and articulated. Furthermore, in Rancière's model, the normative emphasis of the properly political action is a demand for inclusion by the excluded and not, as I argue, the recognition that exclusion is a fundamental and indispensable strategy for properly political action.[8] Instead, I find the position of Chantal Mouffe to be a much more convincing account of the political, and my work should be understood as inspired primarily by Mouffe's left-Schmittian analysis.

Mouffe is an interesting figure because she, in her collaboration with Ernesto Laclau, is connected to the radical break with Marxism in the 1980s, and the emergence of one of its succeeding projects: "radical democracy." In this regard, she is a political theorist that both supports political struggles that emerge from the multiple categories of identity-based oppression, while simultaneously not giving up on a distinctly modern form of understanding politics. In terms of the latter, she draws heavily from the legal philosophy of chief Nazi jurist Carl Schmitt, an ostensibly unlikely and counterintuitive source of inspiration for a radical leftist, to be sure. Clearly Mouffe does not agree with Schmitt's fascist politics, but she very much adheres nonetheless to his definition of the "political":

> Now, for Schmitt, the criterion of the political, its *differentia specifica* is the friend-enemy relation; this involves the creation of a "we" which stands in opposition to a "them", and it is located, from the outset, in the realm of collective identification. The political always has to do with conflicts and antagonisms and cannot but be beyond liberal rationalism since it indicates the limits of any rational consensus and reveals that any consensus is based on acts of exclusion.[9]

For Schmitt, the essence of the political is the antagonistic relation between collective actors defined by the "we/them" qua "friend/enemy" binary. This binary comes into existence, according to Schmitt, via group identity formation based on fundamental components of identity (components outside of rational self-interest) including race, nationalism, religion, and anything else that gives rise to a "we/them" relation.[10] As the essence of the political, this antagonism is posited by Schmitt as the reason liberal democracy is internally contradictory and ultimately impossible. The central contradiction is manifested in the liberal claim that a democratic government is meant to represent the *unity* of a people who are all considered to be *equal*, manifested in an identity between the ruled and the rulers. But what the reality of antagonism shows, according to Schmitt, is that the unity of the people can only be posited when certain groups of people are excluded from its concept, thereby rendering the people unequal and certainly not identical to the ruling regime. Such a principle renders a stable liberal democracy impossible because these constitutive exclusions are bound to lead to eruptions of violence, thereby revealing fundamental political antagonisms; indeed, the possibility of violence is always a condition of the political. It is debated whether Schmitt believed that fascism was a more authentic version of ("organic") democracy than liberalism,[11] but the logic of his position does at least tend that way. Because fascism avows exclusions and represents, as Schmitt suggests, a homogenous and unified population in the form of a conflation of the "nation" and the state, the identity of ruled and rulers is much more plausible under fascism than liberal democracy.

Mouffe draws on Schmitt primarily in terms of his critique of liberalism. In particular, she is concerned with the perceived "post-political" world posited by liberals like Francis Fukuyama. This is imagined as a world in which a general consensus favouring liberal democracy has been reached and, owing to this consensus, all politics going forward is reduced to negotiations amongst experts over technical details related to managing the economy.[12] In this extreme case (the "end of history" thesis), Mouffe asserts that liberal triumphalists have declared the end of political antagonism. But for most liberals the end of history is not an avowed position, but instead the overcoming of antagonism is constructed only as desirable, if not always possible. Mouffe's critique of Rawls, in particular, illustrates the logic of her position. Rawls's procedural conception of justice is based in an individualistic, rationalist conception of human beings who, in the thought-experimental construct of the "original position" operating behind a "veil of ignorance," would agree to a particular notion of institutional justice defined as fairness. For Mouffe, such a deontological position is possible only in the context of a minimalist definition of distributive politics as the only politics appropriate to the public sphere. This type of political liberalism, she claims, relies on:

> relegating pluralism and dissent to the private sphere in order to secure consensus in the public realm. All controversial issues are taken off the agenda in order to create the conditions for a "rational" consensus. As a result, the realm of politics becomes merely the terrain where individuals, stripped of their "disruptive" passions and beliefs and understood as rational agents in search of self-advantage – within the constrains of morality, of course – submit to procedures for adjudicating between their claims that they consider "fair."[13]

Mouffe argues that liberalism can only understand politics in terms of consensus by denying some of the most important aspects of human identity that motivates them to act: the "passions," as she refers to them.[14] One's religious beliefs, one's gender, one's sexuality, one's class position, and one's sense of national identity, are all to be stripped away in the original position, despite the fact that it is these very categories that often constitute the core of political identity and drive individuals to act politically. In other words, these "private" considerations are quite regularly the pivots around which groups are formed. This leads to a further negation of the political engendered by liberalism because it does not recognize that in the political realm, the analyst encounters primarily collective actors, and not individuals.[15] As such, when conflicts break out between actors defined by religious or ethnic differences, liberalism can only deem such actors "irrational" and unable to participate in the deliberative process of rational consensus formation. The lesson to be drawn from recognizing and embracing the importance of private aspects of identity in the antagonistic political arena is that what is considered "irrational" from a post-political perspective is rendered intelligible. As Mouffe puts it: "To negate the political does not make it disappear; it only leads to bewilderment in the face of its manifestations and to impotence in dealing with them."[16]

Mouffe's use of Schmitt to critique liberalism is not employed to challenge democracy, but instead to save it from its current identity with liberalism (and, of course, against Schmitt's association of democracy with fascism). For her, the key is to create a political order that manages antagonisms instead of negating them; one in which the "friend/enemy" duality is replaced by "friend/adversary." This, Mouffe calls "agonistic pluralism" and is meant to provide a new self-conception of democracy (replacing rational-consensus striving) defined by agonism instead of antagonism. In Schmitt's formulation, the relationship between friend and enemy is one of mutual hostility to the existence of the other, and therefore the aim of the political is to annihilate the other. In contrast, the "friend/adversary" binary is one in which the competitors recognize the legitimacy of the other to defend their position, but nonetheless compete for hegemony within a mutually accepted democratic framework. In this way, the aim of competition is not to destroy the other, or the system in which agonism exists, but to fundamentally change the relations of power within it. Mouffe, therefore, incorporates the Schmittian concept of the political into a pluralist-democratic framework:

> Conflict, in order to be accepted as legitimate, needs to take a form that does not destroy the political association. This means that some kind of common bond must exist between the parties in conflict, so that they will not treat their opponents as enemies to be eradicated, seeing their demands as illegitimate, which is precisely what happens with the antagonistic friend/enemy relation. However, the opponents cannot be seen simply as competitors whose interests can be dealt with through mere negotiation, or reconciled through deliberation, because in that case the antagonistic element would simply have been eliminated.[17]

In other words, the structures are familiarly democratic, but the relation among actors is discursively different than those of contemporary liberalism because the goal is not rational consensus, but hegemony.

For present purposes, Mouffe's agonistic pluralism or theory of radical democracy is not of pre-eminent importance. Indeed, I share many of the same concerns regarding "radical democracy" that Mouffe's critics voice against her work, in particular an internal difficulty reconciling the practice of hegemony with the required shared democratic framework of agonistic struggle.[18] Instead, from my perspective the pressing issue is to tease out the implications of one aspect of her Schmittian understanding of the political – the necessity and reality of exclusions in political action. Mouffe's position here is multilayered, and the category of exclusion can be understood in several ways. The most important insight is that exclusions are simply an ontological reality of politics. Because collective actors create a "them" in the process of formulating a "we," they practice a sort of constitutive exclusion. While the actors in a relationship of Mouffian agonism do not strive to destroy their adversaries, nor do they aim to exclude them from agonistic democratic struggle, they do seek to exclude their interests from contributing to the constitution of the order of power relations in society. Mouffe contends that the type of ethical orientation that has come to dominate critical theory denies this, and is constituted by a fundamental disavowal of constitutive exclusion produced in political struggles. This is apparent even in radical leftist circles. I argue that even when Rawls or Habermas are explicitly denounced by, say, self-identified socialists or anarchists, a certain fetishization of inclusion and consensus nonetheless typically abides. In other words, the post-political extends much further beyond liberalism. For critical theory, perhaps the fundamental lesson to learn from Mouffe's critique is that "every order is political and based on some form of exclusion."[19]

Political theorist Jodi Dean is another thinker who has raised concerns with the ethical turn. While Dean uses the language of the post-political, she approaches it from a more Žižekian/Lacanian framework, and characterizes it in terms of the rejection of specific political categories, rather than as a broad ontological generalization. But she also distinguishes between "politics" and "ethics." The term "ethics" is employed by Dean because she has noted its increasing usage in place of "politics" in critical-theoretical literature. This she interprets as symptomatic of a dwindling emphasis on the importance of encouraging *collective* political action, and a rise in individualizing and interpersonal discourses in contemporary critical theory. In a post on her blog *I Cite*, she outlines the character of this shift toward ethics as a series of "crimes" that traditional (modern) political theory is guilty of, which can then be interpreted as prohibitions against particular types of political thought and action. I will cite her post at length here (taking some liberties with the format of the original post):

> Once the New Left delegitimized the old one, it made political will into an offense, a crime with all sorts of different elements:
>
> 1 taking the place or speaking for another (the crime of representation);
> 2 obscuring other crimes and harms (the crime of exclusion);
> 3 judging, condemning, and failing to acknowledge the large terrain of complicating factors necessarily disrupting simple notions of agency (the crime of dogmatism);
> 4 employing dangerous totalizing fantasies that posit an end of history and lead to genocidal adventurism (the crime of utopianism or, as Mark Fisher so persuasively demonstrates, of adopting a fundamentally irrational and unrealistic stance, of failing to concede to the reality of capitalism).

However, she continues:

> But a politics without representation, exclusion, dogmatism, and utopianism is no politics at all. It is instead an ethics. Is it any surprise, then, that under neoliberalism ostensible leftists spend countless hours and pages and keystrokes elaborating ethics? The ethics of this or the ethics of that, fundamentally personal and individual approaches that obscure and deny the systems and structures in which they are embedded?[20]

In terms of her crime #2 – exclusion – Dean is speaking to a common criticism of what is typically referred to as "identity politics," represented by the multiplicity of new social movements that flourished in the late twentieth century. Many groups during this time attempted to assert themselves politically by bringing their marginalized or repressed voices into the public sphere: women, LGBQT communities, racialized minorities, indigenous peoples, and people with disabilities. This was an incredibly important period, both for the Left and for political theory, in general. Indeed, at this time it became increasingly evident that it was imperative for the Left to move away from a mostly white, Western, and heteronormative theoretical position and membership base. This newfound self-awareness radically opened the Left to a re-theorizing of the nature of power and identity, but more than anything it taught the Left to be *inclusive*.

In some respects, inclusivity is obviously an important value to internalize for any progressive political movement. Pragmatically speaking, the more inclusive a social movement, the greater political traction it can create and the more power it can wield (at least to a point; there clearly are diminishing returns). In terms of social justice, inclusivity is important because for far too long the specific interests of certain marginalized groups were not acknowledged on the Left, since it was dominated by white, male, masculinist, and European voices. But there is a fine line between being inclusive and not distinguishing between friend and adversary, which is the condition of properly political organizing; it is a short road from inclusivity to consensus. What happens when the emphasis on inclusivity leads to delusional accounts that "we" constitutes "all"? What happens when there is no longer any recognition of a constitutive outside – a "they," as it were? This was manifest during the period of the ethical turn in a new desire to maximize inclusion, while disavowing that this desire is de facto one for consensus. Such a desire became embodied in grand postmodern categories like Hardt and Negri's "Multitude," or Giddens's "the people"[21] who are situated in the "radical centre" that exists beyond left and right.[22]

Perhaps no contemporary form of critical theory represents this fear of engaging in power more than so-called "post-anarchism." Embedded in Deleuze and Guattari's theory of "nomadicism," post-anarchists conceptualize freedom as resisting power; it does not abide structures or representation, in fact, it creates a normative imperative to actively flee them. With such an avowed desire to avoid power relations, the creation of a normatively acceptable "we" against a well-defined "them," is conceptually unintelligible. The prefix "post" is attached to "anarchism" because thinkers associated with this school are interested in theorizing a political project that is informed by the organizational principles of anarchism, but without the explicit humanism found in the work of classical anarchist theorists like Kropotkin.[23] Richard Day, for example, challenges the logic of Gramscian hegemony and counter-hegemony because it requires the exertion of power relations.[24] Similarly, Todd May invokes Deleuze's idea of "becoming minor" as a curative to power. Becoming minor is a strategy of resistance to domination that avoids asserting one's self or ideas at the top of a hierarchical relationship of power with others, as May claims (referencing Deleuze): "That utilization [of routes, of lines of flight], however, must remain a 'minor' one: the task of becoming-minor is precisely that; it is not a task of making the minor dominant."[25] Lewis Call, on the other hand, relies on a theory of "anarcho-becoming" which finds itself in a constant war with "micro-fascism."[26] And finally, Saul Newman seeks to develop a political theory that can conceptualize human subjectivity and political action (resistance) outside of power relations.[27] He claims, that the task of post-anarchism is to develop an anarchist morality that would allow all identities to take part in resistance. But this begs the question: if all identities are involved, who exactly are they struggling against? It gets no more post-political than this.[28]

In these sorts of discourses, collective actors are constructed not against other actors (i.e., people), but against abstract social structures, systems, or process like "Empire," "becoming fascist," or "hegemony." This type of theorizing is based on a generalized fear of excluding and suggests a depoliticizing logic: if you want to ensure that you eliminate all exclusions, you can do so by avoiding all *distinctions*. In this way, much of critical theory came to deny one of the fundamental realities of the political: all collective identity formation is power-laden in that it is based on constitutive exclusions. There is no Left "we" without an external adversary "they." This actually implies a double negation of the political. First, if all people are constituted as a "we" pitted against a system or structure, and not a "them," the human element of political struggle is erased (the system cannot be considered a "them"). Second, it implies that once the said system or structure has been defeated or removed, all people qua "we" will be better off (as if in the moment of negating antagonisms – which were never acknowledged in the first place – consensus forms and conflict ceases).

The logic of this position can be illustrated by once again returning to Dean's crimes of the New Left as an articulation of the Schmittian conception of the political. Speaking in the context of the Occupy-inspired slogan of the 1 percent versus the 99 percent, she demonstrates how Occupy constructed itself in an exclusionary manner by recognizing an enemy (the 1 percent) with whom there is no potential for dialogue, because the "division goes all the way down – antagonism is fundamental, irreducible."[29] As opposed to a structure or system, Occupy constructed its identity through an antagonistic relationship with *actual, identifiable* people (those in the 1 percent of wealth ownership). This is not to say that political groups should avoid including structures like capitalism as part of the enemy or adversary, but that it is post-political if at the same time those who benefit from the system remain unnamed or inculpable. While Occupy had its own post-political challenges (e.g., consensus-based democracy at General Assemblies), on a conceptual level the 99 percent versus the 1 percent does point to a willingness to practice an exclusion, if not in its practice, at least in its rhetoric. By recognizing that properly political action always includes constitutive exclusions of those marked as adversaries or enemies (depending on the context), actors acknowledge the need to exert power; a willingness to concede their complicity in and desire for unequal power relations. If one claims to act politically in the absence of such guiding principles, I argue, one is positing a false identity between the ethical and political.

Having said all this, one should not overstate the difference between these ethical and political spheres of social action. Indeed, Mouffe has been justly criticized for disavowing that her vision of transforming enemies into adversaries is premised on an (inclusionary) moral judgment and, therefore, some level of consensus-building is inherent to any attempt at hegemonic politics.[30] Indeed, it would be unintelligible not to desire as much agreement as possible; otherwise politics inevitably devolves into an incoherent factionalism. However, one could flip the critique of Mouffe's disavowed inclusionary moral foundation for her theory of politics, and claim that her recognition of *exclusion* as a condition of the political must be treated as an ethical judgment at some level; it must be ethically acceptable to practice exclusion in one's politics, because this is what just power relations requires. While ethics and politics are not identical, they are still inextricably united in all social thought and action. Human subjects are imbued with and, in part, constituted by ethical principles, and those ethics are largely what informs their politics. However, when one becomes engaged in a political struggle, those constitutive and guiding ethics are challenged, perverted, or in some cases, suspended in the face of the reality of antagonism, power, and the demand to *succeed*. Politics possesses a sort of excess that can never be contained by the ethical, and the ethical is unsettled by the excess of the political. In the political there are no assurances of the purity of the ethical, and therefore the ethical requires the ability to anticipate its own contamination in the course of political action. It must be prepared to make consolations, compromises, and suspensions of its own pretences once political demands reveal its limitations. In the absence of such a reflexive predisposition (reflexive in terms of being aware of the risk involved in properly political action), political action is bound to fail, and while *winning* isn't everything when it comes to politics, it is absurd to suggest that it is not a core aspiration of the political. To formulate an abstract ethical model of living together – premised on inclusion or, more properly, *non-exclusion* – followed by a *call to arms*, or an incitement to *create a better world* in the image of that framework, is insufficient for properly *political* theory; it amounts to nothing more than an empty desire for change, an impotent expression of outrage over the state of things.

Returning to Dean's insight regarding the increasing use of the term "ethics" in left-wing discourse, consider the concluding chapter of almost any recently published critical work that attempts to rethink progressive politics by arguing that first we need to reform the dominant forms of *subjectivization*, or our *ethical relations to others*.[31] The abstract ethical in these cases reflects a desire to live outside of power, while the political recognizes the reality of power. In Chantal Mouffe's formulation, the "aim" of the "adversary" in the political realm is a "profound transformation of the existing power relations and the establishment of a new hegemony."[32] In today's political landscape, this requires a Left ready to unapologetically draw lines between us and them as adversaries, a commitment to challenging the false veneer of post-political politics, and a bold plan for rearranging social power. In this respect, the Left can learn a lot from the neoliberal and neo-conservative Right, who have been more than willing and capable of acting politically for a long time now. For example, Thomas Medvetz brilliantly outlines how the American conservative movement has organized itself in properly political terms over the past couple of decades. In order to develop a hegemonic bloc (not Medvetz's term), the Grover Norquist-led conservative right established and continuously reproduced a "we/them" dualism by drawing strong social and political lines for inclusion/exclusion, namely, you can be considered a part of the conservative "movement" if you are avowedly pro-baby, pro-guns, and anti-tax. Otherwise, you're out.[33] Medvetz's essay can be considered an instructional guide to building a political movement and acting (properly) politically.

In summary, the problem with the ethical turn is that, when fetishized, the abstract ethical suspends the political or pretends to be identical to it. Criticizing the "social scientific" thinking of much political theory, Warren Magnusson states: "social sciences leave the political behind (in the domain of the state) or project it into the realm of ethics (where it can be expressed in pious wishes or moral injunctions)."[34] In other words, ethics cannot perform the function of politics. Instead, politics exposes and exceeds the limits of ethics and radically ruptures its promise of living outside of power. It is this distinct character of the political that political theorists should engage with in such a way that it complements and contrasts explorations of the ethical. This position challenges political theory to avoid disavowing that which defines it as an academic discipline – the political.

There is, then, something inherently post-political about most schools of critical theory predominant in academia today. In all cases, from left liberalism to post-anarchism, there exists a sometimes explicitly and other times implicitly overstated normative emphasis on openness and inclusion. Such an emphasis is symptomatic of a desire to live outside of power relations; to avoid promoting a politics that possesses the very essence of the political: "us versus them" dualisms. What has brought the academic and, to a lesser extent, the activist Left to this point? Why does it matter? What, exactly, is at stake for the Left in embracing or disavowing the properly political? What are the consequences of continuously reproducing post-political analyses? Why should we not be satisfied with a politics that is actually an ethics?

Notes

1 Jodi Dean, "The Democratic Deadlock," *Theory and Event* 10(4) (2007): paragraph 7.
2 See for example John Sanbonmatsu, *The Postmodern Prince: Critical Theory, Left Strategy, and the Making of a New Political Subject* (New York: Monthly Review Press, 2003), in which he unmercifully criticizes the New Left of the 1960s that set the foundation for postmodernism and identity politics.
3 I am concerned primarily with schools of "critical" theory, which are constituted by a very diverse set of approaches to politics. However, for a theory to be considered "critical" it must be, at the bare minimum, defined in opposition to or critical of really existing liberal democratic/capitalist regimes of thought. Thus, I do not investigate liberal thought in this chapter (except to the extent it helps clarify Mouffe's concept of the political), despite the fact that liberalism has also been influenced by the ethical turn.
4 Jacques Rancière, *Dis-agreement*, trans. J. Rose (Minneapolis: University of Minnesota Press, 1995).
5 Erik Swyngedouw, "Designing the Post-Political City and the Insurgent Polis," *Civic City Cahier* 5 (London: Bedford Press, 2011).
6 Mark Purcell, "Rancière and Revolution," *Space and Polity* 18(2) (2015): 168–169.
7 Ibid.
8 In the secondary literature on Rancière, it is at times unclear the extent to which his understanding of politics proper is primarily inclusionary (i.e., recognizing the marginalized as legitimate actors within the police), or revolutionary (i.e., fundamentally changing the nature of the police), as Mustafa Dikeç argues in: "Space, Politics, and the Political," *Environment and Planning D: Society and Space* 23 (2005): 171–188.
9 Chantal Mouffe, *The Return of the Political* (New York: Verso, 1993), 123.
10 Carl Schmitt, *The Concept of the Political*, trans. George Schwab (Chicago: University of Chicago Press, 2007), 72
11 See: Paul Gottfried, *Carl Schmitt: Politics and Theory* (Westport: Greenwood Press, 1990).
12 This is also how Slavoj Žižek defines post-politics: "a politics which claims to leave behind old ideological struggles and instead focus on expert management and administration" (Slavoj Žižek, *Violence: Six Sideways Reflections* [New York: Picador, 2008], 40).
13 Mouffe, *Return of the Political*, 140.
14 Ibid., 140.
15 Ibid., 140.
16 Mouffe, "Politics and the Limits of Liberalism," 120.
17 Chantal Mouffe, *On the Political* (New York: Routledge, 2005), 20.
18 Stefan Rummens, "Democracy as a Non-Hegemonic Struggle? Disambiguating Chantal Mouffe's Agonistic Model of Politics," *Constellations* 16(3) (2009): 377–391; Mathias Thaler, "The Illusion of Purity: Chantal Mouffe's Realist Critique of Cosmopolitanism," *Philosophy and Social Criticism* 36(7) (2010): 785–800.
19 Mouffe, *On the Political*, 18.
20 Jodi Dean, "Inept or Unwilling?" *I Cite*, last updated November 20, 2010, accessed December 10, 2013, http://jdeanicite.typepad.com/i_cite/2010/11/inept-or-unwilling.html.
21 Chantal Mouffe, *The Democratic Paradox* (New York: Verso, 2000), 121.
22 Ibid., 109.
23 As Saul Newman puts it, anarchism is just as guilty of essentialism as other types of modern thought because it posits an immutable human nature and natural laws (Saul Newman, *From Bakunin to Lacan: Anti-Authoritarianism and Dislocation of Power* [Lanham: Lexington Books, 2001], 38).
24 Richard Day, *Gramsci is Dead: Anarchist Currents in the Newest Social Movements* (London: Pluto Press, 2005).

25 Todd May, *The Political Philosophy of Poststructuralist Anarchism* (University Park: Penn State Press, 2005), 115.
26 Lewis Call, *Postmodern Anarchism* (Lanham: Lexington Books, 2002), 52–53.
27

> I argue that resistance must not refer to essentialist foundations if it is to avoid reaffirming domination. This is because, as I will have shown, the place of power is inexorably linked to essentialism: universal and totalizing politics that deny difference inevitably flow from essentialist notions. So the next chapter … will try to delineate, using the non-essentialist place I have just developed, a politics of resistance without foundations – a politics which rejects universalizing and totalizing tendencies.
>
> (Newman, Bakunin to Lacan, 10)

28 If there is any doubt that Newman's book epitomizes my charge that the Left has a tendency to treat ethics as if they were politics, one need only examine the title and subtitles of his concluding chapter to *From Bakunin to Lacan*. The chapter's title is "Towards a Politics of Postanarchism." "Politics" is present: so far so good. He also includes two short subsections that contain a variant of the word political in the titles: "Politics in the Age of Uncertainty" and "Politics Beyond Identity." But the clear emphasis of his conclusion is on ethics: "Ethical Limits" is the major sub-divider in the chapter, while "Ethics without Ground," "Anarchist Ethics," and "Ethics of Postanarchism" dominate the text. The point I'm trying to make is that despite what the chapter's title promises to deal with – politics – it quickly devolves into a discussion of ethics and, more specifically, an ethics driven by maximizing inclusion and eschewing power.
29 Jodi Dean, *The Communist Horizon* (New York: Verso, 2012), 100.
30 Thaler, "Illusion of Purity," 795. It should be noted that Thaler's criticism is directed specifically at Mouffe's argument for rethinking *international relations* in a properly political register, and therefore one must consider issues of scale when mobilizing her approach to the properly political.
31 For examples of two critical theorists who are virulently opposed to postmodernism and identity politics, but still supply a weak (read: ethical) conclusion for moving forward with a progressive political project, see Sanbonmatsu, *The Postmodern Prince*; and Stanley Aronowitz, *Left Turn: Forging a New Political Future* (Boulder: Paradigm Press, 2006).
32 Mouffe, *On the Political*, 52.
33 Thomas Medvetz, "The Strength of Weekly Ties: Relations of Material and Symbolic Exchange in the Conservative Movement," *Politics & Society* 34(3) (2006).
34 Magnusson, "Politicizing the Global City," 291.

3 Ethics as a Symptom of Late Capitalism

> The freedom to be happy restricts human freedom if you are not free to be not happy.[1]

The previous chapter distinguished between two modes of conceptualizing politics: the political and the ethical. The conceptual distinction between these two categories centres on the question of power: how is power conceived normatively, who has power and how should it be distributed, and overall what should the Left's relationship to power be? Much of contemporary critical theory contains an imperative to denounce power, refuse to exert it over others, and a deep desire to live outside of it: this is the ethical. The political, on the other hand, acknowledges power relations as both normative and necessary; it recognizes the inherently agonistic nature of politics and acknowledges the necessity of exclusions in its practice.

In this chapter, the discussion of the ethical turn in political theory is extended by exploring the ethical turn as a symptom of changes in global capitalism, from the Fordist mode to post-Fordism. In effect, I argue that the values associated with post-Fordist capitalist relations are mirrored in the normative commitments of the critical theory literature. This is illustrated starkly in contemporary leftist discourses of democracy, primarily in terms of the academic literature, but also in respect to left-wing political activism. Such an exploration can be undertaken by subjecting the ethical turn to a psychoanalytic reading, as outlined by Slavoj Žižek, Jodi Dean, and Wendy Brown. A psychoanalytic approach helps us understand the ethical turn as symptomatic of something greater than, say, simply a fear of reproducing Stalinist authoritarianism in any New Left project, or a generalized fear of excluding marginalized voices. Like the critique of ethical theory in the previous chapter, my concern is not that the ethical turn undermines the Left by fragmenting the grounds for solidarity along identarian political lines, but that the possibility of political antagonism is weakened.

To the extent the ethical turn is, indeed, symptomatic of changes in capitalist organization, it is related both to material political economy and to discursive affect (the way in which a certain desire for the values associated with the ethical turn are engendered in us). In this respect, following Žižek's theoretical framework, the ethical turn is very much connected to the way in which *enjoyment* is produced and regulated by advanced capitalist social relations. The oft-disavowed enjoyment that subjects receive from capitalism, Žižek argues, is identical to the type of enjoyment promoted by ethical theory. Therefore, he posits a non-adversarial, enabling relationship between ethical theory (which he calls "liberal communism") and contemporary capitalism. I conclude this chapter by subjecting the ideal of democracy to a similar analysis, and in the process outline some very basic principles that might work toward politicizing both contemporary critical theory and the Left as a collective movement. This includes a willingness to rethink what has become gospel for the Left: the identity of democracy and ethical values like inclusion. To be successful, I argue that contemporary progressive political movements require an avowed willingness to *exclude*; to determine who is in and who is out of the group and, therefore, in a directly anti-cosmopolitan move, determine who is more worthy of consideration than others (given specific contexts). This implies that the Left should re-conceptualize the inherently limited nature of political community and democracy in such a way as to recognize their spatial and social limits, as well as their constitutive anti-democratic elements.

Žižek and the Cultural Ethics of Capitalism

Slavoj Žižek appears to have very little respect for most of his peers working in the tradition of critical political theory. In fact, he has claimed that outside of a select few,[2] critical academics are the most dangerous type of scholar because, while they might purport to be radical or revolutionary, the actual logic of their positions tend to be quite conservative – not in the sense that, say, orthodox Marxists are conservative leftists, but in the sense that the logic of their politics helps conserve capitalism.[3] While such critical theorists self-identify as radical critics of existing society, for Žižek they are really just expressing left-liberal or cosmopolitan commitments. Here he conflates a number of critical positions (similar to the analysis of "ethical theory" in Chapter 2), into a single category: "liberal communism," which refers to a perspective whose adherents "no longer accept the opposition between Davos and Porto Alegre: their claim is that we can have the global capitalist cake (thrive as entrepreneurs) and eat it (endorse the anti-capitalist causes of social responsibility, ecological concern etc)."[4] When defining liberal communism he has in mind figures associated with the transnational elite, such as Bill Gates, Bono, George Soros, and journalists such as Thomas Friedman. But he goes further than just identifying these elite public figures by including the "new breed of anti-globalist left radicals" whose ideology has become "almost indistinguishable" from the liberal communists (he names only Antonio Negri specifically, at least in this section of *Violence*).[5] Despite this conflation of neoliberals and critical theorists, it is clear that his main target is "postmodernism," broadly speaking (including both the "affirmative" and "sceptical" variants as taxonomized by Pauline Rosenau[6]). Žižek claims that whereas adherents to such a liberal-communist position invariably list capitalism as a source of oppression in the world (along with racism, sexism, and so on), their prescriptive response tends to be a call for more tolerance, respect for difference, and the protection of human rights. While he acknowledges that these are certainly noble goals in the abstract, there is no necessary connection between them and an anti-capitalist position. In fact, for Žižek, not only does postmodernism lack any significant anti-capitalist foundation, but by advocating normative principles that stress tolerance, experimentation, or the value of "transgressive" enjoyment, postmodernism actually *feeds* and complements the contemporary form of capitalism. This is because, from a Žižekian perspective, the cultural logic of capitalism is not what it used to be; it is no longer based in Fordist relations of homogenous mass production and consumption, but in the production of subjects seeking constantly new and unmitigated forms of enjoyment. Most critical academics, he argues, have not re-theorized their mid-twentieth-century critique of capitalism in order to account for this fundamental shift.

Žižek claims that the cultural ethics of late capitalism have changed radically – they are reversed, in a way – since the re-organization of capitalism along post-Fordist lines. In this sense, he agrees with the standard political-economy analysis that mid-twentieth-century capitalism was defined by the imperative that mass production be partnered with the ability of the population to mass consume. This leads to "Fordism," a mode of capitalist regulation that encourages high employment and generous wages for workers in order to avoid devastating economic downturns or crises of over-production. Fordism is defined not just by the ability of capitalist firms to mass-produce goods, but by a highly limited (in material terms) form of mass production: single-run conveyor-belt style production. In other words, Fordist production technologies were limited by their ability to produce only a single (or, at least very limited number) model of a product, albeit in great quantities, in any given factory. The result was that while consumers were offered a significant number of reasonably priced goods to purchase (e.g., washing machines, refrigerators, toasters), the diversity of choices in terms of a particular commodity was limited; everyone could afford a car, as long as it was the Model-T (other models were prohibitively expensive for average consumers). In terms of a cultural ethic, obviously consumerism was the core value that needed to be instilled in populations to ensure Fordism's success. However, such consumerism had to correspond to the production technologies of the time, and therefore consumers required a cultural desire for *sameness*; they all had to want a similar bundle of goods that did not significantly diverge in terms of design or brand-name. This conservative approach to consumption matched well with the generally conservative nature of North American and Western European society during this period. Gendered social roles were strongly taken for granted and most middle-class people aspired to achieve conventional lifestyles defined by the nuclear family supported by a single-income male bread-winner, and the unremunerated labour of a contented housewife. The male head of the family fully expected to work in a single career for his entire life, and retire with a lucrative or moderate pension that would suffice to cover the costs of both himself and his wife in their later years.

Oh, how things have changed. It is now generally agreed that we live in a post-Fordist world. Like its predecessor, the standard political economy model for understanding post-Fordism is related to the organization of production. In the late 1960s, the world witnessed a series of significant advances in production and transportation technology, which revolutionized capitalist social relations. This included mixed-model production and shipping container technologies. These technological advances allowed for a revolution in the logic of production, which has now come to be called "just-in-time production." Just-in-time production negates the imperatives of Fordist production in that it allows for much smaller runs of single-model commodities at reasonable costs, and can produce a much greater diversity of commodity types in vast numbers. This was both a great opportunity and a problem for capitalism, because it now had the ability to saturate the world market with an unprecedented number of new and diverse products, but the existing cultural values of mass consumption were not congruent with the new production potential. The ethic of homogenous consumerism that defined Fordist production had now become archaic. A new consumerist ethic was required to encourage the appropriate form of consumption – one based in a desire for novelty, difference, standing out from the crowd, and, in general, individualized personal expression instead of conforming to conventional social norms.[7]

This is widely considered the genesis of a certain strain of neoliberal cultural discourse used to shift social norms slowly away from the previous, more collectivist, conformist, and conservative set of normative values, and toward more individualist, rebellious, and experimental attitudes regarding enjoyment and the good life. This shift begins in the 1960s with hippy, new age, and radical political youth culture's rejection of the older generation's rigid and conservative worldview, and is now fully established in Gen-X, and Millennial relationships to consumption, work, sexuality, and conceptions of freedom. Neoliberal discourse, it is argued, individualizes successes and failures, "entrepreneurializes" the subject-as-worker, and instils a widespread cynicism of formal political structures and processes. The result is several generations of consumers enthralled by novelty; a desire to express one's individuality and uniqueness through, if not idiosyncratic, at least personalized fashion choices and other commodity purchases. This type of relationship to consumption allows post-Fordist capitalism to continuously produce and sell more and more slightly differentiated products in the absence of any pressing social need for them, unlike under Fordism when products maintained a much higher level of obvious use-value for consumers as they were built to last (versus the intentional obsolescence of post-Fordism). We know on an intellectual level that this form of consumption is unsustainable both socially (in that stagnating wages and growing consumer debt will challenge the very underlining mechanism of capitalist growth) and environmentally (pollution and finite resources). However, this rational acknowledgement of the problem does not seem to matter, and points to the astonishing ideological strength of this relatively new discourse. But this is a well-worn narrative, and there is nothing new for me to add to the huge body of literature devoted to the empirical and discursive aspects of neoliberal consumerism. What I am interested in exploring further is how this discursive constellation is reproduced philosophically in critical social and political theory.

Enjoying Capitalism

For Žižek, this shift from the cultural ethic of Fordism to that of post-Fordism cannot be fully understood by approaching it exclusively from the level of political-economic analysis. The novelty of Žižek's critique is that he submits the entire cultural edifice of capitalism to psychoanalysis. In so doing, the cultural logic of late capitalism is understood not simply as a change in consumer preferences, but instead as nothing less than a radical reorientation of our desire in relationship to enjoyment, and the toppling of a two-millennia-old (Christian) Symbolic Law. This necessarily requires a brief summary of Žižek's Lacanian understanding of the relationship between subjectivity and enjoyment.

For Žižek, in classical Lacanian style, the subject is defined by an irreducible lack at its very core; a lack produced at the moment the subject becomes subject (when it misrecognizes itself as unified or whole). This lack produces desire in the subject in that it continuously strives to achieve the experience of pre-symbolic wholeness, which was violently ruptured upon entry into the Symbolic Order, or the entry into language. At this point of emerging as lack, humans spend the rest of their lives seeking enjoyment in order to fill that constitutive absence, but full satisfaction is impossible because lack is a structural condition of subjectivity; if the subject experiences full satisfaction, subjectivity dissolves into the terrifying pre-symbolic Real. Nonetheless, subjects are animated by the search for enjoyment and become addicted to the "partial" pleasures that, in this case, capitalist culture provides. This type of addictive behaviour, whereby the subject continuously pursues full satisfaction, despite its impossibility, is called "drive." The logic of drive is one in which the subject becomes caught in a closed circuit – circling the object of desire, often resulting in self-destructive behaviour. For Žižek, contemporary capitalist social relations harness this peculiar human tendency by destroying all psychological barriers to the pursuit of enjoyment – all social taboos and, as much as possible, legal prohibitions to enjoyment. The result being that the subject is confronted with an endless set of options for pleasure, and this leads to all kinds of complicated social phenomena.

For psychoanalysis, enjoyment and the prohibition of enjoyment are mediated by the superego, the psychic structure responsible for creating moral imperatives against certain types of social thought and behaviour. The superego operates both ontogenetically (at the level of the individual), and phylogenetically (at the level of the species or culture). Žižek argues that the Fordist cultural superego is represented by Mosaic Law ("The Ten Commandments") and manifested philosophically in Kant's categorical imperative. The Kantian superego imperative is a positive one in that it is duty-based, but negative in the sense that the context of one's duty is largely constituted by a series of prohibitions: the Mosaic Decalogue of "Thou Shalt Nots." Furthermore, one's duty is tied to the moral absolutism of God as Symbolic Authority, or Big Other. In this sense, the moral Law as manifested in the individual's superego is driven by an imperative or duty containing the following logic: "You can, because you must!" This is, according to Žižek, the dominant orientation toward enjoyment that has characterized

Western subjectivity for nearly 2,000 years: one enjoys doing one's duty, even when this duty is based on denying a wide spectrum of human desire, especially the desire for physical and sexual pleasure. In contrast, the new post-Fordist categorical imperative – the "superego injunction to enjoy" – is informed by the logic: "You must, because you can!" The logic is that with God no longer acting as the Symbolic Authority, one must only show fidelity to one's own desire. In other words, with the overthrow of Christian moral prohibitions, the subject is now in a position to enjoy in an unmitigated manner; in the absence of taboos, previously used to justify the inability to fully enjoy, the subject has no excuses not to be enjoying! While the new superego commandment to enjoy comes with its own peculiar set of prohibitions,[8] it is experienced consciously as a radical freedom, one both produced and appropriated by post-Fordist capitalism to sell products, service and, most of all, *experiences*. This produces a peculiar reversal of one of the primary traditional roles of the superego: guilt production. Instead of developing guilt for desiring to transgress moral prohibitions (i.e., the desire to sin), guilt actually accrues in the subject for *not transgressing enough*!

How does all this relate to a critique of the ethical turn? The most obvious connection is that the postmodern deconstruction of traditional cultural values and celebration of transgressive experiences actually *helps* produce the ideal contemporary capitalist subject, which then contributes to the smooth functioning and reproduction of capitalist social relations. Neoliberal capitalism thrives, indeed, *depends* on populations comprised of highly individualized subjects; subjects unhindered by social prohibitions of their desires. To express one's self freely and transgressively – understood to be so politically subversive for the hippies, situationists, and third-wave feminists – is precisely the type of social value that late twentieth-century capital encourages so as to better understand what and how to sell things to people more effectively. After all, post-Fordist production techniques made it possible for counter- or sub-cultural groups to become highly lucrative consumption markets. From Žižek's perspective, it is no coincidence, then, that the various forms of postmodern and identity politics that came to dominate late twentieth-century critical thought emerged simultaneously with a re-organization of capitalism according to neoliberal logics. Such transgressive phenomena and individualized politics are not considered in any way a challenge to capital, but rather as a *symptom* of it. Sanbonmatsu expresses this position well in his critique of "expressivism," which he associates with Michel Foucault:

> The expressivist aesthetic enabled a qualitative deepening of commodity logics in the lifeworld. Foucault's call for an ethic of "care of the self" would become the rallying cry of global capitalism which was happy to oblige by engineering new desires and products for individuals in multiple niche markets.[9]

But it is none other than the arch-postmodernist Jean Baudrillard who expressed it most eloquently almost 40 years ago:

> This compulsion toward liquidity, flow, and an accelerated circulation of what is psychic, sexual, or pertaining to the body is the exact replica of the force which rules market value; capital must circulate; gravity and any fixed point must disappear; the chain of investments and reinvestments must never stop; value must radiate endlessly and in every direction. This is the form itself which the current realization of value takes. It is the form of capital, and sexuality as a catchword and a *model* is the way it appears at the level of bodies.[10]

Just as Marx noted that capital melts all that is solid into air, so too does post-Fordist capitalism radically seek to undermine and dissolve all previous social taboos that frustrate consumption. While it is widely agreed that a transgressive ethic, unaccompanied by a concrete strategy to gain power, is easily co-opted into a consumerist ethic, the reason why Žižek's insights are important is because he situates the source of the problem at the level of the inescapable ontological constitution of subjectivity, as opposed to the more commonly cited source: ideology qua false consciousness.[11] In this respect, it does not matter how much we rationally understand that capitalism is unjust or ecologically unsustainable, as long as it remains our primary source of enjoyment, it will continue with very little contestation. In some respects, the ability to enjoy outside of capitalism has come to appear unintelligible because so-called "post-materialist" values, so proliferate today, are intimately tide to material consumption (if you doubt this claim, I would direct you to think about the perfectly synergistic relationship between yoga, Lululemon, and Ayn Rand).[12]

Enjoying Cosmopolitanism

In political-theoretical terms, this post-Fordist shift in values is reflected in the culture-ideology of cosmopolitanism, considered by some to be a subset of "critical theory." Cosmopolitanism contains a distinctly normative vision of subjectivity. The cosmopolitan subject is tolerant, inclusive toward others, experimental in one's lifestyle, and oriented toward world peace and social equality. Extracting data from a massive global survey, Pippa Norris has explored the demographics of cosmopolitanism. Statistically speaking, she argues, one is more likely to hold cosmopolitan moral and political commitments if one: is male (only slightly more likely than women), lives in cities, speaks English, is North or South American, young, educated, and post-materialist.[13] These characteristics, associated with a wealthier and privileged demographic, imply that there is a distinct class element to cosmopolitanism. Bryan S. Turner explicitly associates cosmopolitan values with a global elite, but he frames them by measuring the intensity of two categories:

1 loyalty to the state; and
2 social solidarity.

Loyalty to the state means simply the level of attachment to and identification with one's country of citizenship, while social solidarity refers to the level of emotive cohesion and sense of collective belonging in any given society. The measurement of both principles falls along a spectrum "hot/cool" (loyalty) and "thick/thin" (solidarity). In both cases, Turner argues that in the postmodern era loyalty has cooled off and solidarity has thinned relative to the political values that developed during the period of history defined by the rise of the modern state. Postmodern-cosmopolitan citizens are defined by cool loyalty and thin solidarity – they are highly nomadic, anti-nationalist, and individualistic, and are embodied in the jet-setting elite of the world. As Turner states: "These post-modern cool loyalties will be characteristic of the global elite … who are geographically and socially mobile.... The post-modern citizen is only moving on."[14]

In contrast, the demographic characterized by hot loyalty and thick solidarity is, defined broadly, the working class. Their values and interest lie in security and sameness; mobility is not a top priority and their livelihoods rely on community ties, as Turner outlines: "those sections of the population which are relatively immobile and located in traditional employment patterns (the working class, ethnic minorities and the under classes) may in fact continue to have hot loyalties and thick patterns of solidarity."[15]

Turner provides no clear declarations about the normative import of this divide between the value sets of the elite and the working class. Instead he makes scattered speculative remarks about the dangers and benefits of each set. Overall, he appears to be more optimistic for the contributions that cosmopolitanism may make to the establishment of a peaceful future. He conjectures that the "ironic" cosmopolitan citizen "may hopefully be less likely to give her undivided support to whatever government happens to be in power,"[16] and might encourage "a more active engagement with cultural issues" like protecting threatened cultures, the environment, and endangered languages.[17] Conversely, he says that the hot loyalty/thick solidarity worldview of the working class may lead to "reactionary nationalism" because members of this group "may well be recruited to nationalist and reactionary parties."[18] The rise in popularity of Donald Trump, UKIP in Britain, and other similarly anti immigrant parties in Europe, appears to affirm Turner's concerns.

His hope is that some level of cosmopolitanism might "trickle down" to the working classes.[19] But if cosmopolitanism is meant to be a "critical" approach to global politics, formulations like Turner's show clearly that it is, at least in its current manifestation, profoundly bourgeois in character. As Craig Calhoun, a more genuinely self-reflexively critical proponent of cosmopolitanism than Turner, states quite baldly: "Cosmopolitanism – though not necessarily cosmopolitan democracy – is now largely the project of capitalism, and it flourishes in the top management of multinational corporations and even more in the consulting firms that serve them."[20] In the face of such a characterization of cosmopolitanism, calling it a "critical" discourse is dubious at best, and disingenuous at worst (I will discuss this in greater detail in the next chapter).

This brings me to the counter-intuitively enabling dynamic of cosmopolitanism discussed earlier. Most of the values associated with cosmopolitanism are almost synonymous with many, if not all, of the values espoused by schools of critical theory: reflexivity, critical thinking, nomadicism, and a general lack of loyalty to the state and place, in general. It is the latter two characteristics that are the most important, at least for the purposes of my argument. The cosmopolitan subject is rootless, as indicated by Turner's identification of nomadicism as a core cosmopolitan value. The cosmopolitan is willing to live wherever opportunity presents itself and feels an ethical compulsion to identify more with the world than a particular nation-state; conditioned to feel guilty when residual nationalist sentiments emerge while watching, say, an Olympic hockey game. The cosmopolitan desires that all people have the opportunity to see the world outside of their small, parochial communities. The cosmopolitan cares about others and knows that exposure to otherness, difference, and unsettling experiences is how individuals grow their uniquely human capacities. In order to promote the cosmopolitan worldview, education must be geared toward inculcating all those who would otherwise remain stuck in tradition and narrow-mindedness with the values of multiculturalism, love for travel and adventure, and a general appreciation for new experiences. Cosmopolitan discourse connects the notion of freedom and ultimately democracy with the values of openness and newness, encapsulated by Nike's crypto-Nietzschean slogan "Just Do It!" In this regard, the cosmopolitan subject acts as a microcosm of neoliberal globalization. From a cosmopolitan perspective, human beings should never really stop moving in their search for new experiences and pleasure, all of which contributes to personal development, mirroring capital's imperative to constantly increase and speed up circuits of investment so as to ensure perpetual growth. The ideal world for the cosmopolitan subject is a radically open and inclusive one: no borders, no barriers to participation in social and political life, no "us and them." It is the paradigmatically "post-political" world as it is governed by a global consensus in terms of moral principles and political organization informed by the spread of individual human rights.

Though this might be a tempting perspective to assume when conceptualizing a more peaceful world, cosmopolitanism ultimately enlarges the scope of inclusivity in a way that dilutes the political. As Calhoun argues, "[b]uilding cosmopolitanism solely on such a discourse of individual rights – without a strong attention to diverse solidarities and struggles for a more just and democratic social order – also runs the risk of *substituting ethics for politics*."[21] In line with Mouffe and Schmitt, such inclusivity can only be realized via constitutive exclusions, which is then bound to lead to a backlash by the excluded; the "part of no part," in Rancière's language.

Fantasizing Freedom

But what does it even mean to be included in the cosmopolitan project? What is the criteria that might satisfy one's demand for inclusion? Political rights? Economic and social equality? Clearly these are the most regularly cited goals of mainstream cosmopolitan movements, but why are they so commonly articulated through a neoliberal vision of the good? The answer, of course, is that contemporary neoliberalism attaches economic, political, and social inclusion to a promise of enjoyment. Ultimately, neoliberal capitalism infuses in subjects a belief that enjoyment is guaranteed in a free market. But this is clearly a false belief, as certain types of freedom are always curtailed by the market. Nonetheless, subjects believe this fiction and disavow experiences that challenge its premise. How does this phenomenon operate on a psychological level? Dean describes this within the psychoanalytic category of "fantasy." Fantasy is the overriding false image of wholeness and consistency that we ascribe to systems or narratives that govern our lives; it is, as Todd McGowan claims, "how subjects and societies organize their enjoyment."[22] Fantasy is the mechanism by which the inconsistencies and gaps in our worldviews are covered over so that we can go on believing; it operates like cognitive dissonance or "fetishized disavowal," in Žižek's terms. In relation to capitalism, Dean argues that one core element of the neoliberal fantasy is that free market competition ensures that "everyone wins" for all the reasons that neo-classical economics support free market capitalism. When two people, motivated by their individual self-interest, come together and make a non-coerced transaction, they both benefit. Extended to the economy as a whole, this logic is encapsulated by "trickle-down" economic principles, so popular with the neoliberal politicians of the 1980s: allow the rich to maximize wealth production through laissez-faire policies and the wealth will trickle down to all, everyone wins! All this, Dean contends, despite the fact that competition by its very definition implies winners and losers.[23]

Of course, no ideological fantasy is able to completely cover over the demonstrative empirical phenomena that disrupts its truth-claims or reveals its inconsistencies. Growing social inequality, increasingly unstable financial markets, and stagnating wages need to be accounted for somehow. As Dean suggests, one of the ideological fail-safes of the fantasy of free trade is quite simple: "If someone loses, this simply indicates that trade was not free."[24] Usually, these sorts of market failures are ascribed to market actors who cheated the system, whether it's insider trading, excessive risk-taking by bankers, unions, welfare cheats, or bloated and corrupt governments. The logic of this position is the same as that which governs the ontological search for enjoyment: when the subject fails to enjoy, it is not because enjoyment is impossible, but because someone else has "stolen" it, stolen the enjoyment the subject deserves. In the face of its structural contradictions, the fantasy of free trade is left undisturbed because the problem is that it was just not free in the first place. The way to address this failure to enjoy is, of course, to make the market more free!

The neoliberal fantasy of competition is interesting to consider within the context of the ethical turn because it represents a disavowed political position. It is avowedly ethical to the extent it is inclusive because everyone wins; no one is left out of the enjoyment it promises ... except, of course, when some don't win. These inevitable failures result in the establishment of discursive antagonisms between the good, honest, hardworking people and the enjoyment-thieves. The latter, of course, must be eliminated so that all can succeed and enjoy. This logic provides the rationale for the indefinite deferral of enjoyment: we'll all enjoy, but not until we've finally removed all the barriers to an authentically free market; not until we've abolished all of those individuals, groups, and institutions that steal our enjoyment! In the meantime, sustained by the fantasy of free trade and competition, subjects of neoliberalism continue to act according to the logic of drive: never fully satisfied, but addicted to the small nuggets of pleasure derived from the very failure of capitalism to fulfil its promise of enjoyment. Strategies for withdrawing the affective investment in the operation (and failure) of capitalism has been identified by some who identify with the "Lacanian Left," as the singularly most significant problem for building a genuinely leftist alternative to neoliberalism.[25]

Desiring Democracy

It is easy to indict contemporary critical theory for sharing an abstract affinity with the cultural values of neoliberal or post-Fordist capitalism, and indeed there is no lack of such indictments in the critical literature.[26] A less well-trodden area of critical inquiry in respect to the relationship between critical theory and neoliberalism is the central position of democracy. If the contemporary Left is defined in part by a desire to live outside of exclusionary political structures, to maximize inclusion and participation in governance, and to denounce hierarchical power relations wherever they exist, how are these demands framed as a whole? Always in the language of democracy, which constitutes the uncritically assumed good at the core of all progressive thought. The category of democracy is the most important value that drives progressive thought forward, and attracts passion and commitment in its adherents, while simultaneously establishing a limit point to its potential or a barrier to its success. Like *objet petit a* in Lacanian theory, the Left circles democracy in a manner that appears to be governed by the logic of drive. The Left acts like an abused wife who stays with her husband because *this time* he really promises to be different. Democracy is the Left's object of desire – an object that by the very structure of its relationship with the Left can never satisfy those who covet it. In the final (psycho)analysis, it is democracy itself that exposes the Left to the affliction of an impossible desire that, in turn, produces a Left compelled to act according to the logic of Lacanian drive. Democracy always lets us down, and yet we still profess our undying loyalty to it.

Why is the Left so enamoured with democracy as an organizational ideal? After all, almost *every* political ideology of any significance today expresses itself through an appeal to democracy – socialist dictatorships, xenophobic (anti-EU) far right-wing populists in Europe, and African nationalists, just to name a few.[27] This observation, which reveals the discursive plasticity of democracy, offers the first obvious answer to the initial question regarding the attachment to democracy: the Left uses the language of democracy out of necessity; no serious political movement that desires influence can do otherwise. It is no stretch to assume that any support-base that left-wing movements currently have would immediately abandon them in droves the moment they denounce democracy; it is simply not an option in contemporary political practice.

However, this does not necessarily explain why progressive political theorists, those mandated and free to think through any and all ideas that may contribute to accessing truth and understanding power – often protected by tenure and academic freedom – have largely assumed democracy to be the foundation upon which all left-wing theory is built. Why do we only deliberate about what democracy *is*, and not so much about whether it is *valuable* or not? Would it not be refreshing or, at least interesting, if some leftist academics began to challenge the inherent worth of democracy (after all, we have a good point of departure in that Nietzsche is widely admired by critical theorists)? Or would such a development be simply frightening? This, of course, is a complicated question to resolve in any authoritative manner, and the answer will be by necessity multifaceted, requiring historical, psychological, and political-theoretical analysis.

Part of the powerful allure of democracy is, of course, that as an abstract concept, democracy is an empty signifier – it has no core, so to speak. As Wendy Brown puts it (citing Etienne Balibar on Spinoza), democracy is unable "to find its own principle" as a political regime.[28] This is because, for Spinoza, the divide between the state and the masses defines all political regimes. Insofar as democracy is defined by the self-rule of the masses, or as positing the identity between ruled and rulers, democracy is unintelligible as a political regime. The closest Spinoza can come to placing democracy within a taxonomy of political regimes is as a "perfect aristocracy" (incidentally, this is how the anarchist George Woodcock defines anarchism, as something akin to "aristocracy universalized and purified"[29]). Democracy in its pure form is, therefore, premised on non-division, and recalls Socrates's scornful depiction of a regime in which every individual represents his own private constitution. When democracy is understood in this manner, it ceases to be "political" in the Mouffian sense because it is, in its ideal-typical form, defined by the absence of fundamental antagonisms and power relations.

Brown goes on to discuss how democracy is, in fact, defined by a socio-political vacuum of sorts, and will always be filled by a "historically available principle – nationalism, racism, xenophobia, cultural chauvinism, market values, Christianity, imperialism, individualism, rights as ends," and so on.[30] This is at once a painfully obvious insight as well as a profoundly important one. There is no such thing as a pure democracy. Every self-identified democratic regime will include an anti-democratic element that serves to stabilize what would otherwise be an unworkable mess of a system. And though this character of democracy is undeniable, it appears to be a truth largely disavowed by much contemporary critical theory. Within the context of the ethical turn, as described in the last chapter, this relationship between democracy and its anti-democratic elements can be understood as symptomatic of the desire to live outside of power relations. Thus, in a reformulation of Brown's critique, the anti-democratic element is always some sort of power relation – democracy in practice is always defined by the projection and circulation of anti-democratic power.

While Brown argues that this may necessitate that we think of democracy as always containing an undemocratic stabilizing feature, it can also be understood as suggesting that democracy always contains an alluring sense of freedom, after all, the absence of a core principle allows the formal category of democracy to be filled in with whatever content one desires. In the case of contemporary critical theory, the values associated with the ethical turn become this content, albeit ranging from its more liberal-representatives to its post-anarchist variants. For the critical political theorist, it is a relatively simple scholarly endeavour to "rethink" democracy in the image of, say, the ideas professed by his or her favourite Continental philosopher. The may include even those thinkers who largely despise democracy – Nietzsche, for example – but only if the anti-democratic element is erased via the process of universalization. So, for Nietzsche, one can "democratize" him by positing a universalized notion of every citizen's right to be an over-man, or by universalizing aristocracy. But far from empowering the "people," this is actually depoliticizing because it denies the constitutive *exclusions* endemic to any political regime. Brown's ultimate point is that the anti-democratic element of any democratic regime must be explicitly *avowed* for democracy to have any meaning:

If democracy inherently lacks a principle of its own, then *any* principle brought to it will:

> necessarily be antidemocratic: if democracy and principle are antithetical, if democracy is innately without a principle of its own, then any principle democracy attaches to must be partially at odds with it. It thus appears that the antidote for democracy's degenerative tendencies is homeopathic – it requires installing another antidemocratic element in democracy's heart.[31]

In a Machiavellian manner, to save democracy, one must be willing to embrace anti-democracy ideologically, while simultaneously calling it democracy for pragmatic/strategic purposes.

Perhaps this fear of an impure democratic system can account for Habermas's shift away from the bourgeois public sphere of the salons and toward that highly abstract and paradigmatically post-political notion of democracy: deliberative democracy. As outlined by Margaret Kohn, over the course of his career Habermas's normative theorizing became increasingly (what I would call) depoliticized, or "cosmopolitanized," by virtue of a progressive "despatialization" of his deliberative model; a despatialization consonant with the ethical turn. Kohn shows how Habermas's earlier work on the public sphere in *The Structural Transformation of the Public Sphere* emphasizes the importance of concrete spaces – the eighteenth-century salons of Europe – for developing democratic practices like public debate and the concept of public opinion. The "public sphere" that we have come to associated with modern liberal democracy, Habermas contended, emerged out of groups constituted of bourgeois individuals that came together in various locations to discuss philosophical matters and important issues of the day. While these groups were highly exclusive in terms of membership – confined to members of the upper and middle classes – they nonetheless provided the template upon which mass democratic publicity would be modelled. As a theorist attuned to the importance of public space, Kohn believes that at this point in his career Habermas's project is significant by virtue of the fact it demonstrates how specific *spaces* – spatially located, physical buildings – were required for a particular type of politics to emerge. Democratic ideas were not spontaneously revealed in the minds of isolated individuals, but were created in a dialogue of equals gathered in specific places, and these places served as microcosms of what would expand to become the public sphere we are familiar with today. This is another way of saying that Habermas recognized the importance of space during a period when most critical theorists were privileging time or history as the master category for understanding political change. However, Kohn claims that by shifting his analysis away from the concrete spaces of the public sphere in his earlier work, to the abstract arena of deliberative democracy in his later research, he obscures power relations in an attempt to create a less exclusionary model for rational consensus.[32] The key insight relevant to my thesis in this book is that, in the earlier work of Habermas, the specific, localized spaces of European salons were shown to be highly *exclusive*, and not open to the greater public. In general, Kohn sees the shift in Habermas's emphasis as symptomatic of something endemic to political theory: a fear of reproducing hierarchical or exclusionary power relations through spatial ontologies: "Although space clearly contributed to political practice, it has not been recognized in contemporary political theory. There is still a widespread suspicion that a political appeal to place is conservative, essentialist, or anachronistic."[33] From my perspective, this points to how space is a problem for deliberative theorists like Habermasians, in that space is a messy political category that disrupts idealist ontological and epistemological commitments in the face of concrete antagonism. Furthermore, the rejection of concrete, exclusionary space can be reinterpreted as a form of a fear of place, because what else are fixed material spaces, if not places. Democracy is not meant to be associated with discrete places, because discrete places are populated by discrete individuals and groups whose identities are bound to their situatedness. Such attachments are necessarily a threat to abstract, universal, and non-parochial deliberation; *place is the anti-democratic element of deliberative democracy*. This line of critique is discussed in greater detail in Chapter 4.

The type of ethical theory I have investigated thus far advances a notion of democracy absent an anti-democratic element. If openness, participation, inclusivity, and a rejection of power relations defines democracy, then this view is tantamount to understanding democracy as its own principle – an impossibility in Brown's model, not to mention Mouffe's concept of the political. For Brown, the lack of an anti-democratic element produces a certain type of "political moralizing" discourse in certain spheres of critical theory and politics. "Political moralizing" is contrasted with "morality in politics," whereby the latter is defined by a metaphysically anchored *telos*, or substantive notion of the good, and the former is characterized by a disavowed desire for this good. This means that in the discourse of political moralizing, morality is invoked against power, but only in a purely negative form (signifying a desire for change but absent a positive alternative vision). Brown writes:

> what form does this impulse take when it has lost its lodging in an abstract principle and vision of the good … when moral claims reduce to moralizing

> complaint? It is when the telos of the good vanishes but the yearning for it remains that morality appears to devolve into moralism in politics.[34]

In relation to power and politics, Brown argues that while morality in politics is always "mistrustful" in its relationship to power, political moralizing

> tends to be intensely antagonistic toward a richly agonistic political or intellectual life. Moralism so loathes overt manifestations of power – its ontological and epistemological premises are so endangered by signs of action and agency – that the moralist inevitably feels antipathy toward politics as a domain of open contestation for power and hegemony.[35]

She even claims that political moralism is born out of a wounded attachment, or a resentment of past injuries:

> As a codification of disappointment or disenthrallment, it seeks to make a world in its own self-image and thus reproves everything tainted with power. In this way, a strange breed of nihilism – opposition to life itself – disguises itself in the clothing of its opposite: righteous political principle.[36]

Moralism is, in other words, a reaction against and denunciation of power by the powerless. Its impotency is due to a lack of a credible political alternative, precisely because such a project would entail engaging with and exerting power. Such a moralizing position can only be articulated through a fetishized desire for democracy.

Democracy as Openness, Democracy as Lack

In terms of connecting democracy to one of the key categories of the ethical turn – openness – one can situate it in respect to the fundamentally political practice of decision-making. While decision-making may appear a banal practice, to "decide" invokes a profound ontological political category: the "decision." In a thoughtful critique of Judith Butler, Dean claims she fetishizes unknowingness in respect to ethical relations with the Other. This is largely because our own self-knowledge (knowledge of self) is always indeterminate. Dean posits:

> If unknowingness conditions ethics then it necessarily conditions politics as well. Our political choices to condemn and denounce, the conditions we pursue through what we exclude, take place under traumatic conditions of unknowability and unpredictability. Our decision for this rather than that will necessarily involve a kind of violence, a foreclosure of the possibility of the future that would have resulted had we decided otherwise. When we intervene politically, we act within situations not of our own making, often in terms of representations and practices we might otherwise trouble or critique. Through our actions, we affect these representations and practices, changing them and ourselves in ways we cannot predict.[37]

To clarify Dean's thoughts, political decisions are always decisions of how *power* will be exerted, employed, or withheld. The moment of decision, a necessary prerequisite for political action, announces an antagonism, an "us versus them," and a willingness to avow this symbolic violence. In addition, Dean continues, because Butler believes that "condemnation involves closure and that closure entails finality and disconnection,"[38] she can only imagine such an act as destroying the conditions for solidarity and understanding. However, Dean opines:

> At the same time, condemnation may work in a different direction. Weakness in one respect may enable another sort of strength, a capacity to form new alliances and connections, to open a space wherein to imagine the possibility of another world. So condemnation and denunciation may produce new links.[39]

Condemnation via the decision may be, then, a requisite moment for determining with whom one will ally; it can produce new networks based on a solidarity of condemnation. Here Dean nicely points to a dialectical conception of openness and closure, and the possibility of the properly political. Radical openness, as an imperative of ethical relations does not preclude closures. Indeed, closures on Dean's account can produce new openings, if openings are defined as reorderings of power relations. This is an important insight, although it may unnecessarily confuse what is really at stake: the normative importance of openness. While decision and condemnation may offer critical theory a new form of openness, it can be quickly demonstrated in contrast that certain options or trajectories are foreclosed at the same time. The main idea to extract from Dean's insights is that in fetishizing openness one inherently disavows an anti-democratic principle operative in all politics, namely, closure; closure, much like exclusion, is an anti-democratic element required for democracy.

How does this relate to the human subject's ontological search for enjoyment? If democracy is an empty container, defined by a fundamental lack, it can be similarly understood as *objet petit a* in Lacanian terms because it cannot find its own principle. On this view, democracy becomes an object of libidinal investment, something that promises us complete enjoyment. But as an object defined by a fundamental lack, that enjoyment is always just out of reach – we can never satisfy our desire through democracy because full enjoyment is impossible. As Dean argues, the logic of our relationship with this particular object becomes something like: "we would be happy (satisfy our desire), if only we had … democracy." Thus, in a classic obsessive/addictive manner, we diagnose the problem of really existing democracy as a lack of democracy as such. Democracy itself, instead of anti-democracy, becomes the allopathic remedy for its own deficiency – *We just need more democracy!* While Dean has written extensively on this subject from a psychoanalytic perspective, in terms of the tension between the ethical and the political, she states:

> Continuing to appeal to democracy, we fail to emphasize the divisions necessary for politics, divisions that should lead us to organize against the

> interests of corporations and their stockholders, against the values of the fundamentalists and the individualists, and on behalf of collectivist arrangements designed to redistribute benefits and opportunities more equitably. *We proceed as if democracy were already the solution to contemporary political problems rather than symptomatic of them.*[40]

Returning to Brown's analysis for a moment, if her deconstruction of democracy is accurate, then pursuing the lack of democracy by striving for more democracy is obviously and categorically self-defeating. More democracy only intensifies democracy's inherent failure as a political regime. What one needs, in other words, is *less* democracy.

The desire for democracy creates a fatalistic (albeit, often in disavowed form) atmosphere for critical theorists, especially for those that consider themselves to be radical or anti-capitalist. Dean describes this outcome well:

> The idea that democracy marks an empty place where things can be otherwise, that democratic procedures incorporates already the keys to revising and reforming the practice of democracy, becomes the conviction that there is nothing but, no alternative to democracy.[41]

In other words, democracy becomes the limit-point of our political horizon.[42] To think beyond democracy is an impossibility, not only because a human good that transcends democracy's limitations is unintelligible given our prevailing Symbolic Order, but it is also considered dangerous.

Attempts to think beyond democracy are considered dangerous for two particular reasons, one psychological in nature and the other a result of deep historical trauma. First, thinking beyond democracy is simply too radical. It would require the dissolution of our selves as political subjects oriented and stabilized by the symbols and rhetoric of democracy. It would be nothing less than an experience of the political Real: non-democracy. Second, to think beyond democracy poses the risk of failure, an anxiety especially pronounced amongst the academic and "internet" Left. In this regard, precisely what haunts the Left is the fear of repeating the same mistake – enacting the same failure – of the twentieth-century Marxist-socialist project. Any thought that contributes to the possibility of inspiring a new Soviet Union, or similar authoritarian state structure, is not an option for the Left. What, then, is the most effective way to ensure that the Left avoids such failure? As mentioned in Chapter 2, the Left must prohibit the conditions of possibility for success *in advance*. In the case of critical theory's relationship to democracy, the strategy for such a prohibition is not so much to invalidate the particular *content* of anti-democratic thinking in its various expressions, but rather to change the very categorical structure of democracy itself, namely, to disavow the political character of democracy and treat it primarily as an *ethical* category defined by openness and inclusion. This returns us to Dean's "crimes" of the old Left: the crimes of representation, exclusion, dogmatism, and utopianism. All these crimes are anti-democratic principles to the extent they require the willingness to engage with and exert power. The New Left's a priori prohibition ensures that they will play no role in addressing the deficiencies of contemporary democracy. Positing democracy as *objet petit a*, but to disavow that democracy always contains an anti-democratic element is the very thing that ensures that democracy will never be achieved. But much like the relationship between capitalism and critical theory, simply recognizing the impossibility of democracy is not enough to reorient the normative relationship between critical theory and democracy.

According to the logic of drive, subjects enjoy the very failure of achieving democracy. We celebrate our inability to achieve democracy in small-scale collective victories or spontaneous shows of solidarity. Whether it is the Occupy Movement, the Zapatista, anti-austerity riots in European capitals, or factory seizures in South America, these events return little morsels of enjoyment upon which democratic drive is sustained. Additionally, there is a purist streak on the critical Left, reflected in its tendency toward factionalism and endless "tendencies" and schisms. The denunciation of impure practices or tenets reflects the partial enjoyment produced by failing to achieve, let alone formulate, an impossible democracy identical to its own concept. The pleasure is one of resentment: "we are not the dogmatic ones, we do not enact the closures and exclusions, and we resent those responsible for such practices." To direct one's hatred toward power, without a willingness to exert power in one's own interest, is a shorthand definition of Nietzsche's *ressentiment*. Although as Nietzsche demonstrated in *Genealogy of Morals*, such resentment can be incredibly productive and lead to the victory of the oppressed, but only once it becomes institutionalized and *politicized* in the form of, say, the Christian Church.[43]

Dean makes an important point about how democracy can once again become meaningful for the Left if it is re-thought in a certain way. She states: "If politicization from the Left is to mean anything at all, it requires politicizing democracy, that is, demonstrating how this organizational form and polemical concept serves highly particular interests and stands in the way of universalization."[44] As counter-intuitive as it may seem, the Left needs to think seriously about embracing certain anti-democratic element(s) of democracy. Anti-democratic thinking can provide a rich and fecund object to explore for progressive political theorists. In this context, "anti-democracy" should not be understood as "non-democratic," as if dictatorship or oligarchy is the only viable alternative to pure democracy; rather, such anti-democratic thinking would be aimed at exploring how other political principles might contribute to greater social equality and the provisions of collective goods, most likely within a formally democratic context. This, of course, is not always appropriate for encouraging political activism. Clearly, promoting non-democracy in the course of anti-capitalist, anti-racist, or anti-poverty organizing would be a foolish, unpragmatic, and self-defeating endeavour. Despite its impossibility, as Yannis Stavrakakis says, democracy is "an inspiration articulating a multitude of radical demands throughout the world, and nothing else seems capable of replacing it – at least for the time being."[45] Therefore, in terms of praxis, the way forward is to emphasize "rethinking" democracy as an organizational form, as most progressive theorists profess to do. The problem is that when the vast majority of left-wing scholars "rethink" democracy, they do so along ethical and not political lines: "deep" democracy, "radical" democracy, "substantive" democracy, "absolute" democracy, and so on. What if, in line with the argument that has been made over the past two chapters, the properly political principles (anti-democratic) that can be attached to democracy in order to politicize critical political theory include exclusivity, non-participation and, especially for thinking the city, loyalty to place? While some critical urbanists like Harvey have taken questions of loyalty to place very seriously (in what he calls "militant particularism"[46]), these principles are so counter-intuitive for so much of the contemporary Left that embracing them may take nothing less than a complete reorientation of the political Symbolic Order. As this book posits the city as the most important site of contemporary left-wing political organization, in the next four chapters a central goal will be to explore how the ethical form of democracy, which dominates critical urban theory, actually leads to the disempowering and further marginalization of already vulnerable urban communities. In contrast, I examine the extent to which a reformed political notion of democracy can inform a politics of resistance that challenges processes of disempowerment and dispossession. In the next chapter, this exploration begins with a discussion of how the ethical form of democracy has manifested itself in "postmodern" theories of the city.

Notes

1 Sara Ahmed, *The Promise of Happiness* (London: Duke University Press, 2010), 193.

2 All across his writings, Žižek shows great deference, in particular, to Alain Badiou. He also regularly demonstrates admiration for the work of Fredric Jameson, Eric Santner, Wendy Brown, and Milan Dolar, among a few others.

3 Žižek has engaged in several well-publicized and bitter debates with famous leftist intellectuals including Ernesto Laclau, Simon Critchley, and, most recently, Noam Chomsky.

4 Žižek, *Violence*, 16. In this quote "Davos" refers to the annual World Economic Forum, a gathering of largely the global elite to discuss how capitalism can fix the world's problems, and "Porto Alegre" refers to the first site of the World Social forum, an annual gathering of progressive activists, academics, and NGOs to discuss alternatives to neoliberal capitalism.

5 Ibid.

6 Pauline Rosenau, *Post-Modernism and the Social Sciences: Insights, Inroads, and Intrusions* (Princeton: Princeton University Press, 1991).

7 See Adam Curtis's documentary *Century of the Self* (London: BBC 4, 2002), for a fantastic exploration of this phenomenon.

8 See: Slavoj Žižek, "A Cup of Decaf Reality," www.lacan.com/zizekdecaf.htm, accessed January 24, 2014.

9 Sanbonmatsu, *Postmodern Prince*, 49–50.

10 Jean Baudrillard, *Forget Foucault*, trans. Phil Beitchman et al. (New York: Semiotexte, 2007), 39.

11 See my discussion of the Chomsky/Žižek "debate" in Chapter 6 for more about this distinction.

12 For background details on the Lululemon–Rand–yoga connection, see: Ian Austen, "Lululemon Athletica Combines Ayn Rand and Yoga," *New York Times*, last updated November 27, 2011, accessed February 7, 2014, www.nytimes.com/2011/11/28/business/media/combines-ayn-rand-and-yoga.html?_r=0.

13 Pippa Norris, "Global Governance and Cosmopolitan Citizens," in *Governance in a Globalizing World*, ed. Joseph Nye and John D. Donahue (Washington, DC: The Brookings Institute, 2000).
14 Turner, "Cosmopolitan Virtue," 141.
15 Ibid., 141–142.
16 Ibid., 142.
17 Ibid., 145.
18 Ibid., 142.
19 Ibid., 141.
20 Craig Calhoun, "Class Consciousness of Frequent Travellers," in *Conceiving Cosmopolitanism: Theory, Context, and Practice*, ed. Steven Vertovec and Robin Cohen (Oxford: Oxford University Press, 2002), 106.
21 Ibid., 107. Italics mine.
22 Todd McGowan, *Enjoying What We Don't Have: The Political Project of Psychoanalysis* (Lincoln: University of Nebraska Press, 2013).
23 Jodi Dean, "Enjoying Neoliberalism," *Cultural Politics* 4(1) (2008): 55–56.
24 Ibid., 56.
25 See, for example, Yannis Stavrakakis, *The Lacanian Left: Psychoanalysis, Theory, Politics* (Edinburgh: Edinburgh University Press, 2007), Chapter 4.
26 Again, see: Aronowitz, *Left Turn*; and Sanbonmatsu, *Postmodern Prince*.
27 The only holdout might be certain strains of political Islam that denounce democracy because it is a human artifact.
28 Wendy Brown, "Democracy Against Itself: Nietzsche's Challenge," in Wendy Brown, *Politics Out of History* (Princeton: Princeton University Press, 2001), 123.
29 Woodcock, *Anarchism*, 34.
30 Brown, "Democracy Against Itself," 124.
31 Ibid., 126.
32 Margaret Kohn, *Radical Space: Building the House of the People* (New York: Cornell University Press, 2003), 9.
33 Ibid., 153.
34 Wendy Brown, "Moralism as Anti-Politics," in Wendy Brown, *Politics Out of History* (Princeton: Princeton University Press, 2001), 28.
35 Ibid., 30.
36 Ibid., 23–24.
37 Jodi Dean, *Democracy and Other Neoliberal Fantasies* (Durham, NC: Duke University Press, 2009), 143.
38 Ibid., 140.
39 Ibid., 141.
40 Dean, "Democratic Deadlock," paragraph 4. Emphasis mine.
41 Dean, *Democracy*, 78.
42 Slavoj Žižek, *Tarrying with the Negative* (Durham, NC: Duke University Press, 1993), 221.
43 Friedrich Nietzsche, *On the Genealogy of Morality*, trans. Carol Diethe (New York: Cambridge University Press, 2007).
44 Dean, "Democratic Deadlock," paragraph 6.
45 Stavrakakis, *The Lacanian Left*, 258.
46 See David Harvey, *Justice, Nature and the Geography of Difference* (Cambridge, MA: Blackwell, 1996), Chapter 1; and *Spaces of Hope* (Berkeley: University of California Press, 2000), Chapter 12.

4 The Open City, or the Ethical Turn in Critical Urban Studies

Novelty itself is a luxury good. Only the rich have enough resources to get bored with having excellent, ordinary food every day.[1]

This chapter explores how the character of critical theories of the city has been affected by the ethical turn in political theory. What does it mean for progressive urban thought and activism when they are subjected to the same prohibitions as those of the "old Left," like the crimes of exclusion and dogmatism? How do the contours of political struggle and social justice in the city change when politics is reduced to moral imperatives for greater inclusivity, dialogue, and openness? What happens to the potential for resistance and organization when solidaristic, parochial, and fixed notions of political communities are replaced with fluid, transient, and cosmopolitan networks of flows? What are the consequences, in other words, of thinking the city as an *ethical* space instead of a site of *politics*?

The central point I work through in the next few chapters is that such thinking has an enabling effect; that is, enabling some of the most deleterious processes specific to the "neoliberalization" of urban landscapes. This facilitatory relationship is very much analogous to the dynamic that links critical political theory and neoliberalism, whereby the very object of critique is unwittingly strengthened by the discourse of the critic. More specifically, it is my contention that much of the critical urban literature shares the very same underlying logic that drives the neoliberalization of the city. Contemporary critical theorists of the city tend to promote the normative ideals of flow, novelty, encounter, inclusivity, and dialogue, all of which actually underpin the very processes they oppose in the neoliberal city. Specific issues that are both criticized and curiously enabled by critical urban theory include the privatization of public space, emphasis on exchange-value over use-value in real estate, and the race to the bottom logic of attracting investment. In particular, what should be considered perhaps the most egregiously destructive process for marginalized urban communities – gentrification – absolutely requires the normative logic of this predominant critical understanding of the city to discursively justify its markedly unjustifiable outcomes. As such, the rest of this book focuses on gentrification more than any other specifically urban process.

But before getting to my critique of gentrification, the present chapter outlines the particular ontological, epistemological, and normative elements of the city as theorized by critical urban scholars who can be associated with the ethical turn. In order, again, to avoid conceptual confusion or present a misleading dichotomy between the "good" modern and the "bad" postmodern. I have coined the term "open city" to describe the various theories of the city that possess the characteristics of "ethical theory" as delineated in the previous chapters. In short, the open city is informed by the values of openness and inclusivity over all others. It is open and inclusive because it posits that all of its inhabitants should have access to its spaces and a voice in its governance. Cosmopolitan conceptions of difference, and both humanist and post-humanist values of becoming, are the ethical values that define the open city. In essence, the open city is a depoliticized city because, in its theoretical construction, it does not recognize the reality of antagonism and other characteristics associated with properly political space.

Henri Lefebvre, the Production of Space, and the Spatial Turn

The theoretical genesis of the open city can be trace back to one of the most influential urban theorists of the mid to late twentieth century, Henri Lefebvre. It is Lefebvre's novel theorization of space, less so than his conception of actual cities, which has most influenced contemporary critical urban studies. His work in the 1950s–1970s serves as the singularly most important theoretical inspiration for the burst of interest in privileging space over time that came to dominate critical urban studies in the waning decades of the twentieth century. More specifically, Lefebvre is best known for both his ontological model of the "production of space" and his normative "right to the city." However, there is a certain ambivalence in clarity and intent of his writing which has led to, if not a radical misreading of his core ideas, at least minor misappropriations of his thought. Whether he was misunderstood or not, at least a passing familiarity with his work is necessary for understanding contemporary critical urban theory.

The importance of Lefebvre's contributions for contemporary critical urban theory cannot be overstated. He is cited ubiquitously, not only amongst Marxist and postmodern theorists, but also by liberals like Susan Fainstein.[2] Lately Lefebvre's political principle "right to the city" has become a rallying cry for various progressive protest movements, from Zuccotti Park to Istanbul, but most contemporary theorists of the city mark the 1974 publication of Lefebvre's *Production of Space* as the germinal moment out of which grew contemporary critical urban theory. In this text, Lefebvre performs a spectacular transgression of Marxist dogma by reorienting his philosophy on the character of *space*, a category that had been systematically de-privileged by Marxism vis-à-vis *time* or *history*. His core insight is that space should not be understood as a passive and empty container of things, but as a dialectically produced embodiment of social relations.[3] This he contrasts with semiotic "discourses" of space, or simple "decoding" of signs which do not interrogate the underlying forces or the concrete social practices that produce spatial organizations in the interests of specific segments of society. This is much like the difference between denotative and connotative signification in semiotics, whereby the former says something literal and uncritical about the object, and the latter transmits ideological meaning, or says something about social relations. Seen in this way, space is always imbued with *power relations* and *ideology*. While what he calls "neocapitalist" space is produced in the interest of capital, unlike orthodox Marxist notions of history, Lefebvre argues that the bourgeoisie's control over space is never absolute; there is always room (called "representational spaces"[4]) for resistance to and re-appropriation of such space, as Soja emphasizes when describing Lefebvre's work: "Concrete spatiality – actual human geography – is thus a competitive arena for struggles over social production and reproduction,"[5] and thus there is "always room for resistance, rejection, and redirection in the nonetheless structured field of urban locales, creating an active politics of spatiality, struggles for place, space, and position within the surveillance and nodal urban landscape."[6] This latter point, I believe, is what contemporary thinkers find so alluring in Lefebvre's work: space always offers an opportunity for immediate resistance that does not rely on waiting patiently for the end of history.

In many respects, Lefebvre's production of space mirrors Marx's argument that the predominant ideology of any given society is the ideology of the ruling class, in that ideology mystifies class relations and obscures the real interests of those exploited by the prevailing organization of production. For Marx, his critique of ideology is mostly confined to the realm of abstract ideas, but it can also apply to a critique of concrete space. When applied specifically to Lefebvre's theoretical innovations, space itself assumes the character of a commodity as outlined by Marx in that the representation of space mystifies the social relations it embodies. While not peculiar to this time period, that space can be perceived as a commodity becomes incredibly important for analyzing "neo" or "late" capitalism because it is defined by a radical shift in the social organization of production. Late capitalism offers new representations that defy the classical Marxist and Fordist paradigms of cities and towns built around factory work. A sort of "base/superstructure" logic is at work in urban space: the character and organization of the city changes to fit the new requirements of a reconstituted late capitalist system.

For Lefebvre, the produced space of neocapitalism is an outgrowth of a new organization of the forces of production, which he calls "urbanization." Urbanization, on Lefebvre's account, is not peculiar to the city, but is nonetheless best illustrated by life therein: "the future of 'man' is not discovered in the cosmos, or in the people, or in production, but in urban society."[7] Urbanization, very much akin to Marx's thesis of the contrast between rural and urban social existence, is marked by a radical shift in both relations of capitalist production as well as the relationship human collectivities have to the production of their built environments. With the gradual withering away of heavily labour-intensive factory manufacturing, and the rise of new communication and information technologies, the built environment (at least in the West) shifted from one that facilitated a relatively small number of fixed production nodes (factories) and a correspondingly low level of delivery circuits (roads, rail, and flight routes), to one in which the city is understood as a single node with an almost limitless set of networks and flows internal and external to it. In this respect, Lefebvre acutely anticipated Castells's theory of "network society."[8] As a result, the mapping of the city and its flows begins to appear much more complex than, say, Engels's Manchester.[9] The flows of capital and labour in the process of urbanization become intensified in quantity, speed, duration, and direction to the point of ostensible randomness and chaos.[10]

Lefebvre frames the restructuring of social space within the classical Marxist framework of an increasing fetishization of exchange-value and exchange relations across the globe at the expense of use-value. The city, for so long exerting a relative autonomy (from a Weberian perspective) from late (monopoly) capitalism and other hegemonic structures like the state, is now increasingly rationalized as a site of exchange, divorced from the needs of its inhabitants. However, according to Lefebvre, and consistent with his tripartite dialectic of space,[11] the city never fully loses its ability to resist the neocapitalist form of urbanization. This means that the normative power of use-value, which Lefebvre encapsulates in the term *oeuvre*, always haunts the late capitalist city.[12] But what sort of image of the city must be projected in order to ensure that this new set of exploitative social relations is mystified so as to appear consistent with the logic of the commodity? The answer is that the city must be represented as a complex and chaotic site of randomness, encounter, unregulated movement and becoming; it must become radically "open." The city must be seen as ungovernable, unpredictable, perhaps even dangerous. In other words, the city must be governed by the logic of the spectacle so that no particular logic of exploitation can be identified easily. Conceptually, urban neighbourhoods and communities appear to lose their coherence and their strong sense of permanence, tradition, and solidarity. This is the new discursive character of produced space for Lefebvre's time, and his category of urbanization is consistent with, if not identical to, what we now call "globalization."[13]

It cannot be stressed enough that Lefebvre understood this shift fundamentally as of mystification and reification, one that needs to be penetrated in order to uncover the violence and exploitation at the heart of what *produces* it. In the context of Los Angeles 20 years later, Edward Soja reasserts and poignantly repeats this imperative of demystifying the urban spectacle:

> Underneath this semiotic blanket there remains an economic order, an instrumental nodal structure, an essentially exploitative spatial division of labour, and this spatially organized urban system has for the past half century been more continuously productive than almost any other in the world. But it has also been increasingly obscured from view, imaginatively mystified in an environment more specialized in the production of encompassing mystifications than practically any other you can name. As has so often been the case in the United States, this conservative deconstruction is accompanied by a numbing depoliticization of fundamental class and gender relations and conflicts. When all that is seen is so fragmented and field with whimsy and pastiche, the hard edges of the capitalist, racist and patriarchal landscape seem to disappear, melt into air.[14]

Therefore, according to Soja, the related problem or temptation for progressive theory is that:

> Spatiality is reduced to a mental construct alone, a way of thinking, an ideational process in which the "image" of reality takes epistemological precedence over the tangible substance and appearance of the real world. Social space folds into mental space, into diaphanous concepts of spatiality which all too often take us away from materialized social realities.[15]

Based on my reading of the literature, I argue that contemporary critical urban theorists have far too often succumbed to the temptation offered by the logic of urban spectacle. Ontologically speaking, Lefebvre's production of space is unmistakably clear: space is always already shifting, contested, and discursive. If the modern understanding of space is defined by space's givenness, fixity, and apolitical nature, then this new framework influenced by Lefebvre is widely understood as the "postmodern" view of space. The problem that emerges is this descriptive postmodern ontology of space quickly becomes associated with a normative one, no matter which social actors such an ontology may serve. Not only does space promise the possibility for human freedom, in a curious way it becomes free itself, like a *human being*. Political scientist Judith Garber's work reveals such an anthropomorphization of space, when she shows that many postmodern theorists tend to over-emphasize the abstract-metaphorical struggle over the meaning of space.[16] She claims that the dominant postmodern view of (urban) space is defined by three fundamental observations:

1 no space is static or asocial;
2 physical and non-physical space reproduces or performs race, sexuality, class, and gender; and
3 metaphorical space is no less "real" than physical space.[17]

In this sense, Garber argues that postmodern theories of space rely too much on abstracting political struggles from their concretely spatial realities. "Over-abstraction," she asserts, "can have perverse results, in that it works against the validation of politics, and especially political *action*, that springs from people's specific positions."[18]

It is important to note a characteristic common to Garber's three insights (that she does not herself explore): the emphasis on movement and change. The first of her observations – no space is static or asocial – by definition alludes to the importance of movement and change in the postmodern perspective of space. The second observation relies on an agentic conception of space – space "reproduces" and "performs" various discursive functions – space "acts." It "acts" in such a way that it produces social injustices based on discursive understandings of social differences. And finally, while the category "metaphor" does not in itself explicitly connote change or movement, when it is contrasted with "physical" space, it implies a sense of impermanence against the fixity of the physical. This last point contrasting metaphorical and physical space, is particularly important because it highlights the postmodern shift toward the fetishization of the image or spectacle of space over the material processes that produce it, and therefore denies one half of Lefebvre's insight into the relationship between space and its socio-economic qua ideological organization and production. Focusing on the disciplinary and potentially emancipatory character of space (as if intervening in spatial relations can in itself lead to greater social justice), is a textbook case of mistaking the symptom for the cause.

All of this discussion of postmodern theories of space amounts to what many contemporary postmodern theorists of the city appear to disavow, despite their leftist predispositions to valorize resistance on the part of the marginalized: while space is clearly not static or apolitical, and it is surely a terrain of political contestation and struggle, there appears to be a peculiar transference of the agentic qualities previously attributed to the working class and other progressive actors onto space itself. Space becomes both the terrain on which political struggle happens and also the agent of the very same struggle. It is another example, then, of how the hard core of Lefebvre's anti-capitalist reworking of spatial analysis has produced in critical urban theory a new logic of spectacle of a sort; one in which the new spatial organization of neoliberal capitalism *reflects* the normative characteristics of the marginalized instead of *repressing* them.[19] This is the most important point to take away in terms of a critique of Lefebvre's contribution to contemporary urban theory: his work has been misappropriated by critical theory to the benefit of global capital in such a way to which critical theorists appear oblivious. In specifically critical urbanist terms, this misappropriation of Lefebvre is intimately connected to the ethical turn, because the values of urban openness and inclusion are also those that underwrite post-political, cosmopolitan critical urban theory, most conspicuously, the literature on the "postmodern" city.

Doreen Massey and Open Space

If one begins with the now uncontroversial claim, originated by Lefebvre, that space is *produced* and not simply ontologically prior to human intervention, the critical scholar must decide what the normative relationship to space is for human politics and activity in general. Giving a spatial turn to the question of openness that I discussed in a more abstract fashion in the last chapter, perhaps the most crucial question in regards to this issue is whether space should be "open" or "closed." Accordingly, if space should be "open," should it be radically or only relatively "open"? What does it even mean for space to be "open"? The "openness" of space has become almost gospel for most critical urban theorists who assert that the more open space is, the more possibilities present themselves for democratic futures. From this perspective, openness and democracy become almost conflated categories. Such a conflation leads (at least when fetishized) to significant problems for popular democratic or progressive political movements. After Lefebvre, arguably the most influential theorist of space in urban studies is Doreen Massey, who penned her seminal work on the topic *For Space* in 2005. Because Massey emphasizes the need for spatial openness, her work has become especially significant for understanding the normative dimensions of space vis-à-vis politics in the city.

For Massey, space is defined by a multiplicity of relations continuously in the process of negotiation, antagonism, and becoming. Space is, therefore, by its very nature *political*: "Conceptualising space as open, multiple and relational, unfinished and always becoming, is a prerequisite for history to be open and thus a prerequisite, too, for the possibility of politics."[20] Within this context, space is understood to be radically unfixed in that it is composed of a multiplicity of *trajectories*, or processes through which phenomena change. Trajectories may refer to animate and inanimate objects, social groupings, or attitudes and ideologies.[21] The point is that all these phenomena change, grow, and diverge in space, and they do so simultaneously. It is, then, logical to conclude (as she does early in her book) that closures of space limit or discourage trajectories. As such, the radical heterogeneity of trajectories as "phenomena-in-becoming" do a certain violence to the integrity of space, and she concludes with what appears to be a normative commitment on her part: "for the future to be open, space must be open too."[22]

However, Massey is quick to acknowledge that an unconditional and uncritical attitude toward the openness of space will also create problems and contradictions for those who want to think the spatial dimensions of progressive politics. Most markedly are the logical contradictions that present themselves when thinking about particular struggles the Left tends to support in the context of the local/global dualism. How is it, she asks by way of an example, that the Left can unwaveringly show support for the Deni people of Amazonia, who want to preserve their way of life by enclosing their communities to the outside world, but simultaneously condemn European nationalists who desire the curbing of immigration?[23] In this situation, when an uncritical support for openness is mapped on to the European context, it is ostensibly logically inconsistent with a defence of the "local," in the case of the Deni. Massey's response to this dilemma is that we must first avoid the allure of simple and naive "spatial fetishization," understood as a position that posits the *form* of space (e.g., the local versus the global) as guaranteeing the normative character of "social, political, or ethical content of the relations which construct that form."[24] All spatial orders are defined by "power-geometries" that identify those benefiting and suffering from their current orderings.[25] This is another way of saying that every situation demands its own contextual analysis in order to identify the forces at work or the character of the operative political negotiations involved in the construction of that space. From this starting point, the responsibility falls on the activist, academic, or community member to engage in the appropriate political action based on issues of power differentials, inequality, and exploitation. On Massey's view, negotiated closures can, in other words, be just as legitimate from a left-critical perspective, as can be an attitude of openness.

I agree that space is indeed defined ontologically by a certain type of openness, heterogeneity, multiplicity, and its constitutive trajectories, but it is a grave mistake to assume that openness is a universally valid ethic for social and political spatial formations (an "is" does not imply an "ought"). If it is true that "for the future to be open, space must be open," the openness of the future can, in some situations, be considered *undesirable* on progressive political grounds. Change and becoming, so characteristic of so much critical thought today, can be challenged by more conservative principles to *remain the same*. The Deni, as Massey's example demonstrates, are perfectly correct in refusing incursions into their territory that would radically alter, if not entirely destroy, their culture. While it may seem obviously just in the case of the Deni, as a general principle such a strategy of exclusion is, in fact, a strongly counter-intuitive and unsettling idea with which to confront the contemporary Left. This principle, which can be expressed as a willingness to exclude or to enact closures, is a profoundly vital one for strategic interventions in the struggle over space. Indeed, an interesting proposal for the Left may be, in fact, the reversal of Massey's general support for openness. That is, instead of: "openness is generally favorable, but sometimes closures are justifiable," perhaps the principle should be "closures are preferred, but sometimes openness can be good too!" This only makes sense in a world in which openness and inclusion have become the catchphrases for a ruling elite. While such a normative position may appear scandalous and anathema to the Left, what if, in line with Brown's work on democracy (and along with "place"), closures and exclusions are precisely the anti-democratic element of democracy urban critical theory has been waiting for?

The Postmodern City qua Open City

It is my contention that, when combined with the normative commitments associated with the ethical turn in political theory, Lefebvre's and Massey's ontologies of space inform the lion's share of the ontological and normative aspects of contemporary critical urban theory. There is no brand of urban theory more illustrative of this claim than that associated with the so-called "postmodern city." As mentioned in Chapter 2, the demise of Marxism and the concomitant rise of postmodern/cosmopolitan political theory and identity politics created profound cascades throughout the humanities and social sciences. The deconstructive impulse to ruthlessly question and unsettle central disciplinary assumptions increasingly became the norm in most disciplines in the 1980s and 1990s. This postmodern turn had a distinctly spatial component as it included questioning long-held assumptions regarding the appropriate locational units for studying social and political phenomena (sometimes referred to as the question of "scale"). In political science, for example, a small but devoted community emerged intent on challenging the assumed centrality, actuality, and normative value of the state and sovereignty in politics. In fact, it is no stretch to say that most of the foundational postmodern thinkers were openly hostile to categories such as these.[26] The challenge to master categories like the state opened up an interesting space for progressive political theorizing in terms of the *site* of politics; if the state was no longer to be treated as a neutral instrument through which progressive ends can be pursued, then where? While political theorists tended to opt for the global level of analysis,[27] critical social theorists and geographers had an answer well prepared: the city. The city was a perfect category for rethinking progressive political action in an environment in which critical political thought was undergoing a serious re-evaluation of its core premises. Not only does the city lack sovereign power but, as I discussed in Chapter 1, it had traditionally proven a strong challenge to the state's hegemony.

It is no stretch to claim that the postmodern turn in *urban* studies was most prominent in the discipline of geography. As Michael Dear (a leading exponent of the postmodern turn) demonstrates, postmodern geographical theory emerged principally through debates over the nature of the city and urban planning.[28] While Lefebvre's 1974 *The Production of Space* is widely considered the seminal work, Dear identifies the first wave of postmodern geography and planning as originating in 1986 with the publication of his own article "Postmodernism and Planning"[29] and Edward Soja's essay "Taking Los Angeles Apart."[30] Later, a series of foundational texts would establish a canon of sorts, relating to the "postmodern city." This includes Soja's book *Postmodern Geographies*,[31] in which he argues, via the case study of Los Angeles, that geography needs to reject the traditional (Marxist) privileging of time as the primary determinant of social relations, and instead reassert the importance of space. Of the postmodern urban theorists discussed here, Soja remains the most Marxist as his analysis is framed explicitly within the relationship between neoliberal uneven development and the production of space in contemporary cities. However, in line with Foucault's category of "heterotopia," he also looks for resistance at the margins of society, in so-called "Thirdspaces,"[32] defined by Soja as "a purposefully tentative and flexible term that attempts to capture what is actually a constantly shifting and changing milieu of ideas, events, appearances, and meanings";[33] the concept of Thirdspace is a hallmark of postmodernist theories of space and it is most commonly used to describe spaces of deviance or resistance to the existing order. Following Soja, in 2000 Michael Dear published his book *The Postmodern Urban Condition*,[34] in which he attempts to work out a postmodern approach to the study of social sciences through an ontology of the city, one informed by "rejection of metanarrative," "distrust of rigid methodology," and the "celebration of plurality." But perhaps more importantly, according to Dear, the core of postmodern planning must be based in an ethic of "dialogue" because "all voices have the right to be heard."[35] And finally, Ash Amin and Nigel Thrift's *Cities: Reimagining the Urban* also creates an outline for a distinctly urban ontology, based on a "transhuman" phenomenology of becoming, extension, and continuous novelty,[36] which produces the city as a "routinely frenetic space."[37]

The principle of openness is very much present in normative discourses of the postmodern city, and this is often contrasted with "order" or "orderliness." The allure of the city is, to some extent, its unruliness and unpredictability vis-à-vis a higher power structure such as the nation-state. For theorists of the postmodern city, this is to be embraced and valorized; it offers unlimited potential for ways of being and becoming, even if it can be disorienting or frightening at times for residents. Such a discourse posits the city as a site of resistance, typified by sentiments like the following by Richard Sennett: "all these aspects of experience [in the city] – difference, complexity, strangeness – afford resistance to domination."[38] To practice an ethical relationship with space is to allow it to flourish in accordance with its nature, or to avoid blocking its ever-becoming. This means that space is free the more it lacks centralized institutions of power and people determine the way they live in an autonomous manner. Critics, such as Don Mitchell, have explored the practical implications of such a position: "Postmodern planning begins from the assumption of a radically complex and anarchic social world and requires that we encourage the *further* disordering,"[39] and this is confirmed by lines like this in the work of Nigel Thrift: "an affirmation of life, can be seen as a means of celebrating the joyous, even transcendent, confusion of life itself."[40] In this respect, the theory of the postmodern city parallels the postmodern understanding of the de-centred subject; the city is to be free in its becoming, as the subject is to be free in its becoming.

However, when it comes to concrete prescriptive analyses, the limitations of the canonical theorists of the postmodern city are put into sharp relief in a similar manner to those of the more generalist ethical theorists who I covered in Chapters 2 and 3. Take, for example, Thrift and Amin. Their book *Cities* is more of an overview of post-structural criticisms of traditional urban studies, rather than a "call to arms"-style issue-based manifesto for resistance in the city. As such, it is difficult to identify what their opinions are regarding specific urban social problems or policies. However, in their less formal writing they demonstrate what can only be called a traditionally cosmopolitan perspective on contemporary political issues. Thrift, for example, publishes regular blog posts for *The Chronicle of Higher Education*. The topics he deals with are manifold, and not detailed or rigorous in any traditional academic sense, but he shows great respect for global "compromise" politics,[41] as well as Britain's place in the EU (with no attention paid to the actual concerns of the British working class).[42] Similarly, Amin has written an editorial "manifesto" for the *Guardian* intended to challenge the growing anti-EU and anti-immigrant ethos in Britain. Consisting largely of cosmopolitan platitudes, he calls for inclusiveness, openness, and diversity in Europe: "Such an ethos," he opines, "would enable us to confront the common concerns of all members of European society independently of their origin."[43] Finally, similar to the content of Amin and Thrift's book, Dear does not really establish a normative position regarding the problems of the city in *The Postmodern Urban Condition*. Instead he only alludes to them in his valorization of the "epistemological politics"[44] and the deconstructive power of postmodernism, as part of his rejection of liberal and Marxist critiques of postmodern geography. Most of his recent normative work has been focused on opposing the erection of walls along the US/Mexican border.[45] In this case, his work reads as not dissimilar to the standard position of the Democratic Party. Overall, the canon of the postmodern city lacks what many would consider essential for a "critical" urban theory, that is, a concrete focus on social justice. This all bolsters Don Mitchell's position when he refers to the postmodern city as the "post-justice" city.[46]

As mentioned earlier, Soja's approach to urban struggle is different than the others in that it remains more explicitly (neo-)Marxist and truer to the normative thrust of Lefebvre's argument. In the absence of a strong post-humanist orientation, Soja retains the language of "justice" unreservedly. But in a twist concurrent with the spatial turn, he introduces a new spatialized dimension to the discourses on justice by developing the concept of "spatial justice." In his book *Seeking Spatial Justice*, Soja argues that spatial justice is informed by the idea that all processes that create just or unjust outcomes will include a geographical element or a re-ordering of space. As he suggests, spatial justice is not meant to replace or pre-empt social or economic justice, but instead to show that the geographical and social are always intertwined in what he calls the "socio-spatial dialectic."[47] In brief, spatial justice is understood as a lens through which to understand an underappreciated aspect of justice. Struggles for social justice are on Soja's account always also struggles over geography:

> Activating this strategically foregrounded spatial perspective ... is the ... recognition that the geographies in which we live can have both positive and negative effects on our lives. They are not just dead background or a neutral physical stage for the human drama but are filled with material and imagined forces that affect events and experiences, forces that can hurt us or help us in nearly everything we do.[48]

Justice for Soja, in general, is the guiding principle of contemporary progressive political action. He sees this category as a "unifying force for social activism" that moves beyond a

> traditional binary, or we/they, politics of economic equality, attached to rigidly defined and often exclusionary channels of oppositional resistance based on class, race, gender, or sexual preference ... instead, the emphasis ... [should be] on an inclusive and combinative rather than exclusive and narrowly channeled political mobilization ... Achieving greater justice here becomes a more encompassing, inclusive, and above all feasible goal than achieving full equality or fomenting revolutionary transformation.[49]

There is a lot to unpack in the above quotation. First, by explicitly rejecting a "we/they" political logic, spatial justice appears to be by definition post-political or just another theoretical manifestation of the ethical turn. However, in this case Soja's motive is to unify social activists who may be divided by their political identifications and, therefore, spatial justice as a category may still employ a properly political relationship to those outside the social activism sphere. However, I think this is unlikely because of the thrust of the clause and sentence that follows his reference to uniting identity-based groups. The second clause of the first sentence asserts that the emphasis of spatial justice should be on inclusivity and "combinative political mobilization" versus exclusionary and parochial approaches. The second sentence reiterates the importance of inclusivity, and adds feasibility to the list of normative characteristics of a spatial justice orientation, because (it is implied) "full equality" and "revolutionary transformation" are unfeasible goals. The basic idea underlying Soja's position on justice, then, is that it seeks to be inclusive and pragmatic; it eschews revolutionary politics and gives up on the struggle for full equality. How, exactly, does this differ from standard, non-spatialized social democratic or left-liberal perspectives on social justice? It does not, as far as I can tell. This is not to say that his position is entirely flawed – as an end goal of political practice, revolution needs to be treated cautiously (a desire for revolution as totality is, indeed, a dangerous, if not impossible, desire), and the Left should always strive to unite diverse groups in struggles for social justice – but it simply does not appear to be *political*. The entire normative thrust of Soja's spatial justice is, in other words, to avoid both living under disciplinary power regimes and exerting power over others.

The emergence of postmodern urban studies, with its novel spatial ontologies, is but one example of a broader trend of theorizing the normative relationship between "openness" and the city. Much like the ethical turn in political theory, this approach to urban theory spans the ideological spectrum from radical anti-capitalist post-structuralism to left-liberal/cosmopolitanism (and even to unapologetically pro-free-market neoliberalism). There is a normative dovetailing in otherwise disparate ideological positions in the emphasis on freedom-as-openness – in all cases, the city is free only to the extent it is open, changing, moving. For Deleuzian insurrectionists, such as the members of the "Invisible Committee," this movement is always one directed away from power (the "line of flight" argument, explored in Chapter 2).[50] For a cosmopolitan or Habermasian, this form of openness is necessary for deliberative democracy (the "town hall meeting") and exposure to difference, as well as a mechanism for discouraging petty parochialisms and intolerance toward, say, immigrants and the neighbourhoods they inhabit.[51] For a communitarian, openness encourages the formation of "public space" and serves as a check against its privatization,[52] while a neoliberal views openness as a precondition for optimally effective capital flows – in a city constantly undergoing decay and revitalization.[53] Much like the Deleuzian example cited above, all these discourse are concerned with power, specifically, the concentration of power. Openness is understood by both neoliberals and post-structuralists, then, as a curative to power – openness dilutes power and allows subjects to avoid being dominated by it, whether the power in question originates in the state or from capital flows. My position remains that this conception of openness is symptomatic of the turn in political theory that I discussed in Chapter 2 – that which shifted the terrain of the political to the realm of ethics. Distinguishing between these two realms of social action – the political and the ethical – is crucial for constructing a theoretical framework that challenges the logic of the "open" city.

Properly Political Theories of the City

Of course, postmodern, cosmopolitan, or otherwise "open" theories of the city do not constitute the entirety of critical urbanism. Just as with any social-scientific academic discipline, predominant theories are always also objects of internal disciplinary critique and resisted by alternative critical traditions. Indeed, a number of prominent scholars share, at least implicitly, many of the same central concerns that I have with postmodern approaches to understanding the city. Particularly prominent in this regard are those associated with the very well-established tradition of Marxist urbanism in geography. The analyses of thinkers like David Harvey, the late Neil Smith, and Erik Swyngedouw, categorically recognize the need to reject the fetishization of openness and inclusivity, which means an embracing of exclusionary politics, at least to an extent. Swyngedouw, for example, explicitly uses the language of post-politics and the properly political when he defines urban planning as governed by a "technocratic consensus" by an "alliance" between the state and capital; a consensus informed by an "inclusive cosmopolitanism" acting as its moral foundation.[54] It is in the work of these theorists that a properly political theory of the city is most developed, although some of their political insights are only implied and require further articulation if they are to fit my taxonomical category of the properly political.

Smith calls the broader theoretical movement that informs post-political approaches to the city as "neo-critical geography," and he claims it is symptomatic of neoliberalism writ large. Neo-critical geography, he suggests, reflects a watered-down capitalist co-optation of radical political ideas that emerged in the mid to late twentieth century (including feminism, queer liberation, and critical race theory) into a harmless and depoliticized pluralist discourse of "diversity" and "multiculturalism." "Once the potent weapon of an oppositional politics," Smith argues, "they are now emblems of establishment neoliberalism largely emptied of radical potential."[55] In his article "What's Left?" Smith focuses most of his energy on scrutinizing the work of Amin and Thrift who propose a radically depoliticized cosmopolitanism as the source of a renewed self-understanding of the Geographical Left; a cosmopolitanism that disavows any past desire for "radical social change" and instead suggests that we "get with our ethical selves, embrace a playful and pluralist agonism, and just let a hundred flowers bloom, the future will surely be rosy."[56]

But it is in Smith's critique of neo-critical geography's relation to power that his properly political sentiments are most strongly implied. Quoting Amin and Thrift, he demonstrates that their New Left will be "heterarchical" in orientation because the world is no longer "hierarchical" in its organization of power;[57] instead, following Thomas Friedman's well know formulation, Amin and Thrift posit the world as flat, thereby contradicting one of the long-standing and founding assumptions of critical geography: uneven development.[58] Once the world has been declared "flat," Smith argues, geography has been rendered post-political, becoming an ally of neoliberalism:

> [i]n the neo-liberal vision, it is fairly clear what political work the idea of a flattened, non-hierarchial earth does. The despatialization of our global purview represents a simultaneous depoliticization: when all places are co-equal, geographical difference may persist – cities versus jungles – but no longer as a vector of gross inequality and no longer therefore as a vector of political opposition.... "Proceed ethically" becomes the strongest of political admonitions when confronted with the question "what is to be done." Politics is flattened into a feel-good ethics.... A moralism of convenience transmutes into a politics of convenience.[59]

It is with this strong foundational critique of post-political thinking that Smith engages in his own political theorization of political struggles in the city.

Smith's mentor, David Harvey, applies a similarly properly political analysis to the study of urban geography (including a comprehensive exploration of the postmodern turn in his seminal *The Condition of Postmodernity*[60]). His guiding premise is that capitalism has always used the city as a central site of investment and rent-seeking behaviour, and that this is especially discernible during periods of crisis. A major strategy for capitalist growth, he argues (citing Appelbaum), especially in twentieth-century America (but also in other parts of the world), has been "building houses and filling them with things."[61] His two favourite historical examples of this strategy are the Haussmanian reconstruction of central Paris in the 1800s, and Robert Moses's remodelling of Long Island in the mid-twentieth century. Thus, Harvey's analysis is very much consistent with Soja's (who devotes a significant portion of *Postmodern Geographies* to Harvey's work). Both understand how the logic of capitalism will produce distinct urban organizational forms in its own interest but, at least for Harvey, this does not imply that radically new strategies of collective resistance must be theorized; strategies that jettison categories like community or historical materialism (that is, strategies requiring ontological and epistemological breaks with existing progressive thought).

It is in relation to his work on the urban commons, however, that Harvey is at his most properly political. He explicitly targets the Left's uncomfortable relationship to power as posing a severe problem for effective political organizing. The contemporary Left, Harvey argues, fetishizes the democratic potential of horizontal power relations over and against enclosure and hierarchy. "Hierarchy," he claims, "is anathema to many segments of the oppositional left these days."[62] The commons, in contrast, is regularly held up as a site of horizontal power relations and universal inclusion and, therefore, a curative to enclosure and hierarchy. However, on his account, this conflation of the commons and inclusion is premised on a fundamental misunderstanding of the nature of the commons, which always includes some practice of enclosure and exclusion. I examine Harvey's work on the commons in much greater detail in Chapter 6, but the gist of his position is that all demands for local autonomy – all attempts to assert the power and legitimacy of a community – are, at least in part, exclusionary and designed to enclose space from outsiders. "At the end of it all," he muses, "the analyst is often left with a simple decision: Whose side are you on, whose common interests do you seek to protect, and by what means?"[63] This is another way of stating Schmitt's formulation of the antagonistic essence of the political.

It is in the realm of conceiving politics that analytical models diverge between the postmodern and the Marxist. One can easily assert that both postmodern and more traditional Marxist theorists of the city agree that cities have been significantly restructured in the era of neoliberalism. That said, the postmodern theorists whose ideas have been criticized in this chapter have a tendency to approach this restructuring as an opportunity to rethink political resistance and action by (disavowedly) using a logic very similar to that of the neoliberal city.

Conversely, Marxists such as Harvey emphasize the importance of penetrating and negating this logic in order to reassert traditional or modern conceptions of collective action designed to "reclaim" the city for the masses. While most leftists today would agree that *orthodox* Marxism is no longer a sufficient position for understanding or for building a progressive political movement, it does serve the Left well to be reminded of its eminently political character in terms of avowing an us-versus-them adversarial worldview. Orthodox Marxism is not sufficient because its particular we/they dualism is not nearly nuanced enough for understanding the way in which social relations of domination produce non-(explicitly)class-based forms of oppression. Additionally, to the extent that Marxism still might promote violence to further revolutionary goals, it should certainly be questioned, or at least approached cautiously. Mouffe is correct (and against Žižek) that significant political change should be pursued through peaceful, preferably democratic means (although this does not exclude militant direct action), as much as humanly possible. The political lesson to learn from Marxist urbanism is, nonetheless, that the city is populated by groups defined by class-based antagonistic relations. While some of these antagonisms may be overcome through dialogue, others are irresolvable outside of genuinely political struggle. Thus, when conceptualizing the city theoretically, the "open" city model is, by definition, a depoliticized one. A properly political understanding of the city involves recognizing closure, exclusions, and antagonisms as not only inevitable, but also desirable.

Conclusion

In summary, the production of space radically shifted Marxist notions of production and class struggle away from exclusively historical analyses that assume factory workers as the subject/object of history, toward spatial analyses and heterogeneous, fluid conceptions of class. Lefebvre's theoretical intervention was crucial for re-conceptualizing progressive politics in anticipation of the globalization of capitalism. However, over time Lefebvre's radically heterodox Marxism, which strongly condemns the society of the spectacle, came to reify and validate the original object of his critique. Lefebvre's observations of how capitalism produces urban space so as to mystify exploitative class relations, in a peculiar way became reified as normative processes by late twentieth-century critical urban theorists. Out of this Lefebvrian analysis of space flows a sort of glorification, if not fetishization, of the indeterminacy, openness, and liberatory promises of space. Again, Doreen Massey's (qualified) slogan encapsulates this fetishization well: "for the future to be open, space must be open." The predominant postmodern position appears to be that the apparent chaos and fluid spaces of the postmodern city can be conceptually rendered as a source of anti-capitalist resistance against the closed and well-circumscribed material structures that are obvious reflections of urban social inequality (gated communities and corporate skyscrapers representing some of the most commonly cited examples). But what must be remembered is that the appearance of randomness and flux is *just as much a product of capitalism as a gated community is*. Just as cosmopolitanism is the ideology of the upper-middle and elite classes, to celebrate the transience, unpredictability, and disorderly nature of the city as a normative ideal, is a position that only someone already secure in their life-situation could believe with any sincerity; someone like Benjamin's *flâneur*, for example. A poor person living in a precarious rental apartment certainly does not desire that the space of their community be "open," if being "open" means the threat of dislocation and dispossession.

The open city is a theoretical construction fed by many of the key insights of what has been called in this book ethical critical theory. These include cosmopolitan commitments – commitments that have had a strangely de-territorializing effect on the city. The city's concrete character, its intimate ties to situated communities, is dispersed and diluted in an ephemeral and floating constellation of almost absolute difference. This is a far cry from the Ancients' conception of the city as an enclosed space in which an identifiable and exclusive community comes together to determine its common affairs. Instead, the open city appears as a sort of agent itself that sweeps up its denizens in a whirlwind that stimulates, on the one hand, self-discovery, self-expression, and creativity, but on the other hand, enacts constitutive exclusions based on race, class, gender, and sexuality. Outside of the "relative fixity" of real estate,[64] there is no permanence in the open city, only movement and change – the ontology of the city mirrors almost precisely the (n)ontology of the de-centred subject. In the next chapter this conception of the open city is situated in another critical narrative that speaks to changes in capitalist cultural imperatives: Paul Virilio's theory of "dromocracy."

Notes

1 Edward Glaeser, *Triumph of the City: How Our Greatest Invention Makes Us Richer, Smarter, Greener, Healthier, and Happier* (New York: The Penguin Press, 2011), 129.
2 Susan Fainstein, "Planning Theory and the City," *Journal of Planning Education and Research* 25(2) (2005).
3 Henri Lefebvre, *The Production of Space*, trans. Donald Nicholson-Smith (Malden: Blackwell, 1974), 136.
4 Ibid., 141.
5 Edward W. Soja, *Postmodern Geographies: The Reassertion of Space in Critical Social Theory* (New York: Verso, 1989), 130.
6 Ibid., 235.
7 Lefebvre, *Production of Space*, 173.
8 Manuel Castells, *The Rise of the Network Society: The Information Age: Economy, Society, and Culture*, Vol. I, 2nd edition (Malden: Wiley-Blackwell, 2010).
9 Friedrich Engels, *The Condition of the Working Class in England in 1844* (London: Oxford University Press, 2009).
10 The key word here is "ostensible" because, akin to demonstrating the mystified logic of the commodity, it is the critical theorist's duty to reveal the logical order underneath the seeming chaos of urban flows.
11 See: Christian Schmid, "Henri Lefebvre's Theory of the Production of Space: Towards a Three-Dimensional Dialectic," in *Space, Difference, Everyday Life: Reading Henri Lefebvre*, ed. Kanishka Goonewardena, Sefan Kipfer, Richard Milgrom, and Christian Schmid (New York: Routledge, 2008).

12 Henri Lefebvre, *Writings on Cities*, ed. and trans. Eleonore Kofman and Elizabeth Lebas (Malden: Blackwell, 2000), 73.
13 David J. Madden, "City Becoming World: Nancy, Lefebvre, and the Global–Urban Imagination," *Environment and Planning D: Society and Space* 30(5) (2012).
14 Soja, *Postmodern Geographies*, 246.
15 Ibid., 125.
16 The theorists she cites in particular are: Watson and Gibson, Rose, Ruddick, and Breitbart and E.-J. Pader. See: Judith Garber, "The City as a Heroic Public Sphere," in *Democracy, Citizenship, and the Global City*, ed. Engin Isin (New York: Routledge, 2002).
17 Ibid., 265.
18 Ibid., pp. 257–258.
19 See for example Don Mitchell's critical insight that too many postmodern geographers see globalized capital as "disorganized" and therefore the changes in cities are "random" (in particular, he accuses Dear and Flusty of promoting this sort of position) (Don Mitchell, "Postmodern Geographical Praxis? The Postmodern Impulse and the War Against Homeless People in the 'Post-Justice City'," in *Postmodern Geography*, ed. Claudio Minca [Malden: Blackwell Publishers, 2001], 71).
20 Doreen Massey, *For Space* (London: SAGE Publications, 2005), 12.
21 Ibid., 59.
22 Ibid.
23 Ibid., 164–165.
24 Ibid., 101.
25 Ibid., 166.
26 Rob Walker, *After the Globe, before the World* (New York: Routledge, 2009); Chris Brown, " 'Turtles All the Way Down': Anti-Foundationalism, Critical Theory and International Relations," *Millennium-Journal of International Studies* 23(2) (1994): 213–236; and the edited volume, Richard Wyn Jones, ed., *Critical Theory and World Politics* (New York: Lynne Rienner Publishers, 2001).
27 Ibid.
28 Michael Dear, "The Postmodern Turn," in *Postmodern Geography: Theory and Praxis*, ed. Claudio Minca (Malden: Blackwell, 2001), 13.
29 Michael Dear, "Postmodernism and Planning," *Environment and Planning D: Society and Space* 4 (1986).
30 Edward Soja, "Taking Los Angeles Apart: Some Fragments of a Critical Human Geography," *Environment and Planning D: Society and Space* 4 (1986).
31 Soja, *Postmodern Geographies*.
32 Mitchell, "Postmodern Geographical Praxis?"
33 Edward Soja, *Thirdspace: Journeys to Los Angeles and Other Real-and-Imagined Places* (Oxford: Blackwell, 1996), 2.
34 Michael Dear, *The Postmodern Urban Condition* (Malden: Blackwell, 2000).
35 Dear, "Postmodern Turn," 21.
36 Ash Amin and Nigel Thrift, *Cities: Reimagining the Urban* (Malden: Polity Press, 2002), 26–27.
37 Amin and Thrift, " 'Emancipatory' City?"
38 Richard Sennett, *Flesh and Stone: The Body and the City in Western Civilization* (New York: W.W. Norton, 1994), 26.
39 Mitchell, "Postmodern Geographical Praxis?" 59.
40 Nigel Thrift, *Non-Representational Theory: Space, Politics, Affect* (New York: Routledge, 2008), 15.
41 Nigel Thrift, "A Growing Global Appreciation for the Value of Compromise," *The Chronicle of Higher Education*, last updated July 9, 2013, accessed March 16, 2014, http://chronicle.com/blogs/worldwise/a-growing-global-appreciation-for-the-value-of-compromise/32369.

42 Nigel Thrift, "If Britain Withdraws from the EU Education Would Suffer," *The Chronicle of Higher Education*, last updated December 20, 2012, accessed March 16, 2014, http://chronicle.com/blogs/worldwise/if-britain-withdraws-from-the-e-u-higher-education-would-suffer/31237.
43 Ash Amin, "A Manifesto for a New Europe," last updated July 14, 2010, accessed March 16, 2014, www.theguardian.com/commentisfree/2010/jul/14/manifesto-new-europe-politics-hope.
44 Dear, *Postmodern Urban Condition*, 285–316.
45 See: Michael Dear, *Why Walls Don't Work: Repairing the US–Mexico Divide* (London: Oxford University Press, 2013).
46 See, again: Mitchell, "Postmodern Geographical Praxis?"
47 Edward W. Soja, *Seeking Spatial Justice* (Minneapolis: University of Minnesota Press, 2010), 4.
48 Ibid., 19.
49 Ibid., 23.
50 The Invisible Committee, *The Coming Insurrection* (Los Angeles: Semiotext(e), 2008); Amin and Thrift, *Cities*.
51 See, for example: Iris Marion Young, *Justice and the Politics of Difference* (Princeton: Princeton University Press, 1990).
52 See for example: Lynn A. Staeheli and Don Mitchell, *The People's Property: Power, Politics, and the Public* (New York: Routledge, 2008); Margaret Kohn, *Brave New Neighborhoods: The Privatization of Public Space* (New York: Routledge, 2004).
53 See for example: Glaeser, *Triumph of the City*; Robert Ellickson, *Order Without Law: How Neighbors Settle Disputes* (Boston: Harvard University Press, 1994); Richard Florida, *Cities and the Creative Class* (New York: Routledge, 2004).
54 Swyngedouw, "Designing the Post-Political City," 21.
55 Neil Smith, "What's Left? Neo-Critical Geography, Or, The Flat Pluralist World of Business Class," *Antipode* 37(5) (2005): 887–899, 891.
56 Ibid., 892.
57 Ibid.
58 Ibid., 894.
59 Ibid.
60 David Harvey, *The Condition of Postmodernity: An Enquiry into the Origins of Cultural Change* (Cambridge, MA: Basil Blackwell, 1989).
61 Harvey, *Rebel Cities*, 130–131.
62 Ibid., 70.
63 Ibid., 71.
64 See: David Harvey, *Social Justice and the City* (Oxford: Blackwell, 1988), 186.

5 Gentrification and the Dromocratic City

The nomad has no passport – or has too many of them.[1]

Hobbes begins his Magnus Opus *Leviathan* by making a peculiar, physics-inspired, observation about human beings: both the natural and moral worlds are explained by bodies in motion; human life itself is only possible when it is predicated on movement. According to Hobbes, then, much like a fish that cannot stop moving, movement is essential to human life (forget the Wolfman, the Hobbesian subject is Aquaman!). But what does it mean to move, and how does this human necessity relate to the concerns of critical political theory? Should humans move as much as possible to ensure that they live a "good," as opposed to "bare," life? Is mobility a core aspiration of political theory? What if we don't really want to move much beyond the involuntary operations of our critical organs? If we answer these questions ambivalently with the liberal statement that people should feel free to move as much as they want, what does this mean for theorizing space? It would appear prima facie that space should be open so that those who would like to move have the ability to do so, and those who do not share such a desire, are not so compelled. This sounds like a simple and uncontroversial principle, who would oppose it? The problem that I have with attaching normative value to mobility is not related to its abstract formulation, but in the way it acts as a disciplinary force in concrete social contexts. In this chapter an argument is presented that states that the predominant left-critical normative attitude toward subjectivity and (specifically urban) space creates a discursive situation in which the decision to move or not to move is decided in advance. Movement is considered imperative and non-negotiable, but only for the most disadvantaged of populations. It is these populations that are most compelled to move but, ironically, those least likely to benefit from compulsory mobility. While this principle can be extended to most realms of social activity, in respect to the spaces of the city, this injunction to move is most pronounced in a distinctly urban phenomenon: gentrification. Movement, as normatively associated with new experiences, the principle of encounter, and experiential learning, acts as a smokescreen for the dissolution, destruction, and dispossession of inner-city communities resulting from gentrification.

But the story does not end there. Not only does the critical fetish of movement in contemporary critical urbanism enable processes like gentrification, the logic of the contemporary neoliberal restructuring of the city promises the *speeding up* of such processes. If speed and movement are normative principles governing the contemporary city, then it is an ideal time to return to Paul Virilio's theory of "dromocracy." Dromocracy is a form of governance that uses the imperative for speed as a technique of discipline and control; a form of crowd control based on dilution and disbursement. The main argument in this chapter is the following: while a critique of dromocracy is not employed explicitly by Virilio to denounce gentrification (and very little, if none at all, of the secondary literature uses it in this way either), as a critical tool, his method known as "dromology" significantly bolsters political-economic accounts of gentrification (like those offered by Neil Smith and David Harvey). The consequence of exploring critical urbanism through a dromological lens is that it shows, quite starkly, how dromocratic normative ideas inform much of both critical urban theory and neoliberal urban planning.

Dromocracy and the "Obligation to Movement"

Recent critical urban planning scholarship, particularly that of David Imbroscio, has noted the central normative role that movement plays in government-sponsored schemes for tackling the most common social challenges faced by inner-city communities. "There is a heavy reliance," he argues, "on moving people through metropolitan space as a means of addressing urban social problems."[2] This emphasis on movement is embodied in what he calls "Liberal Urban Policy" (LUP), an overarching category that includes prominent American urbanist programs like the Gautreaux Project, Move to Opportunity, and Hope VI.[3] At the heart of LUP is the notion that because poor and underprivileged urbanites are "trapped" in communities that lack economic opportunities, what they require by way of government assistance is greater mobility so as to gain access to urban spaces rich with economic activity. By mobility, Imbroscio means not only the ability of the poor to travel to more affluent neighbourhoods for work (for which the government might provide subsidized public transit programs or other subsidy schemes), but also moving in the conventional sense (relocation of one's primary residence). In fact, he claims that most LUP discourses are governed by the idea that poor residents need to move *more than once* in order to create the maximal amount of social mixing and to ensure that no neighbourhoods become too depleted of residents.[4] Thus, LUP can be understood as working within what he calls the "Mobility Paradigm" of urban policy.

This is a classical liberal approach to social issues because it is not designed to guarantee greater equity in terms of *outcomes* for individuals, but instead to create equality of *opportunity*;[5] poor people are provided access to the urban *spaces* that give them the greatest opportunity to find work and escape the cycle of poverty, but they are not directly provided guaranteed employment. While Imbroscio shows that after decades of experimenting with various ambitious LUP programs, the desired outcomes of such plans have not materialized. They have not, for example, increased economic opportunity[6] or "racial balance"[7] in any significant manner. From my perspective, the success or failure of specific manifestations of LUP is of course important for social justice organizing, however, it is not especially relevant to my present argument. What is consequential, is Imbroscio's shrewd identification of one of LUP's most fundamental flawed assumptions: that people naturally want to move and that it is economically rational (and, therefore, *generally* rational) for the poor to desire moving from one neighbourhood to another. LUP operates under the notion that underprivileged people are trapped in their communities and would clearly opt to leave them, given the chance to do so. It naturalizes the assumption that specific places do not matter to people except to the extent they provide economic opportunities. I will speak to the philosophical-ontological failings of these assumptions in the "Philosophical Excursus" that follows this chapter, but for now it is important to demonstrate the alternative type of urban policy that is erased by the naturalization of the Mobility Paradigm. Imbroscio argues that instead of mobility, urban planning should focus on *placemaking*. Thus, instead of moving people to places of greater economic opportunity, the emphasis should be on building within impoverished communities the infrastructure and institutions required to help them become places of wealth and opportunity. For Imbroscio, this means not only building better schools, renovating housing stock, or building public housing, but first and foremost promoting local community ownership of productive assets within inner-city neighbourhoods (in another article he calls this the "Ownership Paradigm").[8]

The tension or, perhaps one could say, the "antagonism" between the logics and power-effects of the Mobility Paradigm and the Placemaking Paradigm is a major axis around which my argument revolves, although I do not use these specific terms. The takeaway of Imbroscio's work is that movement is a political category – it is imbued with a certain social power. While his analysis is limited primarily to the field of contemporary urban policy, it can also be situated in a long historical-philosophical tradition that tracks the evolution of the city's relationship to circulation and individual mobility.

Richard Sennett has documented this history in his excellent book *Flesh and Stone*. In the history of urban planning, he observes, the relationship between human bodies and movement in the city has a long tradition, stretching back to at least eighteenth-century Europe. At this time, inspired by relatively new medical discoveries related to the human body, new imaginaries of the city were germinating in the minds and discourses of the European intelligentsia. More specifically, Sennett claims that it was William Harvey's revelation that the heart pumps blood throughout the body, published in his 1628 medical manual *De motu cordis*, that spurred urban planners to fundamentally rethink the normative nature of cities.[9] In this urban reimagining, a stress was placed on the circulatory character of urban space. As a result, cities were increasingly designed "to function like a healthy body, freely flowing as well as possessed of clean skin,"[10] and, therefore,

> [i]nstead of planning streets for the sake of ceremonies of movement toward an object, as did the Baroque planner, the Enlightenment planner made

> motion an end in itself. The Baroque planner emphasized progress toward a monumental destination, the enlightened planner emphasized the journey itself.[11]

Just as the constant and unimpeded circulation of blood in the body produces the healthy body, these Enlightenment planners posited that so too does the healthy city aim to stimulate its population to move in and around its borders. Urban citizens were considered to be analogous to the blood of a healthy body, whose happiness and, indeed, morality, was a function of circulation and movement.

Writing almost 30 years earlier than Sennett, Paul Virilio (a French contemporary of Lefebvre) connected the fetishization of movement in urban life to the wider socio-economic relations of late-modernity. Virilio is a highly original thinker associated with the small, but interesting, area of social science research known as "speed theory," which emphasizes the contemporary effects of speed on cultural and political phenomena. By situating the phenomenon of "speeding up" in the context of a normative approach to scientific, technological, and infrastructural "progress," Virilio, in effect, denounces speed: "I fight against the propaganda of progress, and this propaganda bears the name of never-ending acceleration."[12] The adjective he applies to such visions of progress is "dromological" – from the Ancient Greek for "race track" – because it relates to "the study and analysis of the increasing speed of transport and communications on the development of land-use."[13]

For Virilio, dromology is first associated with the study of warfare and, in particular, the need for ever-greater speed in military technology in order to overcome the physical and spatial barriers to conquest. But dromology is also concerned with how speed is active in social contexts, especially in the area of policing and discipline. The active excitation of the masses, the enabling and encouragement of constant movement in civilian populations, takes the form of what he calls "dromocracy" – a socially-structural incitement to movement. It is in the revolutionary period of nineteenth-century Europe that Virilio marks the beginning of dromocracy as a type of governance:

> The events of 1789 claimed to be a revolt against subjection, that is, against the constraint to immobility symbolized by the ancient feudal serfdom … a revolt against arbitrary confinement and the obligation to reside in one place. But no one as yet suspected that the conquest of the freedom to come and go so dear to Montaigne could, by sleight of hand, become an *obligation to mobility*.[14]

For Virilio, this is the beginning of an emergent "dictatorship of movement" in Europe – the informal, yet structural "dromocracy" – that enacts a certain violence to space, while serving as an effective form of crowd control. In *Speed and Politics* he states: "As soon as it takes power, the Nazi government offers the German proletariat sport and transport. No more riots, no need for much repression; to empty the streets, it's enough to promise everyone the highway."[15] In this context, the only political resistance to dromocracy or the dictatorship of movement is, quite simply, a refusal to move, as he illustrates through a discussion of the 1848 French Revolution: "In fact, the watchword of these 'workers battalions', as those who would be deported by force to the provinces or drafted into the army were called, was '*we're stayin*' … we're not moving from here!"[16] It is in this vein that, for Virilio, speed qua movement plays an important socio-political role in modern, post-Fordist governance and discipline, while refusing to move emerges as a form of resistance to a compulsory *dromomania*.

Virilio's insights point to a shift in cultural discourse and social values, the importance of which cannot be overstated. Advanced capitalist societies place a high premium on not just the right to mobility, but the normative value of movement itself. Just consider the explosion over the past 40 years in the popularity of leisure travel, working or volunteering abroad schemes, university exchanges, gap years, and so on. Concerning gap years, by some accounts, this practice has become so popular in Australia that those who are unable to, or choose to not leave their homes for one or two years after high school, are looked at with suspicion by their peers. What can one make of all this? There appears to exist a middle-class conception that in order to fully realize one's potential, or to truly squeeze out of life all that one can, one must travel – not exclusively internationally, but also within one's own country, and to a lesser extent, one's city; *Flâneurie* – enjoying the unfamiliar via constant movement and observation – once confined exclusively to the arcades of Paris, has gone global! This is perhaps best encapsulated by Nigel Thrift's post-structuralist theory of human nature, the theme of his book *Non-Representational Theory*. He states (non-critically) in the introduction:

> This is a book based on the leitmotif of movement in its many forms. Thus, to begin with, it would be possible to argue that human life is based on and in movement.… movement captures the joy – I will not say simple – of living as a succession of luminous or mundane instants.[17]

In this case, "joy" can only be "captured" in the process of moving and, therefore, a sedentary life is presumably joyless.

But as I demonstrated earlier, categories associated with enjoyment must never be accepted uncritically as natural or unmediated expressions of our essential humanity. Dromocracy, and the enjoyment it provides, clearly serves an ideological function, one intimately connected to the logic of neoliberal capitalism. While both dromocracy and capitalism possess a structural imperative to movement, dromocracy is defined by a pure normative relationship to motion, capitalist dynamics are more complicated. Drawing on Marx's *Capital*, David Harvey demonstrates how capitalism relies on both "fixed" and "circulatory" capital. Fixed capital refers to any physical asset that is not exhausted in the process of production, but will wear out over time. The classic example of fixed capital is industrial (production) machinery, but also includes the actual factories and other physical infrastructure required for capital accumulation (e.g., airports or shopping malls). In this respect, a dialectical relationship exists between fixed and circulatory capital (as well as between different types of fixed capital), which is another way of saying that effective circulation relies on fixity and vice versa.[18] Neil Smith explains this clearly: "the dynamism of geographical space is equally an expression of capital ... the geographical expression of the constant necessary movement from fixed to circulating capital and back to fixed [...] from use-value to exchange value and back to use-value."[19] So it is incorrect to say that capitalism thrives *absolutely* on movement, because fixed capital is required to facilitate smooth circulation. This is nowhere more apparent than in contemporary cities where the co-called "second-circuit" of capital in real estate has become a significant contributor to the global economy.[20] Therefore, when discussing dromocracy in relation to capitalist processes, I am referring primarily to normative social discourses, i.e., discourses related to people on the move. Clearly real estate capitalism requires a certain level of durability in the houses and condos it constructs. However, in the developers' and mortgage lenders' ideal world, the buyers and renters of real estate would be constantly circulating between them: buying and selling their properties; they would always be on the move, circulating both their bodies and their money.

Within the context of dromocracy, and the "joy" of circulation, a connection exists between the contemporary discourses of self-actualization and mobility. This can be understood as another manifestation of Žižek's superego injunction to enjoy discussed in Chapter 3, but articulated as an imperative to move. As a peremptory edict of the superego, dromomania becomes internalized and subjects are afflicted by guilt if they are not moving enough. Here, again, the logic of critical theory and neoliberalism coincide. As discussed above, capitalism thrives on a certain type of movement – on removing barriers to human circulation, whether it's for business, labour, or tourism. On the labour side of the coin, once such barriers are removed, the training that members of the younger generation received while they were backpacking Europe prepares them perfectly for the new fluid and increasingly borderless economy. Not only are citizens increasingly expected to be willing to move for a job, or to undertake lengthy daily commutes in order to work (as per the new conditions for Canadian EI recipients, for example),[21] they are also expected to willingly move between *jobs*.[22] In this dromocratic world, short-term, non-permanent, and non-full-time contract work becomes the new normal,[23] because "who really wants to work at the same job for their whole life?" In an "editorial" piece entitled "Staying is Settling: Why You Need to Move at Least 5 Times in Your Life," on the website (I kid you not) "Elite Daily" (which describes itself as the "voice of Generation Y"), the dromocratic lifestyle is starkly illustrated:

> Turn around, look at your life and decide right now if this moment, this place makes your pulse race and your heart bend. If there's not a fluttering feeling in the deepest part of your soul, questioning and absorbing everything around you, get out right now.
>
> If you feel comfortable, content and unchallenged ... stand up and walk away. Make plans or don't make plans, but whatever you do, leave this place and find somewhere new.

> [...] Life has a tendency to get stale. Like your favorite food, it loses its edge after a while, that special quality that made you love it so much in the first place. We, like the places we confine ourselves to, become as dull and boring as our surroundings.
>
> New experiences are the reason we live. They are the reason we get up every day, the reason we carry on. While we enjoy comfort, we crave experience. The point of living is not to resign yourself to one part of life, but to continually redefine yourself. It's to baptize yourself, over and over again, in new waters and new experiences.
>
> [...] To truly understand yourself, your purpose and those around you, you must keep moving. You must move at least five times; five times to open your heart and dip your toes into something new, fresh and life changing.[24]

Millions of people are bombarded daily with almost limitless iterations of this ethic on social media. While the above piece was written for a "BuzzFeed"-style content-producing machine website (although with a real author), it would not appear out of place in the writing of Nigel Thrift, Andy Merrifield, or Richard Florida.

When transferred specifically to the realm of critical urban studies, it is also the case that the dominant normative approach to understanding the city characteristic of critical urban studies can be understood as a symptom of the logic of dromocracy – the imperative for speed and motion. What are some of the key recurring concerns of progressive urban activists? Certainly a broad objective is manifested in the desire to break down barriers in cities, which includes encouraging mixed-income neighbourhoods, de-ghettoization, expanding publicly accessible space, and improving transportation options and access. These are all important progressive goals, but when they are posited not alongside a desire for any sort of fixity and stability (which is present in affordable housing activism), they are simply alternative expressions of the demand for openness. Openness always implies freedom of movement and openness constitutes the urban *telos*. On the other hand, a "closed" city is perceived as a site of immobility, uneven power relations, the dominance of capital over people, and the stunting of potential and becoming. A closed city might be understood as one in which space has been privatized, and enclosed from the greater public. But is a call for greater openness really a challenge to the power of urban capital? Clearly, in the abstract, capital flourishes in open environments (fixed capital notwithstanding) – environments in which there are limited barriers to its circulation (after all, this is what "free trade" is all about); and as the controversies surrounding temporary foreign workers in Canada,[25] undocumented workers in the United States, and legal labour migrants in the EU attest, transnational labour mobility greatly benefits capital.

Now, before I am accused of setting up a straw man, it should be noted that most critical urban theorists are thinking of "public" space when they discuss "openness" as a normative category. To the extent that public space is open to all it is therefore considered a curative to the closed, privatized city. In this discourse, central squares and public parks are pitted against gated communities and anti-loitering laws in a battle for democratic control over and access to urban space. There is much truth to this: public spaces have a sort of fixity to them – they have been declared places outside of market relations and the logic of commodification. After all, progressive activists have to constantly fight tooth-and-nail to preserve (let alone expand) public space from the ravenous appetite of capital seeking its privatization. Appeals to public space are powerful and anti-dromocratic in spirit, especially when the spaces are discrete, clearly delineated areas owned by the government or, in some cases, even private entities.

But what about openness in relation to less clearly defined space like urban communities or neighbourhoods as a whole? The seething resentment directed toward the closed and exclusionary nature of gated communities that so many progressive theorists express seems consistent with a normative commitment to openness, but what of other neighbourhoods, i.e., poor inner-city communities? Are they meant to be open as well? My answer to this is that the underlying ontological and normative commitment to openness and inclusivity that informs so much of critical urban studies is compelled by its own logic to respond "yes," of course inner-city neighbourhoods should be open and inclusive. In fact, the vision of the good city that many critical theorists promote is largely based on such communities, or "heterotopias," in Foucault's words. After all, such neighbourhoods are imagined as sites of racialized difference, artistic and lifestyle experimentation, with a hint of the danger and edginess that comes with poverty and criminality. These neighbourhoods express openness in a specific way. While in the eyes of the state, these spaces are often understood as areas to be contained and policed, in the eyes of rent-seeking capital, they are viewed as potential sites of investment, revitalization, and development. Here a perverse logic can be uncovered in the relationship between the discourses of dromocracy, inner-city poverty, and displacement. If mobility is associated with self-actualization then displacement gives the inner-city poor one more movement-based option to improve themselves, that is, to move out! In other words, the discourse of any given revitalization project can be read as suggesting that if the poor and disadvantaged are not free to move they will never reach their full human potential. Therefore, the more that inner-city neighbourhoods are open to new investment and new (wealthy) residents, the better it is for capital. It does not take a huge leap in logic, then, to see how the ostensibly critical commitment to openness on the part of urban theorists may, in fact, discursively enable the forced dislocation of residents required by real estate developers.

Dilution and Concentration

As a political strategy, dromocracy – governance by the incitation to move – strives to neutralize resistance to neoliberal dictates. As a concrete manifestation of dromocracy, gentrification can be framed in terms of "dilution." In effect, if everyone's constantly moving, they aren't really together, which is required for organizing or building a collective claim to a particular place. Once again Sennett provides astute historical-discursive context for this phenomenon. Historically, he argues, there has been a progression in urban planning toward reducing resistance to movement by allowing people to avoid contact with other bodies. When our cities are built to enable and encourage such physical avoidance, it has a de-sensualizing effect on our experience of the city. He claims that freedom from resistance to movement "diminishes sensory awareness, arousal by places or the people in those places. Any strong visceral connection to the environment threatens to tie the individual down."[26] And, of course, this has a class dimension to it, that is to say, the rich and the poor experience dromocracy differently. Sennett explores how, for the eighteenth-century European bourgeoisie, movement became intimately associated with self-realization in the form of experiencing otherness via travel to foreign countries and cities;[27] the *Wanderjahre* can be understood as the eighteenth-century version of the "Gap Year." But the poor, who did not have the luxury of autonomous or leisurely travel, suffered movement as a more base necessity; the poor

> experienced movement in the city in ways which lay beyond the scope of these prejudices. That experience crystallized in the meaning of market movements to the poor: the difference between survival and starvation they measure in the fluctuations of pennies or sous in the price of bread. The city's crowds wanted less market movement, more government regulation, fixity and security. Physical movement in the city only sharpened their hunger pains.[28]

But the effect of dromocracy is certainly not uniform across history. As the internal structure of capitalism changes, so too will the impact dromocracy has on workers and the poor. Sharon Zukin has discussed the significance of social dilution in respect to the post-Fordist relationship between capital and organized labour. She claims that, from capital's perspective, *where workers live* in relation to their place of work, is very much an important question: "Over the years, whether workers should be attached to – or free to float from – their place of employment divided professional economists."[29] In this respect, Zukin shows that the late nineteenth- and early twentieth-century consensus was that workers should live close to factories and other sites of production. In this period entire "factory towns" were built to house labour because this was the most effective way to attract workers away from their farms and hometowns. According to Zukin, this consensus held steady up until as late as the 1970s when professional opinion began shifting toward the desirability of a mobile labour force – one in which individual workers adopted a much more "nomadic" attitude toward employment: "By the 1980s, a neoclassical consensus again endorsed labor mobility. Employers' interest in downsizing firms, reducing excess production capacity, and transferring work from one geographical region to another required that workers be detached from the company."[30] For Zukin, this perspective is inextricably tied to the logic of a globalizing economy, one that increasingly encourages an erasure of the importance of place not just in terms of capital flows, but also the cultural attachments between workers and their geographically-based communities. In the absence of communities constituted by a population united by a shared workplace or industry, the opportunities for organizing and workplace democracy are greatly reduced.

Peter Marcuse makes a similar point in respect to inner-city communities. He explicitly uses the concept of "dilution" to frame his analysis. There is a genealogical connection here as Marcuse's celebrated Critical Theorist father – Herbert – emphasized the social importance of the ghetto as a site of political revolt and organization. Marcuse (the senior) argues that

> ghettos form natural geographical centers from which the struggle can be mounted against targets of vital economic and political importance; in this respect, the ghettos can be compared with the faubourgs of Paris in the eighteenth century, and their location makes for spreading and "contagious" up-heavals.[31]

Therefore, he continues, "[t]he ghetto populations may well become the first mass basis of revolt."[32] By developing the concept of dilution, then, the younger (Peter) Marcuse has identified a strategy in which the political potential of the ghetto is compromised by the creative destruction of urban capital. Ghettos are, on his reading, spatialized methods of social control.[33] They are designed to exclude particular populations from equal participation in society, and to contain their potentially disruptive resistance against this exclusion. Traditionally, he goes on, ghettos operated under a "repressive" model of spatial separation and intense policing. In contemporary times, however, ghetto populations are disciplined via "de-spatialization," or the "dispersion of the population of the ghetto – that is, moving parts of the ghetto population out of the ghetto – while retaining its control functions in a less concentrated spatial setting."[34] This works in concert with "dilution," or giving more privileged segments of the population access to the space of the ghetto. Gentrification is, of course, the most familiar form of such dilution.[35] What the younger Marcuse's analysis shows is that even though market forces are responsible for creating intensely impoverished neighbourhoods in the mould of the traditional image of the North American ghetto (and these ghettos dialectically produce spatialized centres of resistance against the market), they can *also disrupt these centres through despatialization.* In other words, urban capital produces its own adversaries, and then neutralizes them, all through the same market mechanisms. Ultimately, it is much more effective for capitalism to control disruptive and discontented populations by dispersing them, rather than containing such malcontents in intensely geographically-circumscribed areas.

Finally, Don Mitchell extends his critique of postmodern geography to encompass the fetishization of movement and difference, claiming that this fetishization is mirrored in neoliberal planning discourses. His critique of postmodern geography repeats many fairly standard objections that more orthodox leftists have expressed against postmodernism in general, and therefore does not need to be repeated here. However, citing Robert Ellickson's influential 1996 article “Controlling Chronic Misconduct in City Spaces,”[36] Mitchell does build on this standard account by demonstrating how the construction of certain types of (postmodern) heterotopic spaces are, ultimately, also the aim of some of the most neoliberal of planners. Ellickson is an anti-statist (libertarian) legal and property scholar who believes that neighbourhood communities, when left alone, will plan and regulate their spaces more effectively than any central state body will. The nagging problem for such a libertarian approach to urban planning is, as might be imagined, homelessness. The homeless are considered a nuisance that are not regulated by normal urban market mechanisms because where they spend their time is not determined by where they work or proximity to their place of residence. Therefore, because the perceived security and aesthetics deemed desirable by the middle classes can be ruined by the presence of the homeless, even free-market advocates like Ellickson promote at least some minimal government zoning and planning. But, as Mitchell observes, this requires some conceptual gymnastics on his part. In a circular argument Ellickson justifies his regulations by simply not recognizing the homeless as part of the community (because of their behaviour, not because of their status as homeless),[37] rendering them thereby legitimately subject to police discipline and exclusionary zoning regulations. While Ellickson provides a long and detailed argument for his proposed zoning plan, it is unnecessary to explain his reasoning here. What is really important is his conclusion: Ellickson suggests that city centres should be informally zoned so as to create designated “red” zones (roughly 5 percent of the downtown), in which the activities of the homeless would be tolerated, “yellow” zones (about 90 percent of the downtown) – vibrant spaces in which some behaviour associated with homelessness would be tolerated (but no *chronically* anti-social behaviour), and green zones (roughly 5 percent of the downtown) – quiet and secure spaces for the “unusually sensitive” (seniors, families with infants or toddlers, etc.) who would find refuge from any sort of behaviour associated with homelessness.[38]

The point that Mitchell is trying to make with his extensive consideration of Ellickson’s proposals is that the very sorts of urban spaces – like Soja’s “Thirdspaces” – that postmodern geographers see as full of the possibility for resisting neoliberal discipline are, in some instances, very much a *product* of neoliberal planning itself. Reminiscent of Major “Bunny” Colston’s plan to confine drug dealing to a particular abandoned Baltimore neighbourhood (“Hamsterdam”) in *The Wire*, in the case of Ellickson’s plan, the red zones would be intentionally produced neoliberal heterotopias. Mitchell’s critique of Ellickson brings the discussion back to the category of openness when he makes the only unambivalent statement connecting openness to neoliberal urbanism that I came across in the course of researching this book: “Ellickson provides a means to *achieve* the ‘space of extraordinary openness’ that Soja advocates. That his motive might be different from Soja’s is, quite literally, immaterial.”[39] In addition to Mitchell’s critique, I would add that Ellickson appears to mirror some of the fetishization of nomadicism that certain Deleuzian scholars express in relation to urban theory. In order to establish laws that would be considered constitutionally valid, but nonetheless target homeless people, he needs to distinguish between the *behaviour* of the homeless and the *status* of being homeless (laws based on the latter would be unconstitutional in the United States, which is the national context of both Ellickson's and Mitchell's work). He suggests that it is wrong to assume that simply because individuals are homeless they do not make everyday life choices – that is, their status as homeless does not determine the choices they make. In fact, he argues, because the homeless have more free time, and lack family-related and other such social commitments, they have *more freedom* to "move from place to place."[40] Thus, in a bizarre way, the nomadic homeless person is seen to be empowered by their very homelessness in the same way that someone who is independently wealthy is empowered by limitless leisure time. While this position may provide a novel Deleuzian reading of "tramping," so vividly captured in Orwell's *Down and Out in Paris and London*, I argue that this example demonstrates, once again, that the normative emphasis on movement in urban space is revealed to be an important tenet of both critical theory and neoliberal approaches to the city. In this case, Ellickson's neoliberal position mirrors that of anarcho-communists such as the "Invisible Committee." This unintentional dovetailing of the dromocratic normative logics expressed in critical and neoliberal urban theory is nowhere better embodied than in the concept of gentrification.

Gentrification

A huge body of literature exists that deals with the problems associated with gentrification and there is neither space nor reason to review it here in its entirety.[41] As Loretta Lees shows, gentrification research has been characterized by discrete phases of theoretical debate and developments as more data on specific places experiencing gentrification are gathered, different groups of gentrifiers/gentrified are identified, and the global and local economies experience structural changes.[42] Emphases on supply- versus demand-side causation, the influence of public policy on urban zoning and regeneration, and the racialized and class features of displacement have occupied the interest of critical geographers and sociologists over the years. Historically, this marked most gentrification research as distinctly critical in its approach, in that gentrification is treated as a socially unjust process of displacement and dispossession of marginalized populations. Notable in this regard is the work of Neil Smith, Tom Slater, Peter Marcuse, Elvin Wyly, Loretta Lees, David Ley, and Sharon Zukin (at least her earlier work), all of whom emphasize that a coercive expulsion of underprivileged communities is inherent to the process of gentrification. Beginning with the economic downturn of the 1990s, however, interest in gentrification research wavered in general due to the "massive negative equity as the value of real estate plummeted."[43] Now that we are well into the first half of the twenty-first century, there is some concern that this original critical perspective on gentrification is being diluted, as more and more scholars, pundits, and policy-makers unapologetically promote gentrification as a cure-all for inner-city ills. This is most apparent in discourses associated with Richard Florida's "creative class" and a general neo-Jacobsian appreciation for "liveable neighbourhoods," manifesting in what Kate Shaw calls a "displacement of displacement" in critical gentrification research, i.e., a complete disavowal of the population displacement inherent to gentrification.[44] I will touch on some of these debates and developments throughout the present section, but I do not see the benefit of rehashing and/or re-entering the classic debates of critical gentrification studies. Following Tom Slater's advice, I aim to avoid getting bogged down in such debates – especially the consumer sovereignty/production-side debate – thereby distracting my research from the social justice aspect of gentrification research.[45] Instead, I am more interested in answering Lees's call for a renewed "deconstruction" of the "discourses of gentrification";[46] attempting to critique the way gentrification is popularly understood and proposing alternative discursive formations more attuned to the suffering of those displaced. Thus, for the present argument, it does not necessarily matter how or why gentrification happens, but more so how it impacts those affected and how they might resist it. Therefore, even though I won't provide a detailed account of the history of gentrification research, it is necessary to say a few words about my overall normative relationship to gentrification for purposes of clarity.

First, gentrification is a fraught category in that both its cause (redevelopment) and its prevention (allowing communities to avoid displacement) are reasonably desirable (a binary that Slater characterizes as "false choice urbanism"[47]). It is morally and politically ambivalent because, on the one hand, neighbourhood and housing stock improvements are important while, on the other hand, the displacement and dispossession of the most vulnerable communities associated with gentrification is often experienced as a profoundly violent and devastating process. It should be stressed that my conception of gentrification has at its core the process of displacement and, in line with Neil Smith's and David Harvey's theses that gentrification is primarily driven by the logic of capital investment, I understand it as chiefly a process of "accumulation by dispossession," in which even non-owners of real estate are unjustly and, potentially, *illegally* dispossessed (I explain this in greater detail in Chapter 7). Therefore, the present treatment of gentrification is written from the perspective of, or at least in solidarity with, those who are most susceptible to its deleterious effects – poor, non-property-owning individuals and families, who are often racialized and/or suffering from various forms of addictions or disabilities. From this perspective, while gentrification qua revitalization may promise some benefits for residents, it is typically regarded as a disruptive threat to one's livelihood and the character of one's neighbourhood. My emphasis in this chapter is on demonstrating the connection between the normative idea of the open or dromocratic city to the process of gentrification, in so much as the former implicitly, or disavowedly, supports the latter. This section concludes by exploring how some specific principles associated with a genuinely "political" theory of the city might contribute to counteracting this enabling effect.

There is a clear trend in the way that some of the most influential postmodern theorists of the city deal with the problems of gentrification. It is striking, to say the least, how often gentrification is underanalyzed, if not ignored entirely, as a pressing injustice that scholars and activists today should be engaging with in critical urban theory.[48] Take one of the books I identified earlier as part of the canon of the postmodern city: *The Postmodern Urban Condition*, by Michael Dear. In it there is but a single reference to gentrification, and it is in the context of discussing Ted Relph's description of postmodern planning. Gentrification is here listed as a contributing factor to the "collapse of the modernist vision of a future city filled with skyscrapers, megastructures, and other austere icons of scientific rationalism,"[49] and nothing more. Additionally, in *Cities* by Amin and Thrift the authors do in fact speak of a progressive resistance in the city, but it is in no way "political" resistance as I have defined it in this book, but instead a loosely ethical struggle based in a weak Deleuzian antihumanism. As for the issue of gentrification specifically, the term does not show up even once in their entire book! (or at least I did not come across an instance and there is no reference to gentrification in the index). Instead, urban communities are portrayed as almost non-existent by virtue of the fact that the city as a whole is understood as fragmented and autonomous from being. This springs from an overstressed critique of community as nostalgic and conservative, as Amin and Thrift declare: "community cannot and does not exist as a problem now in a way it did for former writers" because of the nature of "distanciation" and mobility in contemporary societies.[50] In a post-human city of encounters and becoming, such traditionally humanist values like community are rendered bereft of meaning, and as such, critical theory surrenders one of the strongest principles mobilized against the forces of gentrification. In fact, in *The Politics of Encounter*, the (erstwhile?) Marxist Andy Merrifield actually claims that urban public spaces, which are "meeting places between virtual and physical worlds between … online and offline encounters"[51] have become "the rest of the world."[52] In this respect, Merrifield argues, an "occupation" can "never be evicted, even when they get evicted. You can't evict a revolution."[53] The muddling of romantic tropes ("you can kill a man, but you can't kill an idea!") and some idealist notion of universal geographical space (time-space compression that flattens the Earth), evacuates Merrifield's words of political content. While his sentiment may give courage to Occupy Wall Street or Tahrir Square protestors, it is nothing less than offensive to victims of actual gentrification, whether the world is aware of their plight or not.

However, there is a hard core of critical urban theorists very much concerned with the unjust effects of gentrification, even if most of the canonical texts on the postmodern city largely ignore it. At least one scholar, Tom Slater, has attempted to explain what he sees as a curious aspect in the resurgence of scholarly interest in gentrification. He considers it curious because this resurgence is characterized largely by what he calls "non-critical" perspectives (while most of the gentrification research of the 1970s and 1980s was markedly "critical"), and he even includes in his research some surprising reversals from anti- to pro-gentrification attitudes on the part of certain influential theorists, such as Sharon Zukin.[54] Slater argues that three trends explain this shift away from critical treatments of gentrification:

1 an obsession with debating methodology (e.g., production-side versus consumption-side theories);

2 displacement ceased to be a central concern of researchers because quantifying displacement is notoriously difficult; and
3 the growing interest of "social mix" development.[55]

Perhaps because my research has focused on more qualitative-philosophical questions related to gentrification, in the course of researching this book, I have had a slightly different experience from that of Slater. In most cases where gentrification is explored in the critical urbanist literature, I have found the authors to be intellectually and morally opposed to gentrification, if not always willing to propose adequately political responses to the problem. Said differently, amongst those critical theorists who write on and clearly oppose gentrification, their opposition may appear weak because they lack the proper normative framework in which it could be strengthened. In other words, the problem may be that in the absence of properly political analyses of cities, it is difficult to incorporate a principled opposition to gentrification when the framework one uses is normatively informed by dromocracy and the fetishization of openness and inclusion. A strong opposition to gentrification that would contribute to the defence of communities against displacement and dispossession, would be one that acknowledges the normative value of exclusion, fixity, and remaining the same (even if these principles are always conditional or context-dependent). These normative positions have become so counter-intuitive for the academic Left, it is no surprise that critical gentrification research has become confused and contradictory.

If gentrification is to be challenged in a properly political manner, it requires the discursive construction of an "us" and "them" that identifies real material antagonisms. This is a tricky matter because there is no consensus in the critical gentrification literature regarding how gentrification occurs or who is responsible for it (which should be expected considering the political nature of the process). However, generally speaking there are two primary schools of thought that explain the phenomenon of gentrification: consumer sovereignty (consumption or demand-side), and production-side (or supply-side) explanations, like Neil Smith's "rent-gap" theory.[56] The former – consumer sovereignty – has two components: a cultural one that suggests changing lifestyle values have made living in the inner city more appealing to the suburbanized middle classes; and an economic one, whereby the cost of rehabilitating older stock in the inner city becomes cheaper for buyers than building new homes in the suburbs.[57] Accordingly, the consumer sovereignty thesis suggests that the combined decisions of rational actor-consumers create an extremely lucrative market for redeveloping downtown neighbourhoods. In contrast, production-side theorists argue that gentrification is caused primarily by urban capital which sees an opportunity for great returns in neighbourhoods defined by superannuated and worn-down housing stock, given the appropriate incentives for investment.[58] Depending on the situation, developers may then lobby local governments to create such incentives in the form of subsidies and other preferential policies.[59]

For the purposes of challenging gentrification, determining which explanation is more empirically true is, at least in respect to my project, not especially important because regardless of cause, the effects are the same for those displaced or dispossessed. However, the discursive narrative that individuals and the public at large *believe* to be true is very important for mobilizing against gentrification, especially in terms of defining a constitutive adversary. For example, if the consumer sovereignty narrative is to be presumed, then the whole process is simply the free market at work in all its creatively destructive glory. Because the free market is constituted by a multiplicity of individuals making self-interested decisions, the villains (from an anti-gentrification position) are these individuals – sometimes referred to as "yuppies" who "invade" vulnerable communities with no concern for their residents. In the case of the production-side school, the free market is not understood to be operating "freely," but instead an alliance of developers and government officials are deliberately producing the conditions that make gentrification possible. Production-side explanations stress that while middle-class condo-buyers are still following their rational self-interest, they are incentivized to do so by other institutions that manipulate the real estate market. In this respect, even though the city officials are clearly complicit, the main villains of the story are developers because they are seen as the most direct agents of urban capital.

It is clear, then, that regardless of how the process is initiated or who is ultimately responsible, the displacement and dispossession the victims of gentrification experience is the same. However, who is perceived as culpable matter quite a bit for political purposes. Both approaches bear benefits and risks. On the demand side of the equation, consumption-based explanations are beneficial for mobilizing a politicized sense of community – an "us versus them" – in which identifiable individuals and groups are marked as adversaries (owners versus renters, wealthy versus poor, etc.). This allows for properly political organizing, aimed at establishing identifiable community interests, rather than a Habermasian public sphere requiring consensus. Of course this strategy also has its risks. Blaming the yuppies or select insiders can lead to severe intra-neighbourhood class tensions. It risks alienating potential allies who understand gentrifiers simply as market actors making rational decisions about where they prefer to live or where they can *afford* to live (especially with the so-called "first-phase" gentrifiers – immigrants, artists, and students). Finally, there is the ever-present danger that what are ultimately class conflicts will morph into racialized confrontations (e.g., Chinese immigrants contributing to the gentrification of Vancouver neighbourhoods). The intersections of class and race do not always break down into neat categories such that racialized populations are always poor, and white people are always rich. The reality is much more complex, even if racialized groups trend disproportionately to the lower end of the socio-economic spectrum.

When it comes to production-oriented explanations, the benefits for organizing resistance are quite clear: anger and principled objections are targeted mainly at institutions, ranging from capitalism itself (the "system") to development firms. This makes for a less personalized enmity and can denaturalize market-led reforms revealing them to be ideologically driven in the interests of a particular class. However, it may also relieve those individuals and groups complicit in gentrification from any causal responsibility. For example, given existing dynamics in market economies, it simply cannot be ignored that home and real-estate owners tend to have dramatically opposed economic interests to those of residential and commercial renters. In other words, blaming the "system" may be considered the "easy way out" because it obscures how members internal to the community actively enable or desire gentrification. One of the most difficult aspects of politicizing a neighbourhood is avowedly identifying adversaries who may very well be one's immediate neighbours.

In conclusion, framing the narrative of an anti-gentrification struggle is a political decision that activists and community members choose in relation to their particular contexts. Considering the properly political implications of gentrification (i.e., that the process is defined by fundamental antagonisms that frustrate pretensions toward inclusion and consensus), it is not surprising that nominally "critical" gentrification researchers have moved away from an emphasis on displacement and class conflict, and toward discourses of "residentialization,"[60] "mixed-income" neighbourhoods, and "regeneration." Neil Smith refers to this shift in gentrification research as "post-political" in that "politics is hijacked today by, at best, an ethics of passive accommodation, at worst a disavowal of politics entirely."[61] Despite differences between explanatory models of gentrification, any genuinely critical analysis of the process requires, at the very least, a properly political framework, and this entails recognizing a fundamental consequence of gentrification: the displacement and dispossession of the most vulnerable urban communities. Regardless of how uncomfortable and difficult it may be, such a political framework entails a clear conceptual identification of enemies – those responsible for enabling the process of displacement and dispossession.

Who are the Gentrifiers? On *Flâneurs*, Cosmopolitans, and Nomads

The values of dromocracy and the ethical turn can be understood as constitutive of a certain type of contemporary subjectivity; a subjectivity that is comfortable with and can take advantage of openness. This is always a normative understanding of subjectivity: How should urban inhabitants use this open space? Why is openness so desirable? In critical urban studies, there are two principal theoretical figures that fit into the category of ideal urban subject: the cosmopolitan and the nomad, both of which are based on the normative value of movement and weak ties to place. Cosmopolitans and nomads are both contemporary and timeless figures; they are ideal types that have both ancient and contemporary manifestations. But as theoretical constructs of contemporary critical theory, they possess a distinctly modern and *urban* progenitor: the *flâneur*.

Walter Benjamin is one of the most original thinkers of the mid to late twentieth century, largely due to his very eclectic intellectual influences. Caught between rival mentors – Gershom Scholem and Theodor Adorno – who competed for his intellectual loyalty, Benjamin produced a set of philosophical texts one part Jewish mysticism and one part neo-Marxist. Thus, Benjamin's writings on the city can be intimidating and disorienting in large part due to his prismatic rhetorical style, and his tendency to think in terms of "constellations."[62]

Nevertheless, it is possible to crystallize a few key insights in his work that can guide the reader toward grasping a Benjaminian notion of the city. In terms of ontology, the city for Benjamin is a site of contradictions and antagonisms – specifically those that constitute the core social dynamics of modernity. The city is the site of the greatest pleasure and the deepest suffering, the most intense artistic creativity and the most vile and vulgar drudgery – wealth and poverty, genius and idiocy, profundity and superficiality – are all to be found comingling in the city. The city encapsulates all that is barbarous in European society, while also containing the potential source of civilization's redemption, dialectically speaking. The city fascinated Benjamin, not so much in terms of its monuments and grandiosity (which to him were testimonies to barbarism as implied in Thesis Seven of "Theses On the Concept of History"),[63] but more so in its "everydayness." This appreciation of the urban quotidian was not due to its banality, but its peculiar vibrancy. As Merrifield asserts, for Benjamin the city was defined by "ubiquitous, dizzy, and noisy presence," which was illustrated by "*movement*: shifting and jarring contrapuntal scenes of traffic—trams, omnibuses, trains, cars, and people, en masse."[64] To truly understand the city from a Benjaminian perspective, one must be able to identify that which is overlooked, covered over, or marginalized, whether incidentally or intentionally. Thus it is through the "fringe" figures in the city that Benjamin sought glimpses into the social dynamics peculiar to urban life. As an, albeit unorthodox, Marxist, Benjamin was particularly interested in the lives and everyday behaviour of the poor, criminals, and deviants – the prostitute, the beggar. These figures, he argues, embody the social contradictions of late modernity, and need to be recognized as such. While his peculiar brand of social awareness in the city is, to this day, still a matter of interest to urban theory, Benjamin's most enduring contribution to critical theories of the city is his epistemology, that is to say, his formulation of how we can come to "know" the city as such.

Benjamin was interested not only in the "down and out" figures marginal to mainstream urban culture, but also was fascinated by the privileged and bourgeois outlier, namely, the *flâneur*; he was so fascinated by this character that he developed an entire epistemology based on its eccentric *phronesis*. The *flâneur* is a figure who is, perhaps, best described as a passionately curious observer of both people and inanimate objects in the city, while simultaneously assuming a detached and disinterested attitude toward the activity that defines him (and it is always a "him"). He is a wanderer – hyper-bourgeois and not wanting for material comfort – who finds every small detail of the city to be pregnant with wonder and delight. The Benjaminian *flâneur* who wanders without intention, actually disrupts the banal routine of the city, redeeming its byways from the "fossilization of habitual routes"[65]; he crosses informal urban borders undetectable by all but himself. But despite his ostensibly superficial "dandiness" (Nietzsche might have consider the *flâneur* the "Last Man"), there is something deep and weighty to the *flâneur* in Benjamin's eyes; he is, as Parker suggests, "a secular pilgrim, a seeker after the profound truths of a temporal-spatial universe that had been made dull and inattentive to the hidden wonders of the metropolis."[66]

The figure upon which Benjamin modelled the *flâneur* was, of course, himself. Not only did he write and publish several texts based on his wanderings in European cities (sometimes high on hashish), but his longest book – *The Arcades Project* – was devoted entirely to his impressionistic observations of Paris as a pedestrian. Thus, it can be said with confidence that Benjamin's epistemology and *Flâneurie* are, quite literally, identical, at least when it comes to understanding the city. Through a phenomenological relationship to urban space, one can learn to read the city like a text, uncover its secrets, scandals, brutalities, and disavowed histories. This peculiarly urban epistemology, so innovative and stimulating, so insightful and critical, nonetheless contributed in no minor way to the emergence in the 1980s of a "critical" theory of the city that celebrates "dandyism" over social organization, novelty over community, and aesthetics over justice.[67] As Magnusson points out, quite often the critical theorist-cum-*flâneur* resorts to revealing "the bizarre patterns of urban life, reminding us of our hypocrisies and misconceptions, and gesturing – sometimes with distaste and at other times with approval – at the politics of this or that," but rarely "engages seriously with urban politics."[68]

Benjamin's contribution to contemporary urban studies has suffered a similar fate to that of Lefebvre's in that his initial insights have been appropriated in a way that obscure his intentions. The figure of the *flâneur* teaches the urbanite how to fully appreciate his (and now, in the twenty-first century, "her's" as well) life in the city – how to enjoy it despite all its social contradictions. His illustration of the wisdom one can accrue via a keen sensitivity to the everydayness of urban encounters is central to contemporary aesthetics of the ironic and the beauty of the quotidian; the "democratization" of beauty, as Susan Sontag might call it.[69] This has opened up a whole new realm of appreciation for urban culture. The *flâneur* also points to the importance of not only moving through the city, but also in the course of this movement taking unfamiliar and always different routes; an appreciation for the new, diverse, and unconventional. To the extent that Benjamin's observations were intended to uncover the injustices in the city, they now serve to reinforce the wonders of the city as a site of novelty, difference, and prosaic beauty. This shows how easy it is for a Marxist sentiment to transform into a cosmopolitan sensibility. As Merrifield suggests, while Benjamin found the materialism of the city abhorrent, he rejoiced in its cosmopolitanism.[70] As the "Marxist nomad"[71] of the early twentieth century, Benjamin became much more influential in liberal and postmodern urban and cultural theory than he did in Marxism. *Flâneurie* is very much at home in cosmopolitan worldviews, and it is the cosmopolitan who is most at home in the open city.

The *Flâneur* is Dead, Long Live the Nomad!

While the *flâneur* is the subject of the open city par excellence, today he is only a marginal figure in the critical urban literature, largely because of his overtly bourgeois character. Very few serious critical theorists would be able to posit such a figure as an inspiration for radical social change, without being disingenuous. At least in the (urban) social sciences, the *flâneur* is a category discussed only to the extent it plays an important role in the historical development of critical urban studies. Nonetheless, his characteristics live on in other approaches to subjectivity associated with city-life – it may even be fair to say that the *flâneur* serves as the "vanishing mediator" of critical urban subjectivity, in that we have to disavow his past importance to the discipline so as not to recognize his contemporary influence.[72] Regardless, *Flâneurie* lives on in contemporary discourses, none more so than cosmopolitanism and post-structural nomadicism. Of the two ethical approaches, cosmopolitanism has been more influential than nomadicism in critical urban studies, and so I will discuss it first.

The cosmopolitan subject shares all the characteristics needed to thrive in the open or dromocratic city. Recall, for example, Bryan Turner's theory of cosmopolitan/postmodern citizens discussed in Chapter 3. The cosmopolitan citizen is defined by cool loyalty to the state and thin social solidarity, and is characterized by the virtues of "irony … distance and reflexivity (coolness); skepticism … care for other cultures … and acceptance of hybridization; post-emotionalism; 'presentism' as opposed to nostalgia; and secularity or an ecumenical appreciation of other religions and cultures."[73] Returning here to Turner is important because he claims that cosmopolitan citizens are most at home in cities, specifically "global" cities.[74] One can connect this position to his normative assertions of the dangers of working-class values and the potential for hope invested in cosmopolitanism, as it suggests that the global city should be seen as the site of a new, more peaceful and tolerant, post-national citizenship. Recall also that the values of Turner's cosmopolitan citizens are more or less synonymous with those attached to what he calls the "transnational elite" class who, in a distinctly urban context, are likewise the gentrifiers. In fact, Loretta Lees has coined a term for such elite figures: "super-gentrifiers," who have "a much less deeply rooted relationship with … [their] … neighbourhood[s] – as with the highly mobile capital they work with, these super-gentrifiers are more mobile too – their identity is arguably more fluid than rooted."[75] And so we come back full circle to the contradictions of critical urban theory: the gentrifying class shares the very same "ethical" or "post-political" values the critical urbanist espouses. Much research has been conducted to assess who exactly is moving into inner-city neighbourhoods and causing the displacement of existing residents. It appears almost unanimous that demographically speaking these gentrifiers are united by a cosmopolitan worldview. Similar to Turner's theories, for example, Matthew W. Rofe has boldly posited an identity between the transnational elite and the gentrifying class.[76] In a more nuanced manner, David Ley has distinguished between a more progressive "first-phase," and more conservative "second-phase" of gentrifiers. He refers to both these demographics as the "new cultural class," very much akin to Richard Florida's creative class, and again they are markedly cosmopolitan in their value sets.[77] Jon Caulfield's work on the motives of gentrifiers bolsters my own observation of the correspondence between the values of critical theory and the new gentrifying class. He argues that an overlooked aspect of gentrification is that often the gentrifiers imagine their return to the inner city as an "emancipatory practice";[78] they view the suburbs as "dehumanizing" and therefore seek out authenticity and diversity in their choice of neighbourhoods. In some respects, the relationship between emancipation and gentrification is connected to enjoying authenticity and liberal tolerance, as Zukin states:

> Appreciating the aesthetics and social history of old buildings in the center showed a cultural sensibility and refinement that transcended the postwar suburban ethos of conformity and kitsch. Moreover, moving downtown in search of social diversity made a statement about liberal tolerance that seemed to contradict "white flight" and disinvestment from the inner city.[79]

Thus, from this perspective, gentrification can be read as in part a symptom of the superego injunction to enjoy discussed in Chapter 3. Cities, at least the best and most successful ones, offer limitless opportunities for pleasure, to realize one's dromocratic impulses via perpetual movement, and to experience the authenticity of difference and diversity.

This raises an uncomfortable issue about the connection between gentrification and critical academics, namely, a good portion of such academics are also part of the class involved in the gentrifying process. While "transnational elite" connotes the super-rich, and therefore does not fit the reality of the structural position of most professors, their cosmopolitan values do not diverge radically from such an elite; or at least Caulfield's analysis strongly implies such a correlation. To my knowledge, no empirical study has attempted to prove that academics specifically tend to be drawn to pre-gentrified or currently gentrifying neighbourhoods, I can only leave my argument in the realm of speculation based on my own anecdotal evidence and abstract-logical deductions. But if true, it provides some explanatory power for the difficulty and ambivalence that accompanies politicizing anti-gentrification research outside of consensus-based or inclusionary models of social justice in critical urban studies. There is, potentially, a performative contradiction in situations where opponents of gentrification are gentrifiers themselves. This is especially the case if we assume that a good portion of these critical theorists are tenured or tenure-track professors and therefore likely to be homeowners. This is in contrast to, say, struggling graduate students and career sessional instructors (or "adjuncts," in the American parlance) who are more likely to be renters. Structurally there is an antagonistic divide here that explains why precariously employed scholars and university-educated inner-city activists are more likely to be more genuinely antagonistic in terms of their willingness to exclude.

Finally, mention should be made of the "nomads." Rosi Braidotti is renowned for developing on Deleuze's theory of nomadology with her category of the "nomadic subject," defined as "a figuration for the kind of subject who has relinquished all idea, desire, or nostalgia for fixity. This figuration expresses the desire for an identity made of transitions, successive shifts, and coordinated changes, without and against an essential unity."[80] This nomadism is not meant in its literal spatial sense, but more so (in the simplest of terms) in relation to one's sense of self. Her position is that all subjects are defined in their becoming by multiple centres, narratives, ethno-geographical sensitivities, and so on. One's identity is inherently rhyzomatic and fluid as it moves through these nodal points, embracing them all, sometimes simultaneously and sometimes selectively. Braidotti's theoretical framework posits the reality of a postmodern age as fragmented, de-territorialized, and diversified – all in part a function of globalized market forces. She does, therefore, recognize that nomadicism is a practice generated by capitalism, and she is critical of neoliberal globalization. But instead of developing a theory that challenges such phenomena by refusing it, she instead states: "The point of nomadic subjectivity is to identify lines of flight, that is to say, a creative alternative space of becoming that would fall not between the mobile/immobile, the resident/the foreigner distinction, but within all these categories."[81] Therefore, the nomadic subject is the perfect subject of neoliberalism, and it is difficult to understand how such a subject does not fit perfectly into Turner's "cosmopolitan class." Clearly Braidotti would deny this, as she states that whereas the "migrant" is amongst the lowest socio-economic class, the "nomad … is usually beyond classification, a sort of classless unit."[82] This appears to be a disavowal of her own class position on the part of Braidotti, for as she makes clear, she is the model upon which her nomadic subject is based: a polyglot, Sorbonne-educated, philosophy professor, with dual citizenship.

Although Braidotti claims that the nomadic subject is not a "metaphor,"[83] and therefore should not be read as glorifying the "glamorous state of jet-setting – integral to and complicitous with global capitalism,"[84] from a spatial perspective it is difficult to understand how it can be understood otherwise. Surely, a cursory genealogy of her use of the term nomad will trace it back through Deleuze to Nietzsche, demonstrating that it begins with the nomadic blonde-beasts of the *Genealogy*. Whether interpreted as referring to lions or barbarians, the blonde beasts are roamers and predators. Yes, Nietzsche projected this description onto human individuals struggling to overcome their fixed selves, but he also genuinely appreciated the empirical-historical, vital, and wilfully powerful nomadic cultures. And biographically speaking, Braidotti makes it clear that nomadicism is more than metaphorical for herself. When asked in an interview "what is your greatest fear," she replied:

> My greatest fear is to become petrified: to become a tree, to put out roots and not be able to move. I have a fear of immobility, of being stuck in one spatio-temporal dimension. It is a variation of a fear of death, a kind of death, of turning to stone and not being able to move again.[85]

When asked about the inspiration for her book *Nomadic Subjects*, she answered: "Yes, I suppose I wrote the book because I was trying to both express and rationalize my own need to continually move.… A lovely form of 'being lightly'."[86]

Conclusion

To conclude this chapter, I feel it is important to say a few words about the argument I made above, connecting academics and gentrification, and in the process wrap up the main theoretical argument I am attempting to formulate. Raising what may be considered awkward observations about cognitive dissonance in critical academic circles is not an attempt on my part to indict or publicly shame home-owning critical theorists, but only to further illustrate the logic of one of my main arguments: the cosmopolitan, ethical, and dromocratic values that drive gentrification are in large part shared by many of those who ostensibly oppose it. Typically, such a topic would be approached as a structural-effect of capitalism, and explained through a political economy lens. This type of explanation would stress the structural position of middle-class individuals and families who should not be blamed for making rational, self-interested economic choices. It is not the responsibility of affluent academics to deny themselves the good things in life (a desirable neighbourhood to live in, owning a home, etc.) in ascetic solidarity with the poor. Instead, critical theorists and activists are responsible for advocating that *all* people have the same sort of opportunities. I fully agree with this sentiment. But it does not change the fact that critical theory has built a theoretical edifice informed by ethical principles that *works against realizing justice for all*, paradoxically *in the name of justice for all*! My argument is that, in order to get to the bottom of the host of contradictions and disavowals present in critical urban theory, one must expand beyond a typical political economy approach and delve into deeper examinations of the affective investment we all have in existing structures of political power. In Chapter 3, I undertook such an investigation vis-à-vis the fundamental fantasies that orient our desire and enjoyment toward capitalism and democracy. In the following philosophical excursus, I outline how Lacanian psychoanalysis is, once again, pertinent to understanding our contradictory and disavowed relationship to things, but this time my focus is specifically on how we understand and enjoy *the city*.

Notes

1 Rosi Braidotti, *Nomadic Subjects: Embodiment and Sexual Difference in Contemporary Feminist Theory* (New York: Columbia University Press, 1994), 33.
2 David Imbroscio, "Beyond Mobility: The Limits of Liberal Urban Policy," *Journal of Urban Affairs* 34(1) (2012): 1–20, 2.
3 Ibid.
4 Ibid., 7.
5 David Imbroscio, "From Redistribution to Ownership: Toward an Alternative Urban Policy for America's Cities," *Urban Affairs Review* 49(6) (2013): 787–820, 796.
6 Imbroscio, "Beyond Mobility," 2.
7 Ibid., 7.
8 Imbroscio, "Redistribution."
9 Sennett, *Flesh and Stone*, 256.
10 Ibid., 263.
11 Ibid., 264.
12 Paul Virilio (interview with Caroline Dumoucel), "Paul Virilio," *Vice*, last updated September 2, 2010, accessed December 4, 2013, www.vice.com/read/paul-virilio-506-v17n9.
13 Paul Virilio, "Architecture Principe," *AA Documents 3: The Function of the Oblique* (London: AA Publications, 1996), 13.
14 Paul Virilio, *Speed and Politics*, trans. Mark Polizotti (Los Angeles: Semiotext(e), 2006), 53. Emphasis mine.
15 Ibid., 49. This is a problematic quotation by Virilio because it appears to gloss over the historical reality of the brutal repression of trade unions and other social bases of working class power by the Nazis. I have included it largely because it demonstrates

well the logic of Virilio's position nicely, even though it is highly exaggerated as an empirical claim.

16 Ibid., 32.

17 Thrift, *Non-Representational Space*, 5.

18 David Harvey, "Globalization and the 'Spatial Fix'," *Geographische Revue* 2 (2001): 23–30.

19 Neil Smith, *Uneven Development: Nature, Capital, and the Production of Space* (New York: Basil Blackwell, 1984), 150.

20 Andy Merrifield, *The Politics of the Encounter: Urban Theory and Protest Under Planetary Urbanization* (Athens: University of Georgia Press, 2013), 10.

21 As of 2013, EI claimants in Canada are required to apply for and accept jobs that are within a one-hour (or more, depending on which city they live in) commute of their place of residence.

22 Accurate data on the average number of careers that individuals will have in a lifetime is spotty, but the average length of tenure per position has dramatically decreased since 1973, at least in the United States. This points logically to an increase in the number of jobs held per person. See: Henry S. Farber, "Job Loss and the Decline in Job Security in the United States," *CEPS Working Papers* 171 (Princeton University: Industrial Relations Section, 2008), 520.

23 For a discussion of this new normal in the context of Toronto, see: Wayne Lewchuk et al., "It's More Than Poverty: Employment Precarity and Household Well-Being" (PEPSO, McMaster University Social Sciences, and the United Way Toronto, February, 2013).

24 Lauren Martin, "Staying Is Settling: Why You Need To Move At Least 5 Times In Your Life," September 11, 2014, accessed November 3, 2014, http://elitedaily.com/life/staying-settling-need-move-5-times-life/751829/.

25 *Huffington Post Canada*, "Temporary Foreign Workers: 18 of 50 Largest Canadian Employers Using Them," last updated April 12, 2013, accessed January 15, 2014, www.huffingtonpost.ca/2013/04/12/temporary-foreign-workers_n_3064389.html.

26 Sennett, *Flesh and Stone*, 256.

27 Ibid., 275.

28 Ibid.

29 Zukin, *Landscapes of Power*, 8.

30 Ibid., 8.

31 Herbert Marcuse, *An Essay on Liberation* (Boston: Beacon Press, 1969), 157.

32 Ibid., viii.

33 Peter Marcuse, "De-Spatialization and Dilution in the Ghetto: Current Trends in the United States," in *The Ghetto: Contemporary Global Issues and Controversies*, ed. Ray Hutchison and Bruce D. Haynes (Boulder: Westview Press, 2012), 40.

34 Ibid., 41.

35 Ibid., 36.

36 Robert Ellickson, "*Controlling Chronic Misconduct in City Spaces:* Of Panhandlers, Skid Rows, and Public-Space Zoning," *Yale Law Journal* 105 (March 1996).

37 Mitchell, "Postmodern Geographical Praxis?" 73.

38 Ibid., 77.

39 Ibid., 77.

40 Ibid., 73. Mitchell makes another interesting comparison by contrasting Ellickson's offensive characterization of homeless people as "more free" with Soja's understanding of heterotopia:

> because contemporary heterotopias (like psychiatric hospitals and prisons) are, as Soja notes, spaces of "deviance," and thus sites for the production of just that "difference" authors like Soja want to promote: mental illness is held up as a site for liberation, not something to be liberated from.
>
> (Ibid., 64)

41 For a comprehensive survey of the literature on gentrification, see: Loretta Lees, Tom Slater, and Elvin Wyly, *Gentrification* (New York: Routledge, 2013).
42 Loretta Lees, "A Reappraisal of Gentrification: Towards a 'Geography of Gentrification'," *Progress in Human Geography* 24(3) (2000): 389–409.
43 Ibid., 389.
44 Kate Shaw, "A Response to the 'Eviction of Critical Perspectives from Gentrification Research'," *International Journal of Urban and Regional Research* 32(1) (March 2008): 192–194, 193.
45 Tom Slater, "The Eviction of Critical Perspectives from Gentrification Research," *International Journal of Urban and Regional Research* 30(4) (December 2006): 737–757.
46 Lees, "A Reappraisal of Gentrification," 404.
47 Tom Slater, "Unravelling False Choice Urbanism," *The City at a Time of Crisis*, April 11, 2014, http://crisis-scape.net/conference/item/180-unravelling-false-choice-urbanism
48 In the two major edited collections devoted to gentrification, none of the canonical postmodern theorists of the city that I discussed in Chapter 4 are contributors. These two collections are *The Gentrification Reader*, ed. Loretta Lees and Tom Slater (New York: Routledge, 2010) and *The Gentrification Debates*, ed. Japonica Brown-Sarcino (New York: Routledge, 2013).
49 Dear, *Postmodern Urban Condition*, 142.
50 Amin and Thrift, *Cities*, 42.
51 Merrifield, *Politics of the Encounter*, 66.
52 Ibid., 67.
53 Ibid.
54 Slater, "Eviction of Critical Perspectives," 739–740.
55 Ibid., 746–751.
56 It should be noted that since the original publication of his rent-gap thesis, Smith has attempted to address critics who claim it is overly one-sided in its economic determinism. He claims consumer choice does, in fact, play an important role in gentrification [see: Neil Smith, "Commentary: Gentrification and the Rent Gap," *Annals of the Association of American Geographers* 77(3) (1987): 462–478]. It should also be noted that there are many variations of explanatory theories of gentrification that attempt to combine the key insights of both production- and supply-side theories. One very good example of such an approach can be found in: Jim Silver, "Gentrification in West Broadway? Contested Space in a Winnipeg Inner City Neighbourhood" (Winnipeg: Canadian Centre for Policy Alternatives Manitoba, May 2006).
57 Neil Smith, "Toward a Theory of Gentrification: A Back to the City Movement by Capital, Not People," *Journal of the American Planning Association* 45(4) (2008): 538.
58 Ibid., 545–547.
59 Ibid., 546, and footnote 2, 547.
60 Slater, "Eviction of Critical Perspectives," 746.
61 Neil Smith, "On 'The Eviction of Critical Perspectives'," *International Journal of Urban and Regional Research* 32(1) (March 2008): 195–197, 195.
62 Walter Benjamin, *The Origin of German Tragic Drama*, trans. John Osborne (London: NLB, 1977), 37.
63 Walter Benjamin, "Theses on the Philosophy of History," *Illuminations*, ed. Hannah Arendt (New York: Harcourt, 1968).
64 Merrifield, *Metromarxism*, 52.
65 Peter Buse, Ken Hirschkop, Scott McCracken, and Bertrand Taithe, *Benjamin's Arcades: An Unguided Tour* (Manchester: Manchester University Press, 2006), 80.
66 Simon Parker, *Urban Theory and the Urban Experience: Encountering the City* (New York: Routledge, 2003), 18.
67 Magnusson, *Politics of Urbanism*, 55.

68 Ibid., 57.
69 Susan Sontag, *On Photography* (New York: Macmillan, 1977).
70 Merrifield, *Metromarxism*, 53.
71 Ibid., 56.
72 The vanishing mediator is a concept that Žižek borrows from Fredric Jameson, and is first explored in *For They Know Not What They Do: Enjoyment as a Political Factor* (New York: Verso, 2008). It refers to a necessary category or figure that mediates between the dialectical transition between opposed concepts. It mediates the transition and then disappears when the new synthetized object is settled. In terms of historical processes, a vanishing mediator is a historically necessary origin for a present reality, that is subject to discursive erasure, because when acknowledged it causes trauma in the present. One of Žižek's favourite examples of the historical vanishing mediator is the relationship between the Terror and the contemporary French Republic. He claims that critics denounce the Terror – the vanishing mediator – without recognizing that it was necessary for the success of the French Revolution; in other words, there would be no French democracy today in the absence of figures like Robespierre's willingness to brutally destroy any pretensions to counter-revolution. The Terror must be denounced because it does not fit the proud narrative of contemporary French democracy.
73 Turner, "Cosmopolitan Virtue," 143.
74 Ibid., 143–144.
75 Lees, "A Reappraisal of Gentrification," 402.
76 Matthew W. Rofe, "'I Want to be Global': Theorising the Gentrifying Class as an Emergent Elite Global Community," in *The Gentrification Reader*, ed. Loretta Lees, Tom Slater, and Elvin Wyly (New York: Routledge, 2010).
77 David Ley, "Gentrification and the Politics of the New Middle Class," in *The Gentrification Reader*, ed. Loretta Lees, Tom Slater, and Elvin Wyly (New York: Routledge, 2010).
78 Jon Caulfield, "'Gentrification' and Desire," in *The Gentrification Reader*, ed. Loretta Lees, Tom Slater, and Elvin Wyly (New York: Routledge, 2010).
79 Sharon Zukin, "Gentrification as Market and Place," in *The Gentrification Debates*, ed. Japonica Brown-Sarcino (New York: Routledge, 2013), 41.
80 Braidotti, *Nomadic Subjects*, 22. For his original work on nomadicism, see also: Gilles Deleuze, "Nomad Art: Space," in *The Deleuze Reader*, ed. Constantin V. Boundas (New York: Columbia University Press, 1993), 165–172.
81 Ibid., 7.
82 Ibid., 22.
83 Ibid., 10–13.
84 Ibid., 10.
85 Rosi Braidotti (interview with Kathleen O'Grady), "A Conversation with Rosi Braidotti," last updated August, 1995, accessed February 3, 2014, http://bailiwick.lib.uiowa.edu/wstudies/Braidotti/Braidotti2.html.
86 Ibid.

Philosophical Excursus

City of Desire; City of Drive

By rejecting dromocracy and its manifestation in the open city as a normative model for critical urban studies, one not only challenges particular values associated with urban life and activism, but also, to a certain extent, the values and principles that underlie much of critical theory in general. These normative and ontological characteristics of contemporary critical theory qua ethical theory were covered in the critiques of Habermasianism, cosmopolitanism, and postmodernism in Chapters 2 and 3. In this philosophical excursus the appraisal of the ethical turn is revisited, but framed in the explicitly psychoanalytic ontological terms of desire and drive – a framework that can be used as the theoretical foundation for an anti-dromocratic and properly political conception of the city. Such a psychoanalytic account relies heavily on Lacanian/Žižekian theories of subjectivity and, therefore, it requires that a good amount of space is devoted to explaining this theory that may appear for many readers unfamiliar and, perhaps, quite difficult and abstract. This diversion is necessary to establish the theoretical foundation for a new critical theory of the city; one informed by what, given the existing theoretical climate, can only be considered fairly unorthodox values and perspectives on the good life. The city of drive, formulated in the second half of this excursus, may appear tremendously counter-intuitive to most leftists today. It is rendered intelligible only when explained in its psychoanalytic theoretical context.

Ideology and Enjoyment

When one considers the social values associated with contemporary critical theory and, in addition, the critical lineage that has led to the crystallization of these values in present-day scholarly and activist circles, it is easy to see how profoundly influential the "early," humanist work of Karl Marx has been. More specifically, a singular idea in the "young" Marx's work stands out as fundamentally germinal: *species-being*. *Species-being* is, for Marx, the normative and ontological nature of man – what distinguishes humans from all other species. It is treated as humankind's *telos*, and the goal of an emancipated and free world defined by a certain type of self-actualization, self-motivation, non-alienation, and full-bodied, erotic enjoyment. While *species-being* has been criticized on ontological grounds by certain critical theorists (primarily post-structuralists)[1] for positing an essentialist, unalienated human nature, something at least akin to *species-being* is almost universally attractive to leftists because of its promise of living outside of power. Who wouldn't want to be free to choose to engage in the contemporary equivalent of hunting in the morning, fishing in the afternoon, farming in the evening, and philosophizing after dinner? Additionally, even though in Marx's philosophy *species-being* means something very technically specific in relation to capitalist social relations, it is easily relatable to most people outside of any sophisticated philosophical context. This is because it expresses very common contemporary human aspirations, at least in advanced capitalist societies: to enjoy life – fully, profoundly, and constantly. In fact, such an emphasis on the relationship between enjoyment and living well is so ubiquitously shared today that it is sometimes difficult to distinguish between its radical left expressions and its standard liberal or neoliberal variants. This poses a dilemma for the left: what does it say about progressive politics if its capitalist opponents express an ostensibly similar vision of the values that should govern humans' life choices? What does it mean when we live in a world in which a quote from *Eros and Civilization* could easily stand in for a Nike slogan?

To begin answering these questions I turn once again to the work of Slavoj Žižek, who approaches contemporary politics through a psychoanalytic lens that frames power relations in terms of the organization of enjoyment. Picking up from the exploration of Žižek's work in Chapter 3, his basic argument is that to understand any stable social system that perpetuates itself without resorting to regular and overtly violent acts of oppression, one must understand how the system provides enjoyment for its members. For Žižek, as a political category, enjoyment trumps rational argumentation, institutional legitimacy, appeals to tradition, or any other commonly cited political principle that explains why individuals support a particular set of socio-political-economic relations. This is important in Žižek's scheme because it challenges a long tradition of Marxist humanism that ascribes a much stronger role to rationality vis-à-vis human agency and political action.

In order to grasp the operative power of enjoyment in contemporary society, one must understand Žižek's reformulation of the nature of ideology. This can be conceptualized as a shift from approaching ideology as Marxist "false consciousness" to a psychoanalytic approach based on the disavowal of knowledge and the valuation of enjoyment. The standard Marxist account of false consciousness posits that in any given society, social discourse – the overarching narrative that legitimates unequal social relations – is produced and circulates in the interest of the ruling class. Consequently, the oppressed classes come to believe things that are structurally opposed to their own interests. Once, however, these classes come to understand through dialectical struggle that their own genuine socio-economic interests are incongruent with prevailing ideology, the ideological edifice crumbles and a new society can be built, informed by fundamentally different class interests. In the false consciousness model, then, the operating logic of overcoming the deleterious effects of ideology is something like: "if only they knew the truth, they would act differently!" In other words, ideology is challenged primarily by replacing false ideas with true ones, leading humans qua rational actors to reject the prevailing ideology in favour of the truth.

For Žižek, this false consciousness understanding of ideology is both politically naive and ontologically flawed. Ideology, Žižek contends, operates according to a much more complex logic. He suggests that all the true knowledge in the world will fail to change a person's behaviour if that person is addicted to the enjoyment provided by a false set of beliefs. In other words, simply knowing that a certain type of behaviour is wrong will not spontaneously compel an actor to behave differently. This new understanding of ideology operates under the following logic: "I know very well what is true, but nonetheless, I act as if I do not know it is true!"[2] Thus, Žižek's new formulation of ideology points to what people *do* and not what they *know*; that is to say, belief (as opposed to knowledge) – the true indication of a functioning ideology – is manifest in *human action* not, as false consciousness suggests, in people's *heads*. One might point to the recent, brief, and mostly contrived (by the internet-Left) "debate" between Noam Chomsky and Žižek, to illustrate the difference between these models of ideology. In a 2012 interview with *Veterans Unplugged*, Chomsky refers to Žižek (along with Lacan and Derrida) as a "charlatan" and a "posturer" who is not a "theorist" because in his work it is impossible to find any

> principles from which you can deduce conclusions, empirically testable proposition where it all goes beyond the level of something you can explain in five minutes to a twelve year-old. See if you can find that when the fancy words are decoded.[3]

Žižek responds by attacking Chomsky's alleged naive empiricism:

> His idea is today that cynicism of those in power is so open that we don't need any critique of ideology, you reach [*sic*] symptomatically between the lines, everything is cynically openly admitted. We just have to bring out the facts of [*sic*] people. Like "This company is profiting in Iraq" and so on and so on. Here I violently disagree.[4]

While neither of the interlocutors addressed the substantive content of each other's theory, a brief reflection on their approaches points to their core differences. Chomsky, who hails from a more analytic philosophical tradition, possesses a strong belief that when regular people have access to the facts, they will act on that knowledge in a liberatory way. This is illustrated by his propaganda model of media outlined in Manufacturing Consent, which claims that the information disseminated by the mainstream media is always distorted due to the layers of filtering imposed by moneyed and state interests. In the absence of unbiased information, regular people cannot access the truth and therefore they accept the status quo. Žižek, on the other hand, argues that in today's world we know very well the truth of our political world (e.g., capitalism is destroying the environment) and that it needs to change, but nonetheless these same people continue to fully participate in it, never challenging the system they know to be fundamentally destructive and unjust. The problem is not that consciousness is false, for Žižek, but that there is an unwillingness to truly believe what we know to be true; we know very well what the truth is, but some psychic mechanism leads us to disavow this truth in our everyday experience.[5]

Thus, to clarify, while I am not equating Chomsky's analytic approach to ideology-as-false consciousness with Marx's version thereof, I am suggesting that they are closer to each other than either is to Žižek's psychoanalytic account. Indeed, Chomsky's understanding of ideology is highly idealist (ideas determine action), and Marx's is materialist (social relations produce subjectivities), but they both assume a centred, rational human actor, with all the inherent qualities of the *species-being* model of human nature. There exists in these models a human essence rationally desirous of being set free and it is unintelligible that something internal and natural to humanity (e.g., death drive) would actively sabotage that rational desire. Instead, the problem must be external: government propaganda, media filtering, or consumer marketing. In contrast, Žižek's psychoanalytic theory points beyond rationality as the major determinant of political consciousness and instead posits one's unconscious relationship to the Real as the source of political behaviour. On a normative level, the logic of Žižek's model of subjectivity points toward a rejection of species-being because species-being can be understood as a type of subjectivity that compels individuals to aspire toward full enjoyment and, therefore, it appears uncomfortably similar to a neoliberal form of subjectivity. To fully appreciate Žižek's radical departure from the more orthodox Marxist account of ideology, it is necessary to understand in detail two central Lacanian categories: "desire" and "drive."

Desire

What sets Žižek's analysis apart from other contemporary critical theorists is his idiosyncratic use of Lacanian psychoanalysis to rethink left politics, anti-capitalist critique, and the functions of ideology. His model of human subjectivity possesses a hard ontological character and therefore must be understood as limiting and determining the possibilities for human behaviour, especially regarding our desire to be "free." What is particularly disturbing from a contemporary critical perspective is the way in which his theory unsettles the *species-being* account of human nature as the vast majority of leftist politics and theory has been based in such an understanding for the past 150 years or so. However, without taking these ontological limits seriously, and this is a bold claim, critical political theory will most likely continue to repeat the same mistakes, and experience the same frustrations that a naive faith in false consciousness often leads. Magnusson expresses a version of this sentiment, albeit from a non-psychoanalytic perspective, in his critique of Marxism:

> a certain despair arises when the analyst recognizes that the people are rarely as united or as progressive as they ought to be and that things keep falling back into the old patterns, which enable the rulers to go on ruling

> more or less as they have done before. The analyst's despair may be offset by arbitrary calls to action – calls that echo the revolutionary aspirations of the past – but just as often the radical critic becomes a *flâneur*: drawing attention to the bizarre patterns of urban life, reminding us of our hypocrisies and misconceptions, and gesturing – sometimes with distaste and at other times with approval – at the politics of this or that.[6]

As with all psychoanalysis, to understand the reality of the present one must return to the very beginning. In the case of Žižek's Lacanianism, this means returning to the pre-symbolic existence of the individual, that is, the brief moment before the individual infant enters into the symbolic realm of language. While it is impossible to directly represent the experience of a new-born (because the world is not intelligible as a set of differentiated symbols until it reacts to and develops language), the traditional psychoanalytic account characterizes it as an undifferentiated wholeness; a bundle of drives and emotions absent self-reflection because no proper "self" exists as of yet. However, Lacan contends, at a certain age (15–18 months) the infant comes to recognize its own image as representing a discrete thing differentiated from other things in the world. This is referred to as the "mirror-stage" of development because it is a result of either literally seeing one's self in the mirror, or caused by some kind of analogous process. Lacan claims that this moment marks the infant's entry into language, or the Symbolic Order, and this traumatic experience will condition the rest of the infant's life.[7] All the significance of this move for gender and sexual identification aside, this experience of entering into the Symbolic Order is fundamentally an experience of loss – loss of an originary, pre-symbolic wholeness. The rest of the subject's life is governed by an unconscious desire to regain wholeness – to fill the empty void that constitutes subjectivity. However, because the ontological condition of being a subject is lack – one cannot be "whole" as a subject – the fulfilment of this desire is impossible. This is another way of saying that despite one's desire the experience of full enjoyment is impossible because it would result in the dissolution of subjectivity and, as such, humans can only ever experience partial enjoyment. This is the fundamental ontological fact that conditions or limits human existence: the inability to achieve full enjoyment.

Lacan postulates the existence of the "split self" in which one's "symbolic" self is simultaneously a product of and source of resistance to the "Real" of the subject. The symbolic self exists in the Symbolic Order, and is comparable to one's "subject position." It is the subject's self-image, as well as a strategy to stay intelligible, unified, and consistent as subject. On the other hand, the Real of the subject is its irreducible core that resists all attempts to be incorporated into the Symbolic. The Real is the pre-linguistic, pre-human, chaotic expression of the individual before it becomes a subject – a simple, inarticulate bundle of drives. The entry of the subject into Language, or the Symbolic, is the moment that the Real disappears from the consciousness of the subject, that is, the Real is the "vanishing mediator" of the subject that mediates between human-qua-animal and human-qua-human. In other words, the moment of consciousness is simultaneously the loss of the Real. This is a moment of misidentification, as the subject comes to understand itself as "autonomous" and "unified" – identical to its symbolic self, locating its centre of rationality in the ego – unaware that it is governed primarily by the dictates of the Real.

The Real manifests itself in a way that constantly threatens the unity of the subject. Unconsciously the subject strives to return to the Real or, more specifically, it seeks the pleasure of the Real referred to as "jouissance." Jouissance – the state of a sublime mixture of pleasure and pain – is precisely that which can never be attained, but is assumed to exist because we are never fully satisfied. It is a desire that can never be satisfied, *an impossible desire*, as it were. If jouissance were ever achieved, it would be tantamount to peering directly into the chasm of the Real of the subject, which would result in the pure devastation of the subject through the collapse of the Symbolic Order (which is required for the subject to remain unified). I have described this elsewhere as being akin to the Judeo-Christian tradition in which seeing the Face of God means certain madness for the witness. In this case, seeing the Face of God produces omniscience, or the pleasure of universal knowledge, and causes madness much like full enjoyment does in Lacanian theory.[8]

According to Žižek's political reading of Lacan, jouissance will manifest itself diversely in different individuals and cultures. While the object cause of desire is always, ultimately, lack, our experience is such that we attach our desire to surrogate concrete objects that we do not possess, but believe that if we were to gain possession of them, we would be happy. Various objects that are always also psychic artefacts correspond, in other words, to the construction of fantasies.[9] According to Lacan, fantasies are the mechanisms through which we organise and control our desires. The "core fantasy" of a subject is what allows it to deal with the traumatic loss of its object (*objet petit a*). For Žižek, the only way a subject can change or become "free" to act – to commit an Act – is to change the core fantasy, which would re-coordinate the Symbolic.[10] In a political register, such fantasies might include "Freedom," "Revolution," or "the End of History," all of which are pure in their fantastic form and, therefore, impossible. Lacan refers to this object-cause of desire as *objet petit a* – that by which one's behaviour is conditioned without fully understanding or being conscious of it. *Objet petit a* corresponds to the Real as a "lost object," something that has been taken away and which the subject incessantly desires to recapture. Since the successful attainment of this object would be a direct encounter with the Real (and by implication, the death of the subject), Lacan understands its pursuit as a sort of death drive or, more specifically, the failure to achieve full enjoyment is sublimated into the death drive which is commonly referred to simply as "drive."

Drive

Drive is a much more complicated and counter-intuitive category than desire. Because the fulfillment of desire is impossible, the act of desiring becomes in a certain way unsustainable or, more specifically, exhausting. As a result, desire becomes drive when the subject fixates its desire on a particular object that stands in for *objet petit a* and achieves partial enjoyment out of *never fully possessing it*. It is not to be understood as a literal, or even figurative desire for death, but more like a tendency on the part of the subject to repeat unhealthy or self-destructive behaviour (from the perspective of subjectivity) centred around particular objects, which results in a sort of "stuckness," or the inability to move one's fixation away from the object. In other words, as Žižek claims, the death drive is "not a biological fact but a notion indicating that the human psychic apparatus is subordinated to a blind automatism of repetition beyond pleasure-seeking, self-preservation, accordance between a man and his milieu."[11] While subjects can never liberate themselves fully from drive and its object of fixation, it is possible (via analysis) to identify *objet petit a* and either moderate the self-destructive behaviour it causes or, indeed, *change the object and its corresponding fantasy*. In Jameson's terms (quoted in Žižek), we are capable of manipulating our desire, or "desiring to desire, a learning to desire,"[12] which is another way of saying that we can learn to desire *better*.

Much like the autobiographical relationship between nomadicism and Rosi Braidotti's fears touched upon in Chapter 5, Žižek relates to drive on a personal level and I think that commenting on this relationship helps to clarify things. In *Conversations with Žižek*, Glyn Daly asks Žižek if his prolific writing (one book per year since the publication of *Sublime Object*) is an example of psychoanalytic drive? He answers:

> Yes, and do you know in what sense? My reference here would be Stephen King's Shining. What people tend to forget is that this novel is basically about writer's block. In the film version the Jack Nicholson character always types the same sentence, cannot start his text, and then the situation explodes into axe killings. But I think the true horror is actually the opposite one: that you have the compulsion to write on and on. That's much more horrifying than writer's block I think. In the same way as when Kierkegaard refers to the human being as an animal that is sick until death, the true horror is immortality; that it will never end. That is my horror – I simply cannot stop.[13]

Žižek is indeed a fantastically prolific writer, and the mind-boggling number of books, essays, and editorials he has produced over the years hints at an almost unhealthy, obsessive-compulsive, addiction to writing on his part. He is also routinely criticized for repeating himself, over and over, from text to text. This has led to charges by his critics that he is a crass commercial opportunist taking advantage of his temporary fame to sell as many books as possible before his star fades. There is no way of knowing if this is true, but if the interview answer he gave to Daly is genuine, then there is at least a more *interesting* explanation for his prolificacy: Žižek receives partial enjoyment from the repetition of writing, despite the fact that it horrifies him and may have self-destructive consequences for his personal life. After finding sections from five of his books reprinted in identical form in *The Parallax View*, in one of her *I Cite* posts[14] Dean ponders why he might engage in such a writing style: Laziness? Mocking academic conventions? Her most interesting theory is provided in a separate post:

> What does he repeat and why? He seems primarily to repeat examples and demonstrations. He sometimes lets concepts drop that haven't quite worked.... And it could be that he repeats theoretical discussions only as he works them out. Once he has his answer, once the theoretical point is thoroughly established, then he doesn't need to return to it. It is already part of the working theoretical system. But this can make matters pretty complicated: he drops what doesn't work and he drops what works.[15]

Whether accurate or not, this theory certainly helps outline the logic of drive. In this case Žižek's writing constantly circulates around an object that he is trying to capture via language. He will, of course, never fully possess this object, but he receives little nuggets of enjoyment every time he finds something that works, and something that does not work, like a series of never-ending cathartic micro-events.

In banal social terms, drive manifests itself in routinized behaviour. Subjects enjoy ensconcing themselves in their daily routines; repeating the same daily tasks and practices with little change. Culturally normative discourses of such routines can be ambivalent. On the one hand, if the daily routine in question is practised within the context of a productive middle-class lifestyle, it may be perceived as part of an honest and contented life. On the other hand, if daily routines are practised by those considered unproductive, or hampered by poverty and substance abuse, then they are perceived as destructive and anti-social. But within a Lacanian psychoanalytic framework both examples speak to the logic of drive. The former – the honest and productive middle-class manifestation – illustrates the way in which drive can contribute to a well-functioning and stable society, thereby confirming that cultural values can coincide with the social effects of drive. Although Žižek does not comment on this specifically, it suggests that the Fordist mode of capitalism was positively complemented by it. However, to the extent that drive manifests itself in the desire for repetition, security, and sameness, it is not a perfect fit for post-Fordist capitalism. The new superego injunction to enjoy batters away at traditional values that valorize simple and unexciting livelihoods. An individual's life defined by boring routine becomes less and less a source of (albeit, never complete) pride and contentment, and more and more a source of *failure* and *guilt*. In the post-Fordist era the enjoyment derived from drive needs to be reoriented to be consistent with the new cultural superego demands. If there is to be routine at all, it is to be characterized by constant and repetitive attempts to enjoy adventurous experiences of the new and unfamiliar.

Desiring the Prohibition of Our Own Desire, and the Freedom Not to Enjoy

Acknowledging the ontological character of drive is deeply unsettling for normative, critical theory. Drive suggests that human subjects by their very nature are stuck in routinized, repetitive circuits of behaviour that mitigate against all the humanist and post-humanist imperatives to experience change and the new as celebrated by critical theory (the superego injunction to enjoy cited in Chapter 3). What does this reveal about humans? First, the very condition of our existence as subjects is that we attain pleasure through failure; because our desire is impossible to maintain it becomes sublimated into drive. Dean has discussed this in relation to the Left's desire for democracy.[16] Second, although liberal democratic subjects will disavow it, the reality of drive is that we desire the prohibition of our own desire. We secretly want to be relieved of the superego imperative to enjoy because it is exhausting, unsustainable. This is used to explain the human tendency to value order/security and leadership over liberty and direct democracy despite the overwhelming cultural imperatives against it. In fact, the more the cultural superego bombards subjects with a normative call for greater participation in politics and self-actualization, the more it creates guilt – guilt of the subject's inability to sustain this exhausting desire. Somehow, the Left must come to acknowledge this ontological reality of subjectivity if it ever hopes to appeal to populations en masse.

If one accepts the reality of drive as the normal state of being for human subjects, one must understand the immense difficulties of inspiring desire for political, social, or cultural change, whether reformist or revolutionary, individual or collective. After all, the logic of drive is that we desire the prohibition of our own desire, which is another way of saying that as a matter of course human beings *tend not to want change even if they think they do*. Lacanian political philosophers such as Badiou, Žižek, and Dean have a formula for change which revolves around the categories of Event and Act, but these categories require only short, intense bursts of collective will that are completely unsustainable in the long term – there is no permanent revolution here; the goal of radical rupture is, as quickly as possible, a return to normalcy. In some sense the radical desire immanent to the Act is always already a disavowed desire for the return of drive; partial pleasures – pleasure in failure – is ultimately what we want, while we live in a culture that constantly demands that we desire beyond it.

A Communism of Drive?

Žižek is an extremely controversial figure on the Left largely, I think, because of his political commentary (and less because of his philosophy). His unpopular political opinions include a spirited defence of Robespierre, claims like Mao did not go far enough during the Cultural Revolution,[17] crypto-Stalinism, and even an interesting editorial comment supporting Barack Obama.[18] I believe that it is possible to separate Žižek's ontology of subjectivity from his stated political positions, and as such I will not be drawing on them in any detail. However, it is good to possess at least a passing familiarity with his politics because it can help clarify my own. In terms of the question of political action, Žižek's philosophy appears a bit muddy as he ostensibly contradicts himself in various places. For example he develops a theory of what he calls "Bartleby ethics," based on Melville's book *Bartleby the Scrivener*, in which activists are urged (paradoxically) to simply refuse participation in the system: the catchphrase is "I'd prefer not to," and he affiliates this directly with Occupy Wall Street. Connectedly, his advice in various writings reads like a reversal of Marx's eleventh thesis on Feuerbach, from "Philosophers have only interpreted the world, the point is to change it" to, effectively, "don't act, just think!" These pronouncements seem to be consistent with a normative politics of drive. However, he is also an avowed proponent of the Badiouian Act/Event construction, which promotes fidelity to the transformative experience of Events that reveal the possibility of radically rupturing the existing political and economic structures. That is to say, in contrast to his Bartleby ethics of refusing to do anything, he also promotes radical action that destroys the ideological apparatus in its entirety! In *In Defense of Lost Causes* he actually concludes the book with a point-form list of principles that the Left should assert dogmatically, and which point to some concrete policies that should be enacted immediately in order to combat looming ecological collapse.[19] In this respect, he appears to be an advocate of a politics of desire – to achieve full enjoyment in a Messianic revolutionary moment. This is, of course, not entirely inconsistent because if his ontology of political action parallels that of individual subjectivity, then the argument is simply that after the collective Act, a new politics of drive is almost immediately established.

In more specific terms, Žižek is a self-described communist, and his normative vision of the future is defined by the absence of capitalism. However, similar to most left-wing thinkers today, he does not provide a detailed plan for such a future. In fact, the first time that I recall him outlining an abstract guiding principle of his vision was in 2013 when I watched the recently released documentary *Marx Reloaded*, in which he says "A communist society is one in which each person could dwell in his own stupidity."[20] Due to Žižek's generally loose rhetorical manner and tendency to use shock humour in his work, one might justifiably pass this off as a joke. However, while this claim is obviously counterintuitive and may appear, quite simply, absurd to anyone associated with the tradition of Western Marxist humanism, I think it is perfectly consistent with Žižek's underlying Lacanianism. This is because a communism "in which each person could dwell in his own stupidity" is a communism of drive. If drive is an inescapable condition of human subjectivity, then *all* societies will be governed by its phylogenetic counterpart. A communist form of drive simply operates in a more materially just and equal political/economic system. Žižek does not fetishize the unattainable desire associated with the *species-being*-as-telos of Marxist humanism – in fact, the logic of his work repudiates it as bolstering the guilt-creation of late capitalism's superego commandment to enjoy. He makes this very clear in *Living in the End Times*:

> How, then, does psychoanalysis stand with regard to enjoyment? Its great task is to break the hold over us of the superego injunction to enjoy, that is, to help us include in the freedom *to* enjoy also the freedom *not* to enjoy, the freedom *from* enjoyment.[21]

In other words, one way to read Žižek's radically heterodox vision of a communist society is that Law liberates us by allowing us to refuse the cultural dictates and incitation to enjoy characteristic of contemporary capitalism. This is because communism would be, assumedly, built on a structure ensuring that people don't starve or go homeless in the process; members of such a communist society are "free" to do what they want, but what they truly want is, by and large, boring routine.

Can we understand Žižek's vision of communism, then, as anything other than a de-eroticized system defined by a prohibition of desire in the name of social equality? In this anti-Nietzschean and anti-Marcusian model, Law works to counter all the cultural imperatives to be more than we are (the very definition of the Real); which is another way of saying that it counters the discursive pressures compelling us toward neoliberal subjectivity. This is a highly counter-intuitive political position for a left-wing political project because it does not promise a future full of the pleasure of new experiences, but one in which subjects are relieved of the discursive requirement to seek out such pleasure. The enjoyment promised in the future is the partial enjoyment of sameness, and routine – the enjoyment of drive. As counter-intuitive as it may appear, approaching critical theory in such a manner is quite productive for avoiding some of the contemporary pitfalls that, all too often, lead to a dovetailing of critical theory and liberal/neoliberal discourses. More specifically, the categories of desire and drive can be used to characterize and rethink critical urban studies when they are applied to various normative conceptions of the city. On the one hand, the predominant depiction of the city – the open city – is one informed by the logic of desire, or the search for an unattainable enjoyment. This corresponds to the "dromocratic" city discussed in the previous chapter. On the other hand, the city of drive recognizes the way in which enjoyment is an ideological category that reinforces neoliberal urban planning principles, and contributes to dromocracy as a form of governance. The city of drive is based in a rejection of the superego injunction to enjoy and its proponents recognize the value and, perhaps, necessity of routine, fixity, and regularity for living well in a collective manner. The city of drive embraces, at least to a certain extent, the monotony and utilitarianism associated with social equality.

Cities of Desire and Drive

As a normative category, the city of drive is best understood in the context of critical gentrification research. After all, gentrification has been shown to be one of the most concrete manifestations of the city of desire, whether it is expressed in terms of openness, inclusivity, or dromocracy. While debates rage over how to explain the process of gentrification, for those opposed to the violence of displacement and dispossession of inner city communities, the core principle for resisting it is largely agreed upon: residents of any given neighbourhood should not be forced to move simply because developers, municipal governments, or yuppies have decided there are better uses for the space they inhabit. This principle of anti-displacement may be informed by moral or legal discourse, but resistance to gentrification is almost always framed in terms of "rights."

Perhaps the most commonly invoked "right" today in critical urban theory and activism is the "right to the city," a concept coined by Henri Lefebvre in

1968. The first and by far most central concept of Lefebvre's work on the right to the city is that of "urban life" or the *oeuvre* of the city. The word *oeuvre* is traditionally used to describe a work of creativity, of art or music or writing. In the case of the *oeuvre* of the city, Lefebvre has in mind a communal project; a collaborative work of social creativity *in progress*. The concept of *oeuvre* in relation to the city is given a particular clarity when he states that: "If there is production of the city, and of social relations in the city, it is a production and reproduction of human beings by human beings, rather than a production of objects."[22] This process of production and reproduction of and by human beings is the project and the purpose of the city and of urban life. It is the *oeuvre* that is created by the inhabitants of an urban space *through* their inhabitance of that space. As Lefebvre puts the matter: "the future of 'man' is not discovered in the cosmos, or in the people, or in production, but in urban society."[23] It is through the *oeuvre* of the city and the production of urban space that man finds meaning. Several prominent contemporary critical urban theorists have built on this loose concept of the right to the city, including David Harvey,[24] Don Mitchell,[25] and Mark Purcell.[26]

The right to the city is a promising category because it raises awareness of the importance of distinguishing cities from other population centres. It points to the growing centrality of cities as places where all the most important human innovations and social conflicts play out. In this respect, the right to the city is a symptom of the growing inequalities and injustices characteristic of the contemporary cityscape; if there were no such injustices, the right to the city would have no resonance. I do not have any strong objections to the right to the city. Given its articulation in a correspondingly appropriate context, I'm sure it can be an effective conceptual and mobilizing tool. But, as Kafui A. Attoh suggests, the diversity of ways in which the right to the city has been formulated in the critical academic literature may be its greatest weakness. In a comprehensive summary of theorists of the concept, Attoh demonstrates that the right to the city's "radical openness" as a theoretical category risks it being rendered incoherent. That said, in Attoh's concern for incoherence, I see an opportunity to distinguish between political and potentially post-political expression of the right to the city. He argues that on the one hand, most theorists of the right to the city approach it as a standard democratic "right" to be included in governance, resources management, etc. On the other hand, certain theorists, especially Marcuse, Bikl, and Staeheli et al., understand it as "a right *against*[27] democratic majority … a right in opposition to democracy."[28] This is because the right to the city in their work is about the right of smaller communities to resist majoritarian interests in their political organization and practices. This divide between "democratic" and "anti-(formal) democratic" expressions of the right to the city are, it would seem, caught in a political struggle for the meaning of the term. The latter expression, I would argue, is really worth developing because it appears to have the most properly political content. That said, for the purposes of my project, I do not consider the right to the city to be especially helpful.

An alternative and more useful "right" that has been discussed to a significant extent in critical urban theory is the "right to stay put."[29] The right to stay put is much more specific in its intention than the right to the city, and clearly more oriented toward resisting gentrification. Introduced in 1984 by Chester Hartman, the right to stay put is in some ways a simple and intuitive principle when considered abstractly. Forced displacement is widely considered unjust – consider the common person's emotional reaction to the plight of refugees of war or famine. It is heart-rending to see images of families, often with many children, forced to leave their homes, taking with them only what they can carry on their backs. However, when extended to the realm of real estate and market relations, displacement is considered less clearly immoral. This is because those threatened by gentrification are most typically non-property owners, and it is assumed that the owners of, say, rental apartments have a stronger right to capitalize on rising property values than residents do to remaining in their apartments. As Blomley suggests, "The argument made by many activists is that such claims ignore the collective constitution of the 'community,' and its moral right not only to continue as an entity but to remain *in situ*."[30] A right to stay put is, then, no less than a challenge to the entire privileging of the exchange-value over the use-value of urban real estate. More specifically, it is a call to resist the dromocratic and cosmopolitan cultural values that normalize gentrification and displacement. The right to stay put serves as an ethical slogan of the city of drive; it encapsulates all that the city of drive stands for. But the right to stay put is left wanting by the fact that it remains suspended at the level of moral imperative, and has very little standing in properly legal terms, at least for non-property owners. It does, however, provide the moral foundation for a properly legal category – common property – which will be discussed in Chapter 6.

Kaleidoscopes and Ballets

Up to this point, the city of drive has been portrayed largely as a normative construction; an approach to understanding the city oriented toward rejecting the superego injunction to enjoy, and instead valorizing the desire for order, fixity, and routine. In order to illustrate that the distinction between the city of desire and the city of drive is more than simply a normative description – that it is, in fact, also an empirical reality – it is helpful to consider one of the more commonly used metaphors for urban space in critical theory: "kaleidoscopes." To provide a few examples, Amin and Thrift refer to "kaleidoscopic urban world[s]"[31] and they claim that the variation of new forms of urban life have given "the mosaic of local worlds that comprise the traditional city … an almost kaleidoscopic spin."[32] In addition, Castells understands cities as "informational kaleidoscopes,"[33] and Soja et al.'s method is in part an attempt to view cities through the "kaleidoscope" of urban restructuring.[34] In this literature a kaleidoscope is understood as a beautiful, colourful, complex work of art – representing the dizzyingly tangled and overlapping series of relations and flows that constitute the contemporary city. Kaleidoscopes present a compelling metaphorical image of the city, a city of flows, encounter, and difference: the postmodern city. It is also an image of artistic creation, circulation, and transactions: the neoliberal city. It promises newness, undiscovered pleasures, and opportunities for reinvention: the creative city. In short, the image of the kaleidoscopic city engages our desire, our desire to desire, and our disavowed impossible desire.

However, when one looks closely at any given kaleidoscope it becomes quite clear that the image is simply a repetition of identical patterns over and over again; there is nothing particularly new about one section to the next because each one is repeated elsewhere. In fact, the prospect of "newness" is impossible because every pattern is a self-contained circuit repeating itself. That newness is impossible is a more apt way to interpret the metaphor of kaleidoscope for an ontology of the city. If each line or pattern in a kaleidoscope represents, to keep it simple for now, a person going about their daily business as if monitored and mapped by a GPS tracker, would not the resulting image resemble a series of self-contained loops of activity? It may be colourful and there may be an intense overlapping of circuits that creates a beautiful pattern when viewed from afar, but when one pays attention to it in detail, are not the activities simply banal and repetitive, even if highly meaningful to those moving? This is the gist of Lacanian drive as applied to urban processes – the city is rendered a de-aestheticized kaleidoscope of compulsive banality.

The kaleidoscope metaphor speaks perfectly to the logic of spectacle – one is bedazzled by the colours and patterns while simultaneously disavowing its regularity and monotony. This critique can be applied to an exploration of Jane Jacobs's celebrated "sidewalk ballet" that she describes in relation to her former neighbourhood in New York. Although she does not explicitly invoke the term "kaleidoscope" in this context (however, she does use the term "kaleidoscope" elsewhere), the metaphor of "ballet" operates in the same way:

> Under the seeming disorder of the old city, wherever the old city is working successfully, is a marvellous order for maintaining the safety of the streets and the freedom of the city. It is a complex order. Its essence is intricacy of sidewalk use, bringing with it a constant succession of eyes. This order is all composed of movement and change, and although it is life, not art, we may fancifully call it the art of the city and liken it to the dance … an intricate ballet in which the individual dancers and ensembles all have distinctive parts which miraculously reinforce each other and compose an orderly whole. The ballet of the good city sidewalk never repeats itself from place to place, and in any one place is always replete with new improvisations.[35]

Is "ballet" an appropriate term to use here? On the one hand, ballet is a very structured dance – choreographed and rehearsed over and over again. This aspect of the metaphor works from my critique of the urban kaleidoscope. But on the other hand, both my initial and most recent readings of Jacobs's discussion of the sidewalk ballet invoked in me primarily a sense of aesthetic wonder; this process is a thing of beauty by virtue of the fact it is not a formally planned ballet, but rather an organic production of intersecting lives. Note that she refers to this order as being defined by "movement and change" – movement, yes, but her empirical description of the players that follows this claim does not, in fact, point to much in the way of change. She refers to a bagpiper who showed up, seemingly randomly, one late night outside her window, but otherwise her ballet is determined primarily by sameness and repetition. Relatedly, she claims that the ballet never "repeats itself from place to place," and that makes sense, but again her empirical description of events suggests that in each discrete place, largely the same events overwhelmingly repeat themselves. Jacobs devotes a long paragraph to naming her neighbours and briefly outlining their morning rituals: Mr. Halpert (appears to be a launderer), Joe Cornacchia's son-in-law who works at the delicatessen, Mr. Goldstein the hardware store owner, and so on. She ends the paragraph by describing (somewhat sentimentally) the moment she leaves for work:

> We nod; we each glance quickly up and down the street, then look back to each other and smile. We have done this many a morning for more than ten years, and we both know what it means: All is well.[36]

Jacobs is a sort of *flâneur* in her neighbourhood – always observing non-eventful interactions with her neighbours. Her observations reveal a profound truth about urban life: it is produced through actions governed by the logic of routine, the logic of drive.

Whatever Jacobs's intent was when she chose "ballet" as her metaphor, it is important to realize that the daily routines of her neighbours that created an eminently liveable neighbourhood were not equivalent to a work of art, if art is judged in large part by the standard of the new. Ultimately, the sidewalk ballet is a product of, not necessarily a "compulsion" to repetitive behaviour (as in the logic of drive), but the intersections and interactions of individuals unmindfully going about their regular routine. Therefore, Jacobs's understanding of the good life in urban neighbourhoods is inextricably tied to repetitive action, and certainly not to adventure-seeking, self-actualization, or nomadicism. In fact, it would seem that the more that individuals who are involved in this ballet might choose to break out of their routines, the less the neighbourhood becomes liveable, at least in the Jacobsian sense of the term. If Mr. Halpert decides not to unlock the laundry's handcart from its mooring one morning, or Joe Cornacchia's son-in-law ceases to stack the empty crates from the delicatessen, or the barber ends his ritual of bringing out his sidewalk folding chair, the "eyes on the street" decrease, and so does a crucial contributing element to the liveability of the neighbourhood. Nomadicism and dromocratic cultural imperatives to enjoy constant movement, in fact, destroy the Jacobsian liveable neighbourhood (even if, over time, they also create liveable neighbourhoods temporarily via gentrification). The liveable neighbourhood, which I am very much in favour of, is established only through the long-term and routinized practice of *sameness*.

The question is does such a neighbourhood – one that produces security ("eyes on the street"), solidarity, utility, and diversity – rely on the recognition of the normative value of something approximating drive? Does such a model of urban living represent, in some ways, a validation of the partial enjoyment subjects receive out of routinized behaviour, and does the continued partial enjoyment of such a scenario require an avowed refusal of the superego injunction to enjoy? Is this how the Left and critical urban theorists should begin thinking about an alternative to the dromocratic city? The next chapter begins to explore these questions by positing a core politico-legal category around which a renewed critical theory of the city can be organized: common property. Common property, as will be shown, is the legal-spatial expression of a politics of *drive*.

Notes

1 See, for example: Newman, *Bakunin to Lacan*.

2 Žižek's most recent articulation of this is in *Less Than Nothing: Hegel and the Shadow of Dialectical Materialism* (New York: Verso, 2012), 997:

> In psychoanalysis, this attitude is called a fetishistic split: I know very well, but ... (I do not really believe it), and is a clear indication of the material force of ideology which makes us refuse what we see and know.

3 Mike Springer, "Slavoj Žižek Responds to Noam Chomsky: 'I Don't Know a Guy Who Was So Often Empirically Wrong'," *Open Culture*, last updated July 17, 2013, accessed October 21, 2013, www.openculture.com/2013/07/slavoj-zizek-responds-to-noam-chomsky.html.

4 Ibid.

5 Todd McGowan frames this tendency in humans to disavow truth in a different way. He claims that "the subject desires not to know and organizes its existence around the avoidance of knowledge" (*Enjoying*, 17). So on this psychoanalytic reading, the truth that subjects refuse to register, is the truth of the unconscious that would upset routinized enjoyment.

6 Magnusson, *Politics of Urbanism*, 57.

7 See: Jacques Lacan, "The Mirror Stage as Formative of the *I* Function as Revealed in Psychoanalytic Experience," *Écrits: A Selection*, trans. Bruce Fink (New York: Norton, 1999).

8 Daniel Webb, "The Unbearable Truth of the Image: Žižek's Re-Reading of Iconoclasm and Peter Brown's Holy Man," *International Journal of Žižek Studies* 4(4) (2010).

9 Such objects are "doubled," they are "strangely split ... the split is within the object itself. The split is not between the empirical reality and the impossible thing. No, it is rather ... both itself and, at the same time, something else" (Slavoj Žižek, *Conversations With Žižek*, ed. Glyn Daly [New York: Polity, 2003], 67).

10 Slavoj Žižek, *In Defense of Lost Causes* (New York: Verso, 2009), 305–306.

11 Slavoj Žižek, *The Sublime Object of Ideology*, 2nd edition (New York: Verso, 2009), 4.

12 Žižek, *Lost Causes*, 196.

13 Žižek, *Conversations*, 42.

14 Jodi Dean, "Reiteration Again," *I Cite*, last updated March 9, 2006, retrieved February 10, 2013, http://jdeanicite.typepad.com/i_cite/2006/03/reiteration_aga.html.

15 Jodi Dean, "Does the Lost Parallax Need Defending?" *I Cite*, last updated June 4, 2008, accessed February 10, 2013, http://jdeanicite.typepad.com/i_cite/2008/06/does-the-lost-p.html.

16

> Instead of a Left attached to an unacknowledged orthodoxy, we have one that has given away on the desire for communism ... It sublimates revolutionary desire to democratic drive, to the repetitious practices offered up as democracy (whether representative, deliberative, or radical).... This Left remains stuck in repetition, unable to break out of the circuits of drive in which it is caught, unable because it enjoys them.
>
> (Dean, *Communist Horizon*, 174–175; see also: Jodi Dean, *Neoliberal Fantasies*)

17 His discussion of Robespierre and Mao can be found in Chapter 4 “Revolutionary Terror from Robespierre to Mao,” in *In Defense of Lost Causes*.
18 Slavoj Žižek, “Why Obama Is More Than Bush With a Human Face,” *Guardian*, last updated November 13, 2012, accessed January 25, 2014, www.theguardian.com/commentisfree/2012/nov/13/obama-ground-floor-thinking.
19 Žižek, *In Defense of Lost Causes*, 461.
20 Jason Barker and Alexandra Weltz (dir.), *Marx Reloaded* (Film Noirs, Medea Film, and ZDF, 2008).
21 Slavoj Žižek, *Living in the End Times* (New York: Verso, 2011), 74.
22 Lefebvre, *Writings on Cities*, 101.
23 Ibid., 173.
24 Harvey, “Right to the City.”
25 Don Mitchell, *The Right to the City: Social Justice and the Fight for Public Space* (New York: The Gilford Press, 2003).
26 Mark Purcell, “Excavating Lefebvre: The Right to the City and Its Urban Politics of the Inhabitant,” *GeoJournal* 58 (2002): 99–108.
27 My italics.
28 Kafui A. Attoh, “What *Kind* of Right is the Right to the City?” *Progress in Human Geography* 35(5) (2011): 669–685, 677.
29 Blomley, *Unsettling the City*, 78.
30 Ibid., 52.
31 Amin and Thrift, *Cities*, 30.
32 Ibid., 43.
33 Castells, *Network Society*, 42.
34 Edward W. Soja, Marco Cenzatti, and Allan David Heskin, *Los Angeles Through the Kaleidoscope of Urban Restructuring* (UCLA, Graduate School of Architecture and Urban Planning, 1985).
35 Jane Jacobs, *The Death and Life of Great American Cities* (New York: Vintage Books, 1961), 50.
36 Ibid., 51.

6 Common Property and the Politicization of Urban Space

Property rights, for too long, have been the exclusive domain of the Right, configured in restrictive and antisocial ways. Reclaiming the commons, then, requires a reclamation of language.[1]

In order to challenge the material and ideological forces that feed into the dromocratic city of movement and change and, in the process, produce alternative foundations for a city of drive, one must choose the most appropriate social arenas for articulating and forwarding one's challenges. This is a question of pragmatics, as opposed to an abstract issue of establishing pure and impure practices determined by ideal-typical considerations (e.g., the most "democratic" approach to achieving goals). Furthermore, organizing and acting politically should always be determined by the context in which they take place. Different modes of action are more effective for different sites or levels of political contestation: the global, federal, urban, rural, workplace, neighbourhood, and so on. The question is, then, what are the appropriate forms of political action for those acting specifically in the context of inner-city neighbourhood struggles against gentrification and other dromocratic forces?

Political activists have several options to choose from. Perhaps the most familiar practice is participating in electoral politics – if you oppose the political status quo then you can support a candidate for office who better represents your interests (whether this includes actively campaigning for said candidate or just passively voting for them). This is most effective if candidates are actually produced and/or chosen by a pre-existing community with shared interests. In the urban political context, an example of such political behaviour would be supporting a pro-business/development candidate or slate of candidates versus those more aligned with inner-city and anti-poverty groups. This is a formal political strategy, but one specifically connected to the legislative aspect of government.

A second mode of political action that an activist might choose to pursue is more informal in character: raising awareness of a particular issue so as to educate and change public opinion. This strategy might be realized through organizing public talks, handing out pamphlets, writing an online blog, and so on. The classic urban example of participating in this sphere of action is making one's voice heard in public town hall meetings. But a more contemporary example is contributing to consultation processes for proposed legislation related to zoning changes, or development projects.

A third option for acting politically – another belonging to the informal political realm – is direct action. As a popular strategy amongst more radical elements of the contemporary Left, direct action is distinguished from other instances of informal political action because it often includes illegal or quasi-illegal activities. In terms of specifically urban political movements, some common direct action activities include housing squats/occupations, tent-cities (like the various Occupy encampments), property destruction, or "policing the police" actions (like Vancouver's DTES "Cop Watch"). Typically, direct action advocates approach their brand of political activity as part of a greater strategy, namely, community organizing designed to create a unified and coherent public that possesses the power to achieve a degree of community autonomy and influence. It is not uncommon for direct action advocates to outright reject participating in formal political structures, like voting, due to various ideological principles they hold, e.g., a principled opposition to representative democracy.

A fourth, formal-political arena for challenging existing political arrangements is the legal sphere. Pursuing political change via legal challenges has proven, in many cases, a much more effective strategy than electoral politics. Some of the most important political developments, whether one agrees with them or not, have been realized by judicial decree – the consequences of Supreme Court decisions being the most paradigmatic. Staeheli and Mitchell provide a good example of such an outcome pertinent to urban space: the US Supreme Court's decision of 1939 in *Hague* v. *CIO*. Without going into the details of the case, this decision ruled on the definition of "public space": who "owns it," and who can use it and for what purposes. It determined that "ownership was less important than customary use, arguing that customary use created public spaces 'wherever the title of the streets and parks may rest',"[2] and that "the people" have a right to assemble in public spaces for political purposes.[3]

All these levels of political action have some merit and, indeed, in terms of challenging the dromocratic city, none of them should be disregarded a priori out of some sort of ideological purity. However, given the nature of gentrification – the urban problem most closely associated with dromocracy – and its treatment in some of the most recent literature on the subject, the most effective strategy for political action lies at the intersection of the legal-juridical realm and direct action. This is because, ultimately, most issues associated with the pursuit of urban social justice are related primarily to regimes of *property*, and property is a highly juridical category. Questions like: who owns what, and who can make use-claims, invoke occupancy rights, and who is included and excluded in conceptions of community are the axes around which various groups struggle to establish their interests and visions of the city. In other words, it is through the lens of property claims that the properly *political* nature of urban conflicts is revealed. However, because the individuals and communities most affected by unjust urban property relations tend to be marginalized, impoverished, and otherwise lacking in crucial resources required to make property-based claims in the legal-juridical arena, direct action in the form of civil disobedience should be considered a legitimate strategy for communicating interests. The following section elaborates on these claims about the normative value of a particular type of political action focused on urban property regimes. However, the bulk of this chapter is devoted to an exploration of a certain type of property – common property – that can form the basis of a new understanding of the city: a properly political city, based on the avowal of certain antagonisms and exclusions.

Why Property?

Urban social movements have long placed property at the centre of their activism. This is not surprising considering that specifically urban issues of social justice are often associated with questions of who has access to both enclosed (e.g., homes) spaces and unenclosed (e.g., parks). While marginalized city dwellers face a litany of everyday difficulties (that most people take for granted as non-issues for themselves), the space where they sleep, where they are protected from the elements, and where they can simply physically *be* at any given moment are near, if not at the top, of their priorities. Because our urban landscapes are saturated with property relations, and those relations determine who can access or be present in particular spaces, understanding and navigating property claims deal inherently with the problem of inclusions and exclusions. Thus, the most universal issues that urban activists are concerned with – gentrification, homelessness, anti-panhandling and anti-loitering laws – are fundamentally issues of property.

Because it mediates access to social space, one can say that property is an eminently political category – political in the sense that it creates the grounds for antagonisms, especially in terms of social equality; radical theorists such as Proudhon have even gone so far as to say that private property and equality cannot coexist.[4] In some cases the antagonisms are between legally acknowledged property owners, but more fundamentally an antagonism exists between owners and non-owners. Property owners typically possess significantly more power than non-owners, because a claim to property ownership is always also a claim to the right to exclude. This reinforces the argument that property is inherently political because inclusions and exclusions are products of the political. In fact, as legal theorist Thomas W. Merrill argues, the right to exclude others from the use of something may be considered the sine qua non of property,[5] and he claims that this goes for all three major property types: private, public, and common.[6] Merrill demonstrates that the American Supreme Court largely agrees with his "single-variable essentialist" understanding of property:

> The Court has said of the right to exclude that it is "universally held to be a fundamental element of the property right;" that it is "one of the most essential rights" of property and that it is "one of the most treasured" rights of property. Although all these statements imply that the right to exclude is not the only right associated with property, no other right has been singled out for such extravagant endorsement by the Court.[7]

Therefore, at the very least, the right to exclude is undeniably a core feature of property as such, and this characteristic is enshrined in law and recognized by mainstream legal scholars (such as Merrill). When *spatialized*, property relations create the legal-physical foundations that may come to delineate antagonisms between those with access to space and those denied access. Referring back to Schmitt's essence of the political, such antagonisms need not always lead to outright, violent conflict; they simply need to establish the conditions of its possibility.

Consequently, it should be no surprise that property relations are an oft-targeted area of political activism. The recent work of Eduardo Moisés Peñalver and Sonia K. Katyal is enlightening in this regard. They call those who engage in illegal or quasi-illegal activism intent on influencing property law "property outlaws" or "property altlaws" respectively. They argue that the practice of civil disobedience vis-à-vis property law is not only a highly effective strategy, especially for those with limited access to financial, legal, and political resources, but also that it benefits law in that it improves legislation by making it come more in line with advances in social values or social needs.

Peñalver and Katyal provide four specific arguments for the significance of property lawbreaking as a form of activism: first, property plays an especially substantial role in the subjective and objective aspects of people's day-to-day lives. It plays a subjective role in that "property ownership is uniquely essential to the construction of personal identity and personhood,"[8] allowing for greater autonomy in everyday life. In short, this means that who we are, and what we can do, is severely limited or enhanced by the way property is distributed socially. For the good of an individual, Jeremy Waldron argues, *private* property is "important for their independence, for their sense of themselves, for their ethical development, for the growth of a sense of prudence and responsibility, for their ability to make good citizens, and so on."[9] In a critique of libertarianism, he observes an inconsistency: from a libertarian perspective, the opportunity to own private property is important enough to form the basis of a human right, while denying that actually *owning* property has the same degree of importance. In Waldron's mind, this appears to be a disavowed contradiction.[10] While in this excerpt Waldron's work speaks to private property exclusively, there is no reason that the benefits accrued by individuals who own private property cannot as well be extended to public and common property. The point of both Peñalver and Katyal's, and Waldron's arguments is that to be denied access to property can cause both psychological (e.g., stigma and a diminished sense of self-worth) and physical (e.g., by lacking shelter) harm.

In terms of property's relationship to the objective aspect of our lives, it constitutes the conditions of use for all the built (and "natural," for that matter) environment. When all space is owned by someone, whether private individuals or public institutions, non-owners move through the built environment always vulnerable to having their space enclosed to them. Second, Peñalver and Katyal argue that property doctrines and distributions have a particularly strong tendency toward inertia and ossification. This is because the whole system of property ownership, at least in liberal democracies, is designed to be stable and predictable (otherwise, it would not perform well its social purpose).[11] Therefore, more so than other areas of law, property regimes require constant pressure is placed on them to change if they are to continue benefiting ever-changing societies. Third, despite its apparent stability, violators of property laws are typically seen as less culpable than those who commit other categories of unlawful acts.[12] This third principle is a pragmatic one. Basically it means that because transgressing property law is popularly understood as more legitimate than, say physical intersubjective violence, it is less likely to damage the fortunes of one's political movement than would, say, murder or kidnapping. Finally, because of the three previously cited characteristics of property relations, Peñalver and Katyal argue that:

> lawbreaking acquires a unique communicative power to reimagine our relationships with the material world and with each other and to provide an informal forum for airing conflicts over resources between owners and non-owners, which the law can eventually shift to accommodate.[13]

In other words, insofar as property is vital to our basic conditions of living, and since it can so easily come to be in contradiction with these conditions, and furthermore because legal transgressions of property relations are perceived as relatively legitimate forms of political action, property lawbreaking can communicate the existence of structural legal injustices and social inequities in such a way that alternative forms of property relations can be made intelligible and palpable to the wider society.

Finally, the argument for privileging property regimes as the focus of political activism can be applied to the specifically urban context. While the law may be mutable and vulnerable to the influence of property outlaws, land and the built environment are much more permanent and fixed in space. This is, at times, a problem for capitalism, especially the neoliberal variant that thrives on circulation and change more so than did Fordist capitalism. Fixed capital, like real estate and toll roads, cannot easily be liquidated in the name of profitability like, say, a flexible workforce or exotic financial instrument. Of course buildings and neighbourhoods can be, and have been over and over again, destroyed and re-developed in the name of economic growth, but this can be very expensive, especially if the initial investment in the property has not been recovered. Thus, urban property – in all its physicality – is an ideal axis around which communities convey to the public at large a set of moral and legal claims that should be harmonized with property law; that is to say, if the letter of property law does not match the normative social reality, then civil disobedience can identify an injustice and demand a reconciliation. What this requires of activists and critical theorists alike is a comprehensive knowledge of property law and the process by which community claims can be moved forward. By understanding the legal nature of property regimes, one can also grasp their properly political characters. In the context of my project, I argue, such an approach to conceptualizing property allows for a renewed *political* theory of the city.

Property and Ownership

The way in which property is conceptualized, organized, and deployed is one of, if not the most, profound determinants of the power relations that characterize contemporary societies. There are many types of property existent in any given political order and, in their dynamic interaction, they all contribute to producing structurally differentiated social groups based on access and ownership. By shifting the emphasis of critical urban studies away from abstract space, and toward property, what exactly distinguishes spatial justice from social justice (in Soja's terms) becomes easier to discern. As Staeheli and Mitchell argue:

> While much research has centered on, and argued over, the nature of public space as *space*, comparatively little has focused on it as *property*. Yet … understanding public space as a set of property relationships is foundational; property is a crucial set of relationships that structure the role, and nature of public space as space.[14]

This is another way of saying that property serves as a major contributor to the production of space. Thus, to the extent that urban conflicts inherently are struggles over space, property regimes should be approached as a central site of struggle.

While property regimes will differ over space and time, it is largely assumed amongst the critical urban studies literature that in at least the advanced industrialized world, the property regimes in place clearly privilege private property over other forms, and that the discourse of "ownership" dominates much of both our intuitive and legal relationships to property. At first glance, neither of these assertions appear controversial to those who identify with the progressive or radical Left. Of course private property is privileged in our legal systems; after all, private property serves as the necessary foundation of capitalist social relations! Connectedly, ownership and alienation of private property produces the dialectic inherent to capitalist growth. How is it even possible to imagine any kind of property, let alone private property, without ownership acting as the central relation between things and people? It is imperative that this second opinion be contested, because it points to an ideological assumption that is widely held, even amongst many critics of capitalism: property is always constituted by discrete objects owned by discrete individuals or groups. This informs the basis of what Blomley calls the "ownership model" of property, and by understanding how it operates one can reveal what it erases (other kinds of existing property) and whose interests it serves.

For Blomley the "ownership" model of property posits that all property clearly and unambiguously belongs to an owner: typically either a private individual or the state. In capitalist liberal democracies, the ownership model privileges private property, with the onus on the state to justify public property, usually based on a perceived essential public need or by invoking national security. Within this framework, private property is popularly understood simply as a relation between things and owners, and does not take into account those affected by this relationship if they are not explicitly and legally acknowledged in the ownership nexus. This is an ideological construct characteristic of positive law, which serves to make legal disputes over property conveniently easy to conceptualize and arbitrate. In Blomley's words, standard property regimes attempt to "purify" landscapes of property by subjecting non-private forms of property to erasure: property is perceived as either private or it is public (state-owned); there is no in-between.[15] The same model applies to public property, although it is slightly more complex in liberal democracies because the general citizenry has some legitimate claim to the ownership of state property. Of course, in practice, the liberal democratic state has the more or less arbitrary power to decide on the use of public property, including its enclosure from the public.

For many a critical theorist, the right of "enclosure" is one of the tenets of the ownership model of property that makes it morally dubious. That is to say, the owner of property is typically understood to have the right to exclude others from the use of their property, to enclose things and space from public use, as discussed earlier. This may appear commonsensical to most of us living in societies in which the ownership aspect of private property is considered sacrosanct, but it is, quite simply, untrue that ownership coheres unequivocally to the right to enclose or exclude. There exists another, long-standing component of our relationship to property that challenges the right to exclude of the ownership model: use rights.

The right to *use* things or space is just as much a property right as the right to enclose. If someone has the right to prevent others from accessing or using property, typically it follows that they have the exclusive right to access and use it. Clearly, this does not mean that all individuals have the right to use all property, all the time. Instead, usage rights are produced and operate primarily through *traditions* of use. Take, for example, public spaces like parks and central squares or plazas. Traditionally, these spaces have been used by the public for explicitly public behaviour, like socializing or political gathering. Regardless of whether these spaces are owned by the government or private entities, citizens have accrued certain use rights to them because they have traditionally been used in a certain way – and note that (at least in the United States) these are rights and not privileges, as established by the aforementioned supreme court case *Hague* v. *CIO*. Consequently, even a private owner of a city park will find it difficult to enclose its space from the public if it has traditionally been open to such use.[16] This leads to a second example of use rights: the legal mechanism of "adverse possession." Adverse possession, also known as "squatter's rights," is based on the notion that "if the owner of a piece of land ceases to use it, and someone else openly and continuously encroaches on that land, title can shift to the encroacher."[17] Thus, usage can not only lead to the transference of title from a private owner to an informal user of property but, alternatively, given a specific set of circumstances (the private owner exerts no effort to prevent the user from utilizing the property), usage rights can be accrued to the users (without legal title changing hands). This simply prevents the owner from excluding the user from his or her traditional use of the property without giving up title.[18] To be clear, the condition of adverse possession described here is that while the owner is present and retains title, because he or she never attempted to exclude the user from using the property in a particular way, the owner loses the right to exclude the user from its use. It is clear, then, that usage rights can disrupt the standard ownership model of property, and reveal that property is always contested and produced through social relations. While scholars like Staeheli and Mitchell focus primarily on the status of "public" property, it is much more productive to approach urban space as a site of usage-based rights by conceptualizing it as a third type of property that disturbs the binary narrative of public/private, namely "common" property.

The Commons versus Common Property

There is a resurgent interest in the category of the "commons" in left political theory today, represented most prominently by Hardt and Negri in their "Empire" trilogy (in particular, *Commonwealth*[19]), but also associated with the work of Alain Badiou, Giorgio Agamben, Jodi Dean, and many others. The commons, traditionally connected to preindustrial agricultural production, oceans, lakes, forests and, more recently, the atmosphere and the Earth as a whole, not to mention intellectual property, is meant to be a space to which no particular individual can claim exclusive ownership or use rights. It is a space that communities understand as open to all for the benefit of all, and its enclosure, privatization, or monopolization is considered an act of violence against the entire community. Karl Marx positioned the idea of common ownership as central to his idea of communism, although he had in mind something quite different than open access to farmland or fishing spots. He envisioned a much more profoundly *modern* commons, one associated with industrial production, entailing the common ownership and usage of machines, factories, and the wealth they produce. Here Marx is pointing toward a less abstract form of commons: common *property*. In "Draft of a Communist Confession of Faith," Friedrich Engels explains the term from a Marxist perspective:

> Private property must, therefore, be abolished and in its place must come the common utilization of all instruments of production and the distribution of all products according to common agreement – in a word, what is called the communal ownership of goods.[20]

This is one of Marx's most alluring and seductive ideas, but simultaneously the most misunderstood. Any hope for its revival requires an asserted attempt at conceptual clarification.

In the popular imagination, and even in some sectors of academia, an enduring tradition of misunderstanding the category of common property lives on. This misunderstanding surrounding common property arises from two factors, one historical and one social-discursive in nature. Historically, because in everyday discourse Marxism is associated with really existing state-socialism, common ownership is often conflated with *public* (state) ownership. But state property and common property are two analytically distinct categories.

Relatedly, in contemporary Western democracies, the commons has been subject to erasure, or been rendered conceptually unintelligible by a legal system which understands property in a rigidly binary manner (namely, private/public, as discussed below). Therefore, a good starting point for defining common property requires distinguishing it from the more familiar categories of private and public property.

As will become apparent, my normative position in this book is, to some extent, dependent on the fact that the formal recognition of common property is well established in common law. Therefore, this section draws primarily from mainstream legal theory, so as to establish a certain level of positivist-legal legitimacy. Property, whether private, public, or common, is traditionally defined by the tripartite relationship between an object (the property), the owner(s) of the object, and non-owners. As outlined by the legal scholar Merrill, therefore, a simple schematic of the three main types of property can be laid out in the following formal legal terms:

> Private property may be said to exist where one person or a small number of persons (including corporations and not-for-profit organizations) have certain rights with respect to valuable resources. Common property may be said to exist where all qualified members of a particular group or community have equal rights to valuable resources. An example would be a common pasture open to all members of a particular village for the grazing of livestock. Public property may be said to exist where governmental entities have certain rights with respect to valuable resources, analogous to the rights of private property owners.[21]

Because property is always understood as a relationship between three terms (object, owner, and non-owner), where Merrill uses the adjectives "certain," "equal," and "certain" rights to define the three forms of property respectively, as discussed earlier, the paramount right shared by all is the *right to exclude.*

In these definitions, property is based principally in terms of ownership. However, in respect to private and public property, their ideal-typical definitions should be understood to differ from common property in that ownership rights are the foundation from which usage rights flow. Just like the owner of a house has the exclusive right to live in it by virtue of owning it, the government has an exclusive right to exclude the general public from using public property because the government owns it (this is only the ideal-typical manner of understanding public property – in practice there are many ways in which government power is limited, depending on the specific uses associated with various forms of public property). In contrast, common property works in a reverse manner. The primary legal basis for common property is not ownership, but *usage* rights that then may, and I stress *may* (because common property exists in a diversity of forms), give rise to ownership rights. Where ownership of common property exists, it is vested in a discrete community of users; this does not mean that every member of, say, a village next to a grazing patch has an equal right to use the patch. In such an example, the "community" is constituted of the shepherds and not the villagers. It is the characteristic of "ownership" that tends to upset critical theorists the most when it comes to property relations because ownership is so closely associated with private property. More specifically, it is the exclusionary social processes and destructive environmental practices it produces, that especially sours critical theorists against property in general. In terms of ownership rights, it has now long been a standard critique on the Left that no one can or should have the right to "own" nature, and when we treat the environment as just another object that can be bought and sold, we instrumentalize it in such a way that we justify its hyper-exploitation.[22] The point is that ownership has come to be widely considered a bad word for much of the political Left – a concern that I am sympathetic to, but one that should not be absolutized because the social effect of ownership varies depending on the type of property in question.

Similar to Merrill's definition, for Blomley: "as an ideal-type, a common property regime is operative when a resource is held by an identifiable community of interdependent users, who exclude outsiders while regulating internal use by community members."[23] It is absolutely crucial to recognize that the right to exclude is fundamental to the legal definition of common property. Interestingly, Blomley goes on to shift the emphasis *away* from the right to exclude and instead focus on the community's right "not to be excluded" from the use of common property;[24] in other words, the normative value of inclusion is prioritized over that of exclusion. This is a post-political move on the part of Blomley, and will be taken up in greater detail in the next chapter. Nonetheless, while Blomley's definition of common property does not include any reference to ownership, the fact that it is partly defined by the right of a community to exclude outsiders suggests it might de facto belong within the ownership model. Avowing the right to exclude gives a certain political character to common property; one that does not exist in approaches to collective property defined by consensus-seeking, expressed often by those who favour "public" over "common" space.[25] However, Blomley is not alone in his approach, as David Harvey also recognizes the exclusionary nature of common property by forwarding a position very much reminiscent of Massey's "negotiated closures" (discussed in Chapter 4), although he comes across as much more committed to the principle of exclusion than does Massey. In *Rebel Cities* he states:

> There is much confusion also over the relationship between the commons and the supposed evils of enclosure. In the grander scheme of things (and particularly at the global level), some sort of enclosure is often the best way to preserve certain kinds of valued commons.[26]

And further, he points to how progressive activists often invoke the need for enclosure without, perhaps, fully avowing it: "In fact a common demand on the left for 'local autonomy' is actually a demand for some kind of enclosure."[27] Speaking to left politics in general, Harvey continues, "[a]t the end of it all, the analyst is often left with a simple decision: Whose side are you on, whose common interests do you seek to protect, and by what means?"[28] Thus, common property can be understood as an eminently political category that recognizes fundamental antagonisms, inside/outside, and friend/adversary binaries. The very important "right not to be excluded," so emphasized by Blomley, should not be considered a right for just anyone who cares to protest their exclusion, but only those who have accrued use rights over time. The right not to be excluded, in other words, can be highly exclusionary!

Urban Common Property

If the commons and common property have typically been associated with pasturelands, croplands and, in more modern times, factories and other industrial sites, how does this model transfer onto urban space? Where exactly do the commons exist in cities? Is it possible to point to and delineate the borders of urban common property? What might constitute the stuff of such a property regime: Parks? Streets? Entire neighbourhoods? To answer this question, one must first understand that common property does not simply exist, just waiting to be identified, but rather is constantly in a state of being *produced*. How is common property produced? Returning to Blomley's definition, it is produced when an "identifiable community of interdependent users" claims use rights to the space or resources in question. In other words, this production of common property is not just a metaphysical process or some sort of post-structural "property relation to come," but is the core of its formal-legal definition: common property is produced through usage. Harvey refers to this as an activity – the practice of "commoning,"[29] and he observes an important distinction between the common and the public, specifically, the process by which the public *becomes* common:

> Public spaces and public goods in the city have always been a matter of state power and public administration, and such spaces and goods do not necessarily a commons make.... To the degree that cities have been sites of vigorous class conflicts and struggles, so urban administrations have often been forced to supply public goods (such as affordable public housing, health care, education, paved streets, sanitation, and water) to an urbanized working class. While these public spaces and public goods contribute mightily to the qualities of the commons, it takes political action on the part of citizens and the people to appropriate them or to make them so.[30]

This is where the study of property relations becomes exceptionally interesting because "commoning" cannot be understood as producing something out of nothing, or as a practice located in a pre-legal space. Where commoning occurs, most intensely in cities, is always a space already saturated with property relations – that is to say, private and public property is always the object of commoning. Take for example, a hypothetical primarily commercial street in a busy Canadian city. This street contains multiple instances of public and private property (shops, patios, sidewalks, post offices, and so on). If it is to be "commoned," it does so not by the transference of titles to the community, but through the creation of moral and, potentially, legal communal usage rights. Through traditions of use, all space defined in a relatively well-circumscribed neighbourhood area that has been established through traditions of community use are potentially rendered common property. Matt Hern illustrates this well in his discussion of the potential for commoning in Vancouver:

> This speaks to the fundamental difference between public spaces and common places, and this is one of the core themes of this book: how can a city, this city, become a city of common places. Public space, and lots of it, is crucial but we have to realize that we need more than that. People move through public space – but common space is where they stop, what they learn to inhabit, and make their own.[31]

While Hern is not arguing from a formal-legal position when he distinguishes public and common space in this way (movement versus stopping, respectively), he discursively reinforces a strategy for commoning that may have some legal force. When residents move through public space *asocially* (i.e., without any social purpose beyond getting from point A to point B), they do not contribute, at least strongly, to producing an "identifiable community of interdependent users," like they might in a more overtly social use of space (i.e., when a community is formed that inhabits the space in a particular way). This is another way of saying that if a community desires a legal claim to spatial common property, that community is best served by establishing clear and decidedly social uses in the space in question.

Blomley makes a similar case when he argues that an entire urban neighbourhood could conceivably be claimed as common property:

> For activists, the injustices wrought by gentrification and displacement extend beyond the denial of the property rights of individual residents to the use of their hotel rooms. Development pressures challenge the collective entitlement of poor community members to the use and occupation of the *neighbourhood as a whole*.[32]

Thus, the legal property binary private/public is not only unsettled due to the introduction of the common, but the character of the particular instances of private and public property are *internally* unsettled in such a way that property becomes private and common, or public and common, *simultaneously*. Zuccotti Park, as it was appropriated by Occupy Wall Street, is a perfect contemporary example of such an internal unsettling brought on by commoning, but historical examples abound in places governed by common law, perhaps the most paradigmatic being the aforementioned traditional use of walking paths across privately owned farmland in rural England.[33]

Commoning has several properly political characteristics and, therefore, should be of great interest to critical political theory and urban activists alike. First, it is a strategy that transcends the ethical or moral sphere of social action and can be articulated in the formal political-legal realm. In the case of gentrification, for example, the entire discourse of the evils of displacement can be shifted toward a discourse of *dispossession*.[34] The importance of this principle for legitimizing common property claims cannot be overstated, and it is something that Blomley stresses as well. Consider the case of renters or small business owners forced to move from their homes and neighbourhoods due to the rise in value of real estate. While outside observers of a struggle against gentrification might sympathize with the plight of underprivileged tenants evicted from their homes, in the absence of an intelligible legal basis designed to challenge this process, these observers can only understand such displacement as a regrettable instance of the natural logic of investment and development. However, if community members are understood as legal *owners* of the space, then the moral injunction against *displacement* becomes a legal entitlement against *dispossession* – a much more powerful discourse for legitimating resistance. Blomley expresses this well:

> [T]he tendency now, in these neo-liberal times, is to think of the interests of the poor through a Dickensian frame of welfare and charity. Preventing displacement and homelessness is a "good" thing to do. Evictions from a hotel are lamentable, but little more. Viewed through the frame of the commons, however, we are forced to use a language of rights, entitlement and justice. Capital is not simply investing in *terra nullius* or "developing" an empty shell. Title to the site has not been quieted, with property rights fully vested in a single, identifiable owner.[35]

Furthermore, depending on the laws of the specific jurisdiction, commoning can be played out in the courts. Commoning is a practice favourable to marginalized communities because it requires only limited resources compared to other forms of political activism. This is because, at its foundation, commoning is enacted through the simple repetitions of everyday living. In a way, commoning is the legal effect of Jane Jacobs's street ballet. Everyday banal routine, conducted unconsciously by regular people going about their business, is what produces common property. For commoning to be successful as a form of activism, of course, an intelligible community must be created to forward its claims and this requires committed organizing and mobilizing. Additionally, communities require access to legal representation, which is always conditioned by its costs. However, such legal representation can, arguably, be achieved with relatively minimal financial resources compared to, say, outrightly purchasing property for community use.[36]

Creating Community

For commoning to be both effective and to cohere to its legal definition, an identifiable community must be present. In urban situations there are several ways to conceive of communities: city or neighbourhood-wide, identity-based (the queer community, the indigenous community, the immigrant community), class-based (the homeless, workers, the middle class, the elite) and, of course, communities overlap because individuals belong to a multiplicity of urban communities. However, when gentrification is the particular issue threatening a community, it is geography or space that will serve as the prime determinant of collective identity, with the others playing crucial complementary roles. It is not unfamiliar to hear inner-city activists and city official or developers invoking the "community" when promoting or challenging urban initiatives that will impact a specific neighbourhood, as if a unified population with homogenous interests exists therein. Discursively speaking, this is an important move to make for either group because public support will typically and intuitively side with what is perceived as the interests of the majority. However, the reality is that if you actually believe your own rhetoric in such a situation, you are fantasizing about a political space outside of the reality of antagonism. Gentrification most certainly benefits some people who live in poor neighbourhoods, most prominently property owners, while it clearly hurts others, notably, residential tenants and small business owners who lease commercial space. Thus, when creating a community opposed to gentrification, it will always be built via a constitutive exclusion of those who support destructive redevelopment or the redistribution of vulnerable populations. While this may seem obvious, it is telling how often the description of such communities in the critical urban studies literature disavow such exclusions and instead almost exclusively focus on external adversaries or enemies like condo developers.

On the topic of community, it does not matter only how those vulnerable to displacement and dispossession conceive of themselves, but also how the representatives of urban capital do. That is, there exists a deliberate discursive framing of community by municipal governments and real estate developers. A typical pro-development narrative is that the not yet gentrified inner city is constructed as a space of danger, criminality, poverty, homogeneity, and one lacking culture and community. From the outside, the inner city is perceived as a sort of prison full of inmates seeking desperately to break out, living lives of intolerable poverty and insecurity. What is most interesting due to its contradictory character is that the not-yet-gentrified neighbourhood is *also* constructed as a space of *transience* – defined by a nomadic and shifting population – despite the discourse that it is *almost impossible to escape*. On the one hand, denizens of the inner city lack the ability to escape their intolerable confines. On the other hand, the population is ever-shifting and homeless. It is represented as *terra nullius*, in both population and certainly in terms of property; no one really lives there, nor does a community with strong roots in the space exist because everyone is just passing through.[37] This contradictory narrative is a discursive requirement for reinforcing the idea that the inner city lacks community and solidarity, and therefore justifies gentrification via economic development or forced relocation. After all, residents of these neighbourhoods desire only to get out, and neighbourhood revitalization simply expedites the process! In this context, neoliberal discourse creates the conditions that make gentrification appear acceptable (economic renewal), and progressive political qua ethical theories legitimize the real material outcomes of gentrification (displacement and dispossession). Take for example Iris Marion Young's opposition to the "ideal" of community. She claims that such a mode of identification is exclusive in that it constructs a "we" and a "them." As such, Young believes this leads to a discursive situation in which it is difficult to build relations of mutual respect with others: "The desire for community relies on the same desire for social wholeness and identification that underlies racism and ethnic chauvinism on the one hand and political sectarianism on the other."[38] Instead, she argues that we should work toward a "politics of difference" in an "unoppressive city" defined by "social relations without domination in which persons live together in relations of mediation among strangers with whom they are not in community."[39] Here Young illustrates perfectly the kind of "ethical" critical discourse that can be used unintentionally to justify gentrification. She is right that such an ideal of community can have racist and other chauvinistic outcomes; there is always a risk of genuinely unjust exclusions, but it is up to the community itself to deal with such possibilities. It is certainly not the community members' duty to discursively dissolve the community simply because it might become intolerant toward others in the process. What is most important for anti-gentrification movements is, then, to emphasize that communities exist even in some of the most ostensibly barren and blighted areas of the inner city. It is much easier to challenge radical redevelopment in neighbourhoods conceived of as *terra populi*, and much more difficult when seen to be *terra nullius*.[40] While commoning is the process by which such a discursive struggle to prove the very existence of a community takes place, it is the invocation of common property that can give legal grounding for usage or ownership rights to the space the community inhabits.

Hardt and Negri's Metropolis

To conclude this chapter, I will make a few comments regarding one of the most influential and striking critical-theoretical explorations of the urban common, namely, the ideas of Hardt and Negri in their book *Commonwealth*. Of all the critical theories of the city I have worked through, their normative approach connecting urban space and common property contains virtually *everything I have been critiquing throughout this book*: the post-political, confusing ethics for politics, fetishizing inclusivity, the commons without exclusion, democracy minus an anti-democratic element, and positing the city as a site of politics without antagonism. In short, Hardt and Negri's work embodies all that I believe must be rejected in order to re-politicize theories of the city, the central goal of my book.

On a purely theoretical level, Hardt and Negri's *Commonwealth* demonstrates how the discursive use of common property and the commons can appear properly political, while simultaneously being employed in a distinctly post-political manner. *Commonwealth* is a dizzying overview of, among other issues, academic and activist approaches to understanding the relationship between the production of value and the commons. Much of the book reads like a survey of contemporary critical theory as it relates to contemporary "alter-globalization" and other progressive political movements. In this respect, *Commonwealth* is similar to Day's *Gramsci is Dead*,[41] albeit Hardt and Negri's work is much more abstract-philosophical in character. What sets this text apart from other similar projects is that the authors situate the city, or the "metropolis" (as they refer to it), as the site containing the most revolutionary political potential. Every topic of major concern for my project is discussed in *Commonwealth*: the commons, property relations, urban space, gentrification, critical theory, and the political. If it devoted more space to discussing the empirical actions of a specific political movement or instance of progressive mobilization and resistance, it might negate the need to critique more standard empirical case studies like the ones discussed in the next chapter. But Hardt and Negri's exploration of the Zapatistas, the Black Power Movement, and the Bolivian social movements that brought Evo Morales to power are quite cursory in nature and, therefore, cannot be used as conventional case studies.[42] As such, *Commonwealth* is, arguably, the most pronounced example of critical theory that misconceptualizes the city as an ethical category while simultaneously claiming it to be political. Virtually every criticism I have directed at critical urban theory in this book can be illustrated by a close reading of *Commonwealth.*

To begin, Hardt and Negri's emphasis on the importance of the commons in urban space is to be lauded for its inclusion in a book that is otherwise very broad and abstract in its political theorizing. Unfortunately, their distinctive construction of the category of the "common" is the symptomatic example par excellence of the ethical turn in critical theory, or the hegemony of post-politics. In *Commonwealth*, Hardt and Negri set out to re-conceptualize the common so as to make property relations intelligible in the "post-industrial" world. In advanced economies no longer dominated by unionized factory work, they argue that the emerging commons is characterized by creative and intellectual labour. Using the language of the "multitude" of "altermodernity," they view the common as (in addition to the terrestrial commons) "those results of social production that are necessary for social interaction and further production, such as knowledges, languages, codes, information, affects, and so forth."[43] As such, the common is "an inexhaustible source of innovation and creativity,"[44] and it is this type of common that capitalism now attempts to "desocialize" by processes of containment and co-optation – through enclosure by copyright and patent protections.[45] The authors see this as a destructive process because it blocks the effective production of ideas and creative practices, thereby stunting the innovation required for further growth (much like Marx argued that feudalism hindered the economic potential of capital).[46] The internal contradiction of the logic of post-industrial capitalism is depicted here as one between the need for ideas and creativity to be free to flourish, and an industrial economic-legal system that does everything in its power to discourage this potential. On Hardt and Negri's account, the new "biopolitical" form of the common threatens the continued existence of capitalism because industrial production is no longer the primary source of growth.

Hardt and Negri present an interesting, if not entirely compelling, picture of the relationship of the common to left politics. However, for the purposes of my argument I am not concerned with the role that the common plays in Hardt and Negri's (what might be called) implicit historical teleology (i.e., because the current economic system no longer fosters maximal economic growth it will be replaced by one that does). Instead, the importance of their work to mine lies in where they locate the overwhelming amount of commons geographically: the "metropolis."

Hardt and Negri refer to the metropolis as "[o]ne vast reservoir of common wealth."[47] They claim that "the city is the source of the common and the receptacle into which it flows";[48] the authors do not consider this, in itself, to be a new development; for a long time, at least since the Industrial Revolution, the city has acted as the most intensive site of common accumulation. The difference, they suggest, is in the *type* of common that is now being produced in cities. Consistent with most theories of post-industrial globalization, they claim: "Today we are witnessing a shift … from the *industrial* to the *biopolitical metropolis*."[49] While they do not provide an explicit definition of biopolitical metropolis, they come closest when they state:

> The city, of course, is not just a built environment consisting of buildings and streets and subways and parks and waste systems and communications cables but also a living dynamic of cultural practices, intellectual circuits, affective networks, and social institutions. These elements of the common contained in the city are not only the prerequisite for biopolitical production but also its result.[50]

Not only do Hardt and Negri explicitly shift away from the tradition of thinking the commons primarily in terms of agriculture or ecological categories, but they also seek to rethink the nature of the common in cities. The city, as a site of the common, becomes firmly established as the place in which most progressive or revolutionary potential is contained because this is where value, or "common wealth," is created. They cite real estate as a core constituent and beneficiary of such value. This is not a novel insight as when Hardt and Negri say that the common creates value, they are simply articulating what orthodox economists call "positive externalities." In line with consumption-oriented theories of gentrification, they claim that various types of individuals, social groups (often marginalized), small businesses, and public works interact to produce dynamic and interesting urban milieus or neighbourhoods that become highly desirable in which to live. Consequently, in these very same locations, rent-seeking capital accumulates real estate simply in order for it to valuate, but in contrast to the residents who produce the common, capital produces nothing. It is the poor, they suggest, who produce the common that then valuates[51] and, therefore, rent-seeking capital should be understood as largely parasitic and unproductive in this type of urban context: "Rent operates through a *desocialization of the common*, privatizing in the hands of the rich the common wealth produced and consolidated in the metropolis."[52] Referring to the clichéd investment slogan "location, location, location," Hardt and Negri assert, "Location is merely a name for proximity and access to common wealth."[53]

It might seem apparent, then, that by recognizing the crucial relationship between the commons and the metropolis, Hardt and Negri have established the basis for re-politicizing the city in critical theory. But actually, their analysis falls short because their overall normative position remains suspended in the ethical sphere of human action, and fails to reach the status of the properly political. Because their entire political theory is based on maximizing inclusion they thereby avoid the dirty realm of power relations, or the properly political. In this way Hardt and Negri's conception of the city conforms seamlessly to the open city model (especially the Deleuzian-inspired types) explored earlier in Chapter 4. Take for example this illustrative quotation from *Commonwealth*:

> The politics of the metropolis is the organization of encounters. Its task is to promote joyful encounters, make them repeat, and minimize infelicitous encounters. This requires, first, openness to alterity and the capacity to form relationships with others, to generate joyful encounters and thus create social bodies with ever-greater capacities. Second, and perhaps more important, it requires learning how to withdraw from conflictive, destructive relationships and to decompose the pernicious social bodies that result from them. Finally, since so many of the spontaneous encounters are not immediately joyful, this politics of the metropolis requires discovering how to transform conflictive encounters, as much as possible, into joyful and productive ones.[54]

For Hardt and Negri, despite citing the metropolis as a discrete place, their desire is clearly for a global commons – a "global space"[55] – one with no exclusions, and no hierarchical relations of power. The closest to a friend/enemy relationship in their work is the dualism Multitude/Empire, which delineates a "we" (all) and an "enemy" (the system); and when there is no adversary there is no politics. Mouffe critiques Hardt and Negri's earlier book, *Empire*, in a manner consonant with my own position: "*Empire* in fact is no more than an ultra-left version of the cosmopolitan perspective. Far from empowering us, it contributes to reinforcing the current incapacity to think and act politically."[56] Their city is one defined as an arena outside of agonism or antagonism and therefore outside of politics. Regrettably, this turns their very insightful claim about the urban commons into another instance of moralizing; a Utopian protest against the injustices of capitalism, suspended at the level of ethics, with no corresponding political project.[57] Mouffe confirms this:

> Their idea of an "absolute democracy", a state or radical immanence beyond, where a new form of self-organization of the multitude would replace a power-structured order, is the postmodern form of longing for a reconciled world … where the political would have been eliminated.[58]

However, Hardt and Negri are far from unique in their approach. In contemporary critical theory, approaching the commons as a site of maximal, or even universal, inclusion is not unusual because it is an approach very much influenced by work done on the "global" commons. As a normative position the global commons appears morally commonsensical and it is not in any way risky to support such a position publicly. After all, it is easy and non-controversial to claim that all of humanity should have access to clean water and breathable air!

But this expedient position ignores the long tradition in which localized commons are not only sites of inclusion, but very much also places of regulated *exclusions*. For some, like Hardt and Negri, using the singular noun "common" instead of commons or common "property" may be an attempt to avoid invoking the ownership model of property in their research, which thereby implies exclusions. A genuinely political position would argue that explicitly and unapologetically characterizing the commons in terms of usage-cum-ownership property rights, is paramount for conceptual delineation, community organizing, and rhetorical political purposes. The unwillingness to avowedly invoke the exclusionary aspect of the commons or common property is a recurring problematic feature of many an empirical case study in the critical urban theory literature.

Notes

1 Nicholas Blomley, "Enclosure, Common Right and the Property of the Poor," *Social Legal Studies* 17 (2008): 326.
2 Staeheli and Mitchell, *The People's Property*, xii.
3 Ibid., 5.
4 Jeremy Waldron, *The Right to Private Property* (New York: Oxford University Press, 1990), 323.
5 Thomas W. Merrill, "Property and the Right to Exclude," *Nebraska Law Review* 77(4) (1998): 730–755, 730.
6 Ibid., 749. Later in this chapter, this claim is nuanced in order to show that in some cases common property does not adhere to this definition. However, the right to exclude is clearly a cardinal aspect of most forms of property.
7 Merrill, "Property and the Right to Exclude," 735.
8 Eduardo M. Peñalver and Sonia K. Katyal, *Property Outlaws: How Squatters, Pirates, and Protesters Improve the Law of Ownership* (New Haven: Yale University Press, 2010), 26.
9 Waldron, *Private Property*, 408.
10 Ibid., 392.
11 Peñalver and Katyal, *Property Outlaws*, 29.
12 Ibid., 30.
13 Ibid., 26.
14 Staeheli and Mitchell, *The People's Property*, xx.
15 Blomley, *Unsettling the City*, 322.
16 Occupy Wall Street's occupation of Zuccotti Park provides a useful example of such a situation. As a privately owned public space open 24 hours a day, the owners of the park were not legally able to prevent the occupation. This position was supported by the NYPD.
17 Blomley, *Unsettling the City*, 94.
18 A classic example of this is the right to use walkways through farmers' fields in England.
19 I examine *Commonwealth* more closely at the end of this chapter.
20 Friedrich Engels, "Draft of a Communist Confession of Faith," *Marx/Engels Selected Works*, Vol. 1 (Moscow: Progress Publishers, 1969), 47.
21 Merrill, "Property and the Right to Exclude," 733.
22 Martin Heidegger, "The Question Concerning Technology," in *The Question Concerning Technology and Other Essays*, trans. William Lovitt (New York: HarperCollins, 1977); Max Horkheimer, *Eclipse of Reason* (London: Continuum Press, 2004).
23 Blomley, "Enclosure," 318.

24 Blomley, *Unsettling the City*, 153.
25 See, for example, Kohn, *Brave New Neighborhoods*, 10.
26 Harvey, *Rebel Cities*, 70.
27 Ibid., 71.
28 Ibid., 71.
29 Ibid., 73.
30 Ibid., 72–73.
31 Matt Hern, *Common Ground in a Liquid City: Essays in Defense of an Urban Future* (Edinburgh: AK Press, 2010), 59.
32 Blomley, *Unsettling the City*, 52.
33 Harvey provides three more contemporary examples of public spaces that have been commoned: "Syntagma Square in Athens, Tahrir Square in Cairo, and the Plaza de Catalunya in Barcelona were public spaces that became an urban commons as people assembled there to express their political views and make demands" (Harvey, *Rebel Cities*, 73).
34 Blomley, *Unsettling the City*, 92.
35 Blomley, "Enclosure," 325.
36 As the example of the South Central Farmers' struggle to purchase their community garden in LA shows, sometimes even having sufficient funds is not enough to attain desired land. See the documentary film: Scott Hamilton Kennedy (dir.), *The Garden* (Black Valley Films, 2008).
37 Blomley, "Enclosure," 321. Waldron provides a similar opinion when he states:

> Of course, those who hold this view do not necessarily deny that poverty and radical inequality are matters of considerable concern. It is a pity perhaps that so much of the wealth of the society is concentrated in so few hands, and that so many go hungry or have no chance to make a decent life for themselves. But it is not a concern connected with the right to property.
>
> (Waldron, *Private Property*, 390)

38 Young, *Justice*, 302.
39 Ibid., 303.
40 Blomley, *Unsettling the City*, 93.
41 See my critique of post-anarchism in Chapter 2.
42 In addition, and curiously, very few of the social movements they discuss are actually based in urban areas.
43 Michael Hardt and Antonio Negri, *Commonwealth* (Cambridge, MA: Harvard University Press, 2011), viii.
44 Ibid., 111–112.
45 Ibid., 258.
46 Ibid., 143.
47 Ibid., 153.
48 Ibid., 154.
49 Ibid., 154.
50 Ibid.,153–154.
51 Ibid., 156.
52 Ibid., 258.
53 Ibid., 156.
54 Ibid., 255.
55 Ibid., 247.
56 Mouffe, *Return of the Political*, 107.
57 It should be noted that in one sense Hardt and Negri acknowledge their lack of a political project. Their brand of political theory is one that posits that the "multitude" itself will determine the future course of communist politics. In their opinion, it is not the job of critical academics to act as prophets of the revolution: "there is no place for a vanguard here or even intellectuals organic to the forces of progress in the Gramscian

sense" (Hardt and Negri, *Commonwealth*, 118). The role of the academic is to follow the multitude's lead and encourage it – or help it come into being by proposing institutions proper to its desires. There is certainly some wisdom in this approach, but surely it can also be understood as a strategy to avoid political commitments. Consider this quote: "In our view, the other to power … is best defined as an alternative production of subjectivity, which not only resists power but also seeks autonomy from it" (ibid., 56). Once again, a new subjectivity appears to be the pre-condition for a successful revolution, and this new subjectivity is to be collective, universal, and inclusive of all humanity.

58 Mouffe, *Return of the Political*, 115.

7 Immanent Critique and Disavowing the Urban Political

As a form of critique, Slavoj Žižek's model of ideology (as described in the Philosophical Excursus), in which he rejects the logic of false consciousness in favour of a manifest disconnect between human knowledge and action, provides an effective technique for identifying the symptoms of disavowed political positions. He claims that when subjects think and avow something to be morally right and empirically true, but appear to disavow this knowledge in their actions, this is symptomatic of ideology at work. The importance of Žižek's intervention is that he shifts the question of ideology from a matter of conscious belief to one of embodied, unconscious enjoyment; he reverses the location of "false consciousness" so that what one "knows" at the level of consciousness is, contra Marx, genuinely that which is in one's interests. Mystified "false" knowledge, then, is not a matter of consciousness but revealed in action as a betrayal of conscious knowledge. While radical leftists may *think* they oppose capitalism, they don't really *believe* it, because they are addicted to the enjoyment it provides (just like everyone else). Žižek's theory is clearly useful for identifying disconnects between theory and action, but it is also a potent method of textual analysis – for seeking out and highlighting performative disavowals in normative academic work. Such a method is traditionally called "immanent critique."

Approaching an object via immanent critique is akin to Marx's deconstruction of the commodity form: the commodity's outward appearance mystifies the inner social dynamics that produces it. When analyzing a written text in this manner, the explicit assertions of an author can be said to obscure the underlying disavowed ideological meaning of the work. In the case of post-political or ethical theorizing, for example, the outward use of properly political terms (like antagonism or community) may elude the author's disavowed post-political commitments. This mystification is not intentional on the part of the author, which is why one can use the term "disavowed" to describe the underlying normative orientation. Therefore, immanent critique is not intended to catch anyone in a lie, or to cast aspersions on anyone's sincerity, but instead it aims to uncover deeply buried assumptions of which an author may be largely unaware.

In many respects this entire book has been an exercise in immanent critique of critical urban political theory. I've aimed to show that many critical urban theorists who think they are formulating properly political analyses of urban phenomena are, in fact, working in a post-political framework. If one is interested in approaching critical urban theory specifically in this manner, I argue, the most effective strategy is to work through the relevant texts and pay special attention to any mentions (or absences) of key political categories as outlined throughout this book: the political, antagonism, inclusion/exclusion, and democracy. But more specifically, I contend, an immanent critic of critical urban literature should look to the way in which these political concepts have been expressed through a sustained analysis of *property regimes*. By centring the critique on property and, specifically common property or the commons, authors are by definition (if not expressly) legitimating *exclusion* as a political tactic in the name of social justice.

Because this book is concerned first and foremost with political theory, I have thus far focussed primarily on abstract theories of urban space and politics. However, immanent critique can be even more enlightening when applied to the mismatch between normative critical theory and actual, empirical examples of urban conflict. It is in the realm of case studies that scholars often reveal a disavowed values-mismatch, or are demonstrably unaware that their empirical descriptions of events, while factually accurate, actually contradict their normative insights drawn from them. Such an immanent critique shows how critical theory all too often *describes* properly political action while simultaneously *ascribing it an ethical logic and content.* These sorts of denials, defined by post-political principles, occur in situations where such a hegemonic normative framework exists that it becomes almost unintelligible for the actions or attitudes of valorized actors to diverge from it. But this is precisely the case with much contemporary critical urban theory as applied to the ethical turn and the open city. The normative commitment to openness and inclusivity, which informs the hegemonic understanding of the city, has become so overwhelmingly commonsensical to the critical urban theorist that she or he cannot recognize it when communities and activists act politically, based on antagonism and exclusions.

Thus, in this final chapter, I shift my focus away from the largely abstract theorization of the various schools of critical urban theory and explore the way such theory has been applied concretely in the service of explaining specific struggles over urban space. In each case, the literature I have chosen deals with the political categories emphasized throughout this book. I have also chosen the work of theorists that I greatly admire, have learned from, and am sympathetic to. In this way, I hope to avoid straw-man arguments or curt dismissals based on any latent sectarian bias. I consider all four theorists – Nick Blomley, Andy Merrifield, and Lynn Staeheli and Don Mitchell (as a pair) – to be working in the theoretical milieu I identify with: one influenced by Marxist political economy, but not dogmatically so; sympathetic to postmodern and post-structuralist insights, including intersectionality, without fetishizing them; and genuinely concerned with promoting social justice as understood in a fairly typical social-democratic or democratic socialist manner.

Blomley: From the Right to Exclude, to the Right not to be Excluded

Of all the critical urban theorists whose work I have studied in the process of creating this book, there is no one that has been more singularly influential on me than Nicholas Blomley. It was Blomley's book *Unsettling the City* and his essay "Enclosure, Common Right and the Property of the Poor," that introduced and convinced me of the importance of approaching the city as a site of common property. His research demonstrates just how regularly appeals to common property are invoked in urban struggles for control over communities. With a special focus on Vancouver, Blomley explores several high-profile cases in which communities explicitly rejected the ownership model of property in order to protect usage claims to buildings, parks, and neighbourhoods, and the political lessons that can be drawn from them all. However, despite recognizing that common property is defined by exclusive use rights, and that activists use the language of exclusion in order to assert these rights over particular spaces, Blomley still appears reticent to acknowledge that this might be considered part of a normative logic of resistance. Instead, he tends to emphasize the inclusionary potential for a politics of common property that might challenge the logic of exclusion characteristic of private property regimes. As mentioned briefly in the last chapter, his work tends to emphasize the "right not to be excluded" over the "right to exclude" when discussing common property.

One particular case that Blomley has done extensive work on is the struggle over the Woodward's department store in Vancouver's downtown eastside (DES). This case study goes a long way toward highlighting how a discourse of common property can be translated into a strong moral and legal ownership claim to community space, how it can politicize communities and how, despite all this, I argue, that critical theory can still produce post-political conclusions.

According to Blomley's account, the Woodward's department store was opened in 1903 at the corner of Abbot and Hastings streets, in the DES of Vancouver (often referred to as "Canada's poorest area code"). It served as a central space for day-to-day community life, especially shopping and socializing. It was a community touchstone and a site of memories, events, and activities that lent it a special meaning in the neighbourhood. The business closed in 1993 and the space was sold to a condominium developer who planned to erect a complex of 350 market-priced residential units. This began a long struggle over how the space should be used, and who had claims over it.

The community itself, defined for the moment as everyone who lived or conducted business in the DES, was split over the issue. On one hand, many local business owners welcomed the condominium project as they considered it an opportunity for an influx of money into the impoverished neighbourhood. Not surprisingly, however, the majority of long-term residents (often living in residential hotels, or "SROs") and community activists were horrified by the prospect, and instead advocated for the development of social housing in this space. The type of discourse Blomley ascribes to these activists in the defence of their claim to the space is important. Woodward's, they argued, was given its history and meaning by the community through the way the locals had *used* the space.[1] It was a place open to the public, providing both a social space and, in a more banal sense, Woodward's was simply a convenient place to shop (which was something in short supply in the DES). Therefore, from the perspective of the long-term residents, any private owner that intended to build something there that would enclose the space from the community, contribute to gentrification (preventing long-term residents even the *ability to live* in their neighbourhood), or simply not consider the particular interests of the community, lacked the moral and legal authority to appropriate that space. In other words, the community claimed a right to that space as common property, based on a shared tradition of use and meaning.

Blomley explains that the space itself became a contentious issue within formal political bodies over the next 15 years, as progressive provincial governments and municipal councils instituted policies favourable to the community, as quickly as business-friendly governments reversed them. This is notable because the battle over Woodward's was only effective to the extent that the community had allies in government, and it did not reject conspiring with officials out of some form of ideological purity. The community was willing to, unapologetically, employ the much-maligned power structure of "representation" (one of Jodi Dean's "crimes" of the old Left) toward its ends in the form of an ad hoc "Committee of the Downtown Eastside." As with all forms of representation, this required determining those who would be included and excluded in the construction of "the community": in this instance, not everyone living in the neighbourhood was considered equal, with the right to an equal voice. Those supportive of the condominium development were excluded, for example, while anyone in favour of low-income housing was welcomed. If Blomley's description is accurate, this struggle was not approached conceptually as operating in a Habermasian public sphere nor a Rawlsian Original Position. It was based *explicitly* on a willingness to *exclude* – a willingness to acknowledge fundamental political antagonisms that divide the community.

How might one frame this struggle in terms of the theory I have explored throughout this book? Appealing to the "right to stay put," the basic thrust of the activists' rejection of the condominium proposal was as follows: this is our community, we have lived here for generations, and therefore we claim a right to live here and use the space; like Virilio's Worker Battalions, we will not be moved. This is not a multilayered, obtuse, deconstruction of social norms that only a professor of cultural studies can appreciate. It is a simple demand to ensure that one has the ability to continue living in one's community and not be gentrified. As a result, the activists and residents fought not informed by abstract cosmopolitan principles of inclusion, multiculturalism, or experimental living, but on genuinely political principles of:

- Exclusion: by naming enemies – for example, Kassam Aghtai (the condo developer involved with the first redevelopment proposal), community business elites who favoured the development, municipal politicians who enabled it, and the prospective wealthy condo-owners ("yuppies" as the locals referred to them).

- Fixity and particularity: by asserting that the neighbourhood was the site of struggle, not the city of Vancouver. Not all Vancouverites had claims to that neighbourhood, but only those who lived there, *in that particular neighbourhood*, and had contributed to the construction of its traditions (and even this was limited to those mentioned above).
- Representation: by making alliances in electoral politics, and by creating a community with limits and leaders (e.g., the Committee of the DES).
- Loyalty/patriotism: by expressing a deep attachment to the neighbourhood (a "militant particularism") and an unwillingness to disavow the community simply because it was considered poor or dangerous.

The discursive position was very simple: this neighbourhood contains a community that refuses to be dissolved or dispossessed and this community has no interest, at least in the case of how the Woodward's space would be developed, in being unconditionally open to others, experimenting with ways of being, or buying into the disingenuous paternalism of market-driven community development.

Consider, then, this struggle in terms of the politics of common property. Community activists made claims that rendered common property conceptually as a hybrid of usage and ownership models of property. It is usage-based due to the processes and traditions that inform the legitimacy of claims to particular spaces, but ownership-based in that these claims are exclusionary and fixed in the moment they are made. The community invoked a right to exclude outsiders and even specific insiders who were interested in enclosing the space, and its conception of the neighbourhood was not so much a space of becoming which should be left open to potentially radical change, but a (relatively) closed community with the right to preserve its traditions (without completely foreclosing the possibility of self-interested and self-directed change, of course). The struggle over Woodward's exposes the way in which the story of property can be told in such a way that it exists *simultaneously as private and common property*. When the Woodward's store was operating, the community developed a certain claim to how the building was used. When it was abandoned, the community similarly understood the *building/space/land* as commonly owned, despite the fact that the building and land *were also privately owned*. This illustrates not only how the dichotomous purity of the property regime can be upset by the introduction of common property, but also how specific objects subject to it can become *internally* unsettled (as described in Chapter 6).

Ultimately, in 2008, the struggle over Woodward's ended in a compromise agreement. After extensive consultations with the community, the new developer who purchased the site built a multi-use complex that included 536 market-priced units, 125 single-bedroom and 75 family non-market-priced units, a daycare, an office of the National Film Board, spaces for community and non-profit organizations, private shops, and more. Whether this can be considered a victory of sorts for the community who actively resisted the original development plan, is still very much a matter of debate. Gentrification of the DES continues today and some activists have shown that it appears to emanate from the site on which Woodward's used to stand.[2] This suggests that even mixed-income housing is not desirable for the most vulnerable members of, at least, this community.[3] Indeed, DES activists such as Jean Swanson have called social mix "a euphemism for destroying low income communities,"[4] and Blomley argues that social mix in reality almost always results in rich people moving into poor areas and rarely the other way around.[5]

To act in a properly political manner does not require unconditional victory; indeed it does not require any success at all. In the case of the Woodward's building, 15 years of committed political organizing and struggle changed the power relations in a way that benefitted the community. More specifically, it strengthened the community's bargaining power when it came to formal negotiations. The result was that the original redevelopment plan was altered significantly, and the community achieved at least some of its demands. In the final analysis, the redevelopment was "slowed" or "stalled" due to over a decade of concerted community activism which, at least in terms of conceptualizing these urban processes, challenged the logic of the open city – to increase the speed and intensity of creative destruction. The struggle over Woodward's shows that common property can be considered a strong bargaining chip, not only for preserving and protecting access to spaces, but also for cultivating such space. It is a fundamental mistake to treat inner city communities as uninterested in improving the material conditions of their neighbourhoods. As Newman and Wyly state, the notion that communities have to choose "either long-term disinvestment and neglect or gentrification and displacement" is a false choice.[6] The type of politics of common property outlined in this book, which was shared by DES activists, does not close space from improvement, but can be used to negotiate improvements in line with community interests.

Finally, the Woodward's example shows that for the politics of urban common property to be properly political, it benefits from moving beyond reactionary ethical forms by developing a sophisticated understanding of the position of common property in existing legal frameworks via rights-based claims that are more than abstract and moralistic in nature. This is important for the perceived legitimacy of the claims. Recall from Chapter 6, that while many people may sympathize with victims of gentrification, it is often difficult for them to understand how things could be different because those displaced do not own the homes in which they live. It is difficult, in other words, to shift one's perspective away from thinking about real estate in the logic of primarily market-based relations. But articulating a politics of common property, in legal terms, can alter the terms of debate: from the informally moral wrong of displacement, to the formally *illegal* practice of *dispossession*. In this respect, one can both accentuate and challenge Engin Isin when he says that a new understanding of rights-based claims in the context of the city should focus "less on legal rules and more on norms, practices, meanings and identities."[7] In the language of common property, norms, practices, meanings, and identities are critical, but as a means of *establishing legal rules* that formally *recognize the legitimacy of communities' claims to their property and space*. The struggle for common property is not a metaphorical struggle, but an attempt to articulate through existing law a set of rights that have been heretofore subject to erasure.

For all the great insights that Blomley captures in his study of the Woodward's struggle, even he falls into the trap of post-political thinking. Almost all the elements of rejecting a post-political understanding of struggle against dromocratic imperatives in the neoliberal city are there: recognizing antagonism, opposing dromocratic imperatives, and claims to common ownership of urban space. But despite all this, Blomley does not wholeheartedly embrace such a political approach to the movement he clearly supports. This is evidenced by what might be called an understated but crucial aspect of his critical intervention in debates over urban common property. While he *defines* common property in the standard tradition – as based on communities with exclusionary use rights – his *emphasis* when discussing common property is the poor's right *not* to be excluded from its use. In "Enclosure," he states this quite clearly in two separate sentences: "The developer's right to exclude is countered by the claim that the poor have a right to not be excluded";[8] and "If private property is based upon the right to exclude others from the benefits of a resource, common property can be understood as the right to not be excluded from the use of a thing."[9] By turning the emphasis away from the right to exclude toward the right not to be excluded, Blomley actually depoliticizes the category of common property; he turns what would be defined as a community constituted by antagonism into one that should be considered inclusive. It is implied, then, that all actors have legitimate claims to the space and therefore it is difficult to understand how the normative frame for politics could be other than consensus-seeking.

How else might we understand Blomley as giving into a post-political or ethical temptation here? One of his most important insights is that common property is not simply a tool that can be used by the poor to make claims on their communities but, on the contrary, it is the *rich and privileged that make the greatest use of common property discourses.* Wealthy communities typically have much greater influence on the governance and development of their neighbourhoods, and the claims that prevent, say, a social housing project from going up, or to keeping density low, are effectively the same as would be used in the inner city to fight gentrification. While this is often referred to as NIMBYism, it has proven successful and ultimately it appeals to the character and traditional use of communities. Rejecting such a discourse on behalf of the poor because it has often been used to exclude them, reflected in the naive cliché "if you use the tools of the enemy against them then you become like them," is an unpragmatic and "ethical" mistake because it connotes a desire to live outside of power relations, or a fear of exerting power. If becoming like your enemy means accruing power, only someone who already possesses power or security would oppose this in principle. A line from Kohn epitomizes this post-political position as a reticence to engage in power relations:

> Despite these compelling features, I am hesitant to adopt the term commons and instead want to defend the more familiar (but discredited) concept of the public. The main reason for my choice of terminology is that the term commons can legitimately be applied to forms of joint ownership that are still extremely elitist and exclusive.[10]

Kohn is absolutely correct in her observation, but this is no reason to reject a politics of the commons. On a philosophical level, one might ask the question: If contemporary cities are increasingly becoming defined by closed, gated, or "carceral" communities, which exclude outsiders, why shouldn't poor communities be allowed to treat their neighbourhoods in a similar manner? Why should "everyone's" voice be heard in city planning only when it comes to the inner-city or impoverished neighbourhoods? It has been shown time and time again that the rich and powerful can and do appropriate the normative imperative of "inclusivity" for their own interests. So, really, what do the poor stand to lose by invoking exclusionary claims to urban space?

There is no doubt that adopting such an exclusionary political stance can be intense and uncomfortably confrontational in practice. Just consider the sentiment behind regularly invoked anti-gentrification slogans like "Yuppie Scum, Fuck Off!" It is difficult to imagine a more antagonistic attitude than this; it goes far beyond what Mouffe has in mind when she advocates agonistic pluralism, because it leaves out a mutually acknowledged legitimate framework in which the struggle takes place. But, nonetheless, "Yuppie Scum, Fuck Off!" is a recurring sentiment in anti-gentrification struggles, and was certainly present in the fight over Woodward's in the DES. Incidentally, I do not think such an absolutist and belligerently antagonistic position is typically helpful for anti-gentrification movements (because such movements still need allies), even if it is morally legitimate in some or most situations. But it is no doubt *political* in a Schmittian sense, and if such an intense sentiment is shared by enough people who identify as a community, it can certainly contribute to a strong anti-gentrification campaign, even if it marginalizes potential allies. But more than anything, when that much *anger* and *resentment* builds up in a marginalized community, it attests to the presence of severely asymmetrical power relations, and a significant portion of the population that feels powerless in the face of compelled eviction from their neighbourhood. The character and rhetoric of any given anti-gentrification struggle will differ depending on several factors: the nature of the threat, as well as the class, racialized, and gendered makeup of the population, and other vagaries of the existing political climate. What does not change, however, is the fundamental ontology of the political, whereby the "us" is threatened with displacement and dispossession by a "them."

Who Owns Public Property? Staeheli and Mitchell on Urban Gardens

In Chapter 6 I showed that there exists a widespread conceptual confusion regarding the difference between common and public property. It is important that a distinction is made between the two because of the false private/public property dichotomy and corresponding erasure of the commons that Blomley describes: if land, buildings, or other urban spaces are not clearly state-owned then the assumption is that they are privately owned. The result is that common property is erased discursively in the process. Perhaps this is why many critical urban theorists privilege the public over the common: the public is more readily intelligible, both intuitively and legally. However, from a progressive political perspective, contributing to the erasure of common property regimes in this way is disadvantageous, even if it is done in the name of securing access and use rights to public spaces for underprivileged and marginalized people. When used to defend use rights to a discrete, unambiguously state-owned space like a city park, appealing to the rights associated with public space can be effective and pragmatic (although, less so if the issue is the pending dismantling of the park by the City. In cases like this, common property is a better legal category for protecting the space). But when the object of contested ownership is composed of several discrete places, or ownership is simply unclear due to overlapping property regimes, the principles of public property can be at best limiting and post-political (e.g., because it then grants universal access to a larger public, instead of a limited community), and at worst unintelligible. Only common property, in all its nuanced legality, can provide the foundation for legitimate ownership or use rights for such spaces. In cases where common property is mistaken for public, it detracts from both the conceptual intelligibility and the moral suasion of the argument required to justify community ownership.

Lynn A. Staeheli and Don Mitchell's cases studies in *The People's Property?* provide great examples of how common property can be either mistaken for public property or how public property is favoured because of its presumed socially inclusive character. Their book is driven by the questions "who owns what?" and "how is the 'who' of ownership constituted through property regimes?" The preoccupation of the book is with the private/public divide as it relates to space and property:

> While much research has centered on, and argued over, the nature of public space as *space*, comparatively little has focused on it as *property*. Yet as we will argue throughout this book, understanding public space as a set of property relationships is foundational; property is a crucial set of relationships that structure the role, function, and nature of public space as space.[11]

From the authors' perspective, the public is intimately associated with the concept of the "people," but the two categories should not, in any way, be understood as always identical. What they mean by this is that the public is a highly regulated space constituted by legal inclusion and exclusion of certain people, as they state: "The struggle over who can *be* on public property is a struggle over who is and *is not* to be included as part of 'the people'."[12] Struggles for access to public space are, then, processes of creating the means for a certain public to be considered the people. If this sounds familiar, it should, because it is precisely the same process by which property is made common, or the procedure by which it is "commoned," to use Harvey's term.

They answer these questions of the relationship between public space and the people via a series of case studies drawn from across the United States, including public spaces in Washington, DC, Santa Fe, San Diego, and Syracuse. But for present purposes, Staeheli and Mitchell's work that is of most interest is a case study that features a very popular urban phenomenon in the context of critical urban studies: the community garden. While this is not discussed by Staeheli and Mitchell, it is worth noting that urban community gardens are places greatly appreciated by critical urbanists. In my, albeit impressionistic, reading of the broader literature, one can point to several reasons for this appreciation. First, because public gardeners are frequently produced in abandoned lots, they are a wonderful example of the creative appropriation of urban space. Second, because the "communities" involved in their creation regularly include a mixture of progressive activists and underprivileged city residents, they often become more than simple places of horticulture, and instead also come to represent sites of progressive organizing and resistance to the power of urbanized capital. Third, urban gardening is typically conceived of as an inherently progressive social practice, especially in terms of food security and sustainable agriculture. Fourth, community gardens are innately *communal*, and therefore contribute to the creation of community, something that most critical theorists believe to be deteriorating in the neoliberal city. Fifth, when communal gardens are threatened by redevelopment plans or any other manner of re-appropriation, some communities have demonstrated their passion and commitment to the sites by organizing sustained resistance campaigns, even becoming causes célèbres in some cases, like the South Central Farmers' struggle in Los Angeles (the subject of a well-known documentary).[13] But for the purposes of my argument, communal gardens are important primarily because of the way in which all of the above considerations contribute toward understanding the production of discrete sites of common property and the potential for properly political action. There may be no better example of unused public or private space made "productive" in a distinct manner, and by a discrete community, than a public garden.

Staeheli and Mitchell explore exclusively the struggles for maintaining the existence of communal gardens in New York City. In the 1970s, due to processes of disinvestment and deindustrialization, they argue, many urban core NYC neighbourhoods suffered mass abandonment of commercial and residential properties. The City purchased many of these properties, but with no short-term plans for redevelopment. In the absence of any proposals for revitalizing the affected neighbourhoods, activists and residents began improving the land themselves by creating gardens intended for community use. These gardens were scattered across the city, and while some failed to work as intended, others flourished as successful community projects. According to Staeheli and Mitchell's narrative, these gardens operated with no opposition from the City (the City actually condoned them) through the 1970s and 1980s until the City decided it was time to redevelop the land in the 1990s. This set off a protracted conflict between the City and the gardeners, a struggle not unlike the battle over Woodward's in Vancouver. The biggest difference between the two struggles is that whereas the Woodward's building was privately owned before the community commoned it, the NYC gardens were publicly owned. The practice of commoning, or "publicizing" (as Staeheli and Mitchell describe it) these public spaces was otherwise almost identical:

> The gardeners imagined the gardens as places where people could work together – even while recognizing and valuing difference in class, race, age,

> gender, and citizenship – in the building of an inclusive community and in developing a voice that could be heard in the city as a whole.... what was critical to the rights claims of the gardening community was that the gardens were spaces that the residents of marginalized and abandoned areas had actively made … The common refrain was that the gardens may have been owned by the City in a narrow legal sense, but they had been made by the residents themselves … The gardeners argued that as residents of the neighborhoods and as people who had devoted countless hours transforming the lots from junk piles into green spaces for work, play, and gathering, they had a fundamental right to the land and a fundamental right to the city they had made.[14]

In respect to the type of development that should take place on this land, Mayor Giuliani and the City argued that there was a greater need for housing, and this included subsidized homes, rather than gardens. The gardeners did not disagree with this sentiment, but instead pointed out that there was more than enough *unused* abandoned space for new housing stock. Additionally, the gardeners asserted that the City's expressed interest in building homes was secondary to their main, concealed motivation: to destroy the spaces that were used for progressive and, in some cases, radical political organizing. This targeting of public gardens implies the importance of physical space for building a community of resistance in the neoliberal/dromocratic city, and Staeheli and Mitchell recognize it as such. They argue that the immobile character of land "is a considerable problem for capitalism, which relies on the full exchangeability and therefore the physical circulation, of things."[15] And make no mistake, these gardeners understood their gardens to be sites of exclusion. Acknowledging an antagonism between rich and poor, they were not considered spaces for all New Yorkers to congregate, as the authors acknowledge:

> The point is significant, as the gardeners claimed a right to public space for communities that were otherwise deprived of the resources of the city. They did not, for example, make the same sort of claims about the necessity of gardens for the wealthiest areas of the city. Rather, their claim was that as marginalized communities, they had a particular communal right to the space in which they could organize, mobilize, and seek empowerment.[16]

As such, in the case of community gardens, Staeheli and Mitchell consider the practice of exclusion a legitimate tactic because it was exercised in the name of creating a democratic public, rather than to discriminate against an identifiable group.[17]

Eventually the conflict ended with an agreement in 1999 to save several of the gardens by transferring ownership from the City to two Land Trusts ("The Trust for Public Land" and "The New York Restoration Project"). Staeheli and Mitchell are suspicious of this move because land trusts "operate in the murky region between public and private. They own land as private entities, yet they claim to do so in the public interest,"[18] and therefore ownership is transferred to private entities. This alienates ownership from the gardeners themselves and situates ultimate control of the gardens in "distant, more bureaucratic agencies."[19] In short, the authors argue that there is no guarantee that the land trusts will share the same type of vision and limited sense of "public" for the gardens as was established when the gardens were created as public space by the community. Ultimately, at the time of writing, Staeheli and Mitchell report that none of the gardeners felt that the trusts had significantly restricted the functions of the gardens. However, they did suggest that an atmosphere of uneasiness and concern for the future was present among the gardeners, precisely because the property relations had changed and the land trusts had become such powerful actors in the city.

Staeheli and Mitchell's analysis describes and avows all of the principles that I consider important for politicizing urban space: antagonism, exclusion, fixity, and emphasizing the central role of property relations. Indeed, the actors in their case studies regularly appear to embody these properly political values. Nonetheless, they insist on using the language of public rather than common. They appear to be uneasy with the concept of common property because it is "so much weaker" than public property in American law.[20] Staeheli and Mitchell's concern appears to be more of a "feeling" than a legally-informed judgment; echoing Iris Marion Young's sentiment discussed in the previous chapter, they seem to fear "community" and "community property" because it invokes a certain insularity and parochialism. For example, within their exploration of the exclusions enacted by the owners of a shopping mall in Syracuse they opine:

> While many definitions cocoon community members in feelings of belonging, protection, and mutuality, most definitions also recognize the role of community in excluding non-members, and the obligation of community members to conform to communal norms. Community, in other words, may be a tool to discipline people in their relations with other people and institutions. From the perspective of a community, it may be acceptable, then, to set a norm of civil behaviour, and to exclude people who do not conform to that behaviour ... by making other community members feel uncomfortable.[21]

From their perspective, the "public" should be prioritized because it has greater potential for building democratic "publics."

Thus, Staeheli and Mitchell appear to stress the political importance of language choices when framing a conflict over urban space/property. Does it all boil down to determining the framing terms to which communities will respond most favourably? There is a strong juridical argument to be made for stressing the public because it is better established and recognized in common law. More generally, public property is clearly the more familiar and intelligible property type for virtually all members of liberal democracies. And theorists like Staeheli and Mitchell, and Kohn, make strong populist arguments in favour of the inclusive character of *public* property. In the ethical-discursive environment in which we live today, such an appeal to inclusivity plays well, not only among marginalized communities, but also middle-class and policy-making circles. But, given certain circumstances, the right to public property may very well be the type of appeal that the Left should be slowly deprivileging, at least at the local level. If public space and public property cannot become disassociated from post-political or ethical understanding of community and politics, then the only currently available option with legal standing is common property. As my critique of Blomley and Hardt and Negri hints, perhaps the common is also becoming associated with such a discursive understanding. If so, distinguishing the public and common conceptually may indeed be the most immediate task required of the critical urban theorist. It seems clear that whether the discussion is situated in the context of public or common property regimes, in order to conceptualize urban space and politics in a manner that genuinely challenges the neoliberal, open, ethical, or dromocratic city, critical theory needs to *politicize* itself.

I contend, however, that there is more at stake than a simple matter of semantic coding. Choosing to use the language of common property over public will be determined to some extent by the scale and function of the space and the interests of the affected community. Staeheli and Mitchell open their book with a brief description of the 2006 mass protest in Chicago, in which 100,000 documented and undocumented immigrants and their allies marched through the streets demanding to be recognized as part of the American public. By physically occupying space, they "asserted themselves as part of the public – the *people* – of the United States."[22] At this scale of political activism, it is unintelligible if not impossible for those involved to base their demands on a right to *exclude*. Such a movement can only be oriented toward moral and legal inclusion, by virtue of the fact that American citizenship is a universalized limit-category of belonging. It follows that to the extent exclusionary politics is being practised, it is in the context of the American anti-immigration movement bent on limiting access to both American territory and citizenship. While this counter-movement is conservative and reactionary, it is nonetheless *political* to the extent it is premised on a right to exclude and an us/them dualism. It is understandable, then, that a leftist might balk at supporting any political movements based on a right to exclude, considering how ugly and dangerous such mass movements can be. But when one shifts the scale of and the issue of concern for a particular struggle, this reticence is oft proven unjustified. Following Harvey's comments on scale, when one considers much smaller group formations, like community gardens, *the entire point* of organizing is to produce an *exclusionary* space. Conceptually, this type of commoning should be considered analogous to support for First Nations sovereignty, or Massey's example of negotiated closure vis-à-vis the Amazonian Deni, not to mention asserting exclusive use-rights within neighbourhoods in order to fight gentrification. While clearly not all social exclusions are socially just or politically progressive, all properly political action involves exclusions, a lesson the Left would be well served to acknowledge in their struggles to establish common ownership of urban space.

Merrifield: Overlapping Consensus and Urban Negative Dialectics

Andy Merrifield is one of the most prominent names in critical urban geography. He has published a number of highly regarded books and articles related to the theory and practice of urban political struggle from a neo-Marxist perspective. His work touches on all the important beats that compose the pulse of critical urbanism, including the master theorists (Lefebvre, Benjamin, Castells, and Harvey), the critical concepts (right to the city, production of space) and empirical processes (gentrification, inner city movements, globalization). However, one familiar with his whole body of work will encounter in his academic trajectory a subtle shift away from a more empirically grounded, political economy approach, to relatively contained and localized struggles (as in his 2002 book *Dialectical Urbanism*), to a much more theoretically abstract and Lefebvrian rejection of traditional notions of urban space, accompanied by an increased emphasis on hugely spectacular urban events, like the Arab Spring and Occupy Wall Street (as in his 2013 *The Politics of the Encounter* and 2014's *The New Urban Question*). In this respect, one might argue that his evolution as a scholar has been akin to Habermas's move from a theorist of public space, to one of deliberative ethics, as Kohn documents so insightfully. A strange "despatialization" occurs in Merrifield's more recent work as he rejects the category of the city and instead embraces "planetary urbanization." This move, in his own words, shifts geography away from "the ghost thinking in terms of absolutes – of entities with borders and clear demarcations between what's inside and what's outside. It suggests, instead, something new, something futuristic, something that embraces urban becoming."[23] He refers to planetary urbanization as "formless" and "open-ended" and, therefore, "transformative politics presumably needs to be likewise."[24] The problem with such ideas is, I argue, if there is no form, there can be no exclusion, and therefore Merrifield's founding premises forecloses the possibility of politics proper. Additionally, notwithstanding his shift from Marxist political economy to Marxist-inflected Evental analysis, one aspect of Merrifield's work that remains consistent is his commitment to a sort of ethical cosmopolitanism when considering the politicization of the city.

It may be that the diversity of Merrifield's influences muddies his analysis but, on my reading of his work, there is a clear tension between his cosmopolitan ethics and his, albeit weak, Marxist class analysis, and it is reflected by the case studies he develops in *Dialectical Urbanism*. That is, in the course of exploring specific inner-city struggles, his normative position does not, I contend, wholeheartedly embrace the political lessons that his case studies provide. Merrifield espouses an ostensibly typical ethical vision of critical urban praxis when he advocates a "negative dialectic" of the city, a term borrowed from Theodor Adorno but never really acknowledged as such. Merrifield defines this "negative dialectic" as a constant struggle that neither plans for nor reaches a utopia but nonetheless moves forward, creating itself and its goals in the process. His position is consonant with dromocratic imperatives when he references Dostoevsky's ethic that "human beings eternally and continually build roads for themselves, leading somewhere, no matter where, and that the main thing isn't where it leads, 'but just that it leads.' Urban dwellers and critical urbanists need to internalize this spirit."[25] In sloganized form, the spirit of Merrifield's negative dialectic might be something like: "what you struggle for doesn't matter, as long as you struggle." His position might be considered ostensibly properly political because, to the extent it involves struggle, it implies agonism, but it is agonism without any concrete desire for hegemony. Regardless of whether this theory is ethical or quasi-political, his case studies appear to contradict some aspects of his normative vision without him acknowledging it. Much like Blomley's study of Woodward's, Merrifield's descriptive analyses of inner-city movements show that they do not share such a negative-dialectical ethic, but instead form struggles more characteristic of the Mouffian political.

For example, in Chapter 3 of *Dialectical Urbanism*, "Them and Us? Rebuilding the Ruins in Liverpool," Merrifield examines the way in which, in the 1980s and 1990s, class and racialized divisions in the impoverished district of Toxteth in Liverpool prevented potentially progressive development schemes (that he thinks would have genuinely benefited the community) while avoiding mass gentrification. The community of Toxteth is intensely poor and considerably diverse in ethnic terms, as Merrifield illustrates: "All Liverpool council communiqués to Toxteth residents come translated in six languages"[26] (Arabic, Bengali, Chinese, Somali, and Urdu). The gist of the story Merrifield discloses is that in an attempt to address the decades of physical degeneration and blighting, chronic violence, criminal activity, and periodic riots that afflicted the area, the City of Liverpool devised a redevelopment plan for the Granby neighbourhood (widely recognized as the poorest and most violent area in the Toxteth district). This included a Compulsory Purchase Order (CPO)[27] passed in 1997 for all the residential units in the Granby Street area. Housing was purchased for £17,000 per unit, with a promise that all displaced residents would be relocated in the area if they requested to do so.[28] However, as of 2001 (Merrifield's book was published in 2002), no new construction had commenced and, as Merrifield states, the "entire Granby neighbourhood resembled the South Bronx in its darkest days of the late 1970s. Ruins were everywhere. Street upon street was boarded up and derelict, uninhabited and uninhabitable."[29] Thus, according to Merrifield's narrative, through the lens of critical gentrification studies, the situation Granby finds itself in is an anomaly of sorts. Despite mass dislocation of its population due to the CPO, the story of Granby represents a clear case of a neighbourhood that somehow still succeeded in being *neither revitalized nor gentrified.*

Merrifield is interested in exploring the inter-community dynamics that failed to lead to meaningful regeneration of the neighbourhood. He returns to the initial 1994 municipal discussions that brought community members together to discuss redevelopment plans. Interestingly (for a Marxist), he conceptualizes the negotiations in a Rawlsian framework of "reasonable pluralism," which is pursued by identifying an "overlap of consensus" amongst different stakeholders.[30] Recognizing that the diversity of groups could not be expected to share a singularly unified set of interests, the Rawlsian method seeks to identify shared interests that may serve as germinal for, in the case of Granby, building a redevelopment plan that would benefit all segments of the neighbourhood. In Merrifield's opinion, this proved to be impossible as there existed a paucity of trust between the various neighbourhood groups; tensions were simply too strong between owners and renters, blacks and whites, and various subgroups within the larger black community (in particular, tensions between older, British-born groups and newly established immigrants, especially Somalians). In addition, the residents shared a general suspicion of the city's motive for the proposed redevelopment. In respect to the inter-ethnic divides, Merrifield provides a standard Marxist criticism of identity politics: by defining their communities in narrow and parochial (ethnic) terms, the population of Granby was unable to organize in an effective political manner because their mutual distrust blinded them to any shared inter-ethnic interests. For Merrifield, the overlap in consensus should have been built around class: "if these groups have anything in common then it's the common trait of poverty; they're all members of the working class, they all have to sell their labor power as a commodity to make ends meet."[31]

The first important lesson that can be gleaned from Merrifield's description of Granby is that, far from acting apolitically, the various groups involved in the negotiations were acting in a paradigmatically Schmittian political manner: by creating a series of "us" and "them" dualisms, based in what would be considered largely "private" aspects of identity (in this case, race). However, on Merrifield's retelling of the events, it does appear true on the surface that their political activity was ineffective because they did not overcome their particular antagonisms that would enable them to crystallize around Mouffe's fundamental political antagonism "Left/Right" (defined by class, in this case). Here he is not saying that the community should have avoided antagonisms, but that it organized itself based on false group lines. In this regard, Merrifield intimates a need for effective political action similar to the sort that I have advocated throughout this book. However, where his analysis is left wanting a genuinely political character, is in his a priori assumption that the search for consensus should inform the Granby community's politics. In the course of outlining the various collective actors involved in the deliberative process, he does not identify a single villain in the narrative, or an "adversary" around and against whom the community could coalesce. Typically, in such situations, a leftist would indict neoliberal municipal governments and developers as such adversarial figures, and it is safe to say that Merrifield would be sympathetic to such a construction (perhaps he feels that it goes without saying). But capitalist developers are examples of easily vilified outsiders because they are not indigenous to the neighbourhood. The true test of a willingness to act politically concerns identifying adversaries *internal* to a community. It is naive to assume that all residents internal to a neighbourhood such as Granby can be understood as part of a homogenous group in terms of class, and that identifying adversaries outside the physical borders of the neighbourhood exhausts the antagonisms. Perhaps most glaringly, even if all residents are relatively poor, home and other property-owners will typically possess (sometimes radically) opposed interests to that of renters or the homeless. In this respect, the traditional Marxist class breakdown between wage-earners and owners of production sputters in the face of a more immediate antagonism: the renters and home-owners of Granby may be mostly working class, but they are divided by ownership/non-ownership of real estate. Quite simply, Merrifield does not appear to consider this a possible source of antagonism. This is a performative absence on the part of Merrifield. In fact, property itself is nowhere posited as a political category, at least in this specific case study.

Another insight for progressive politics that racially diverse neighbourhoods like Granby highlight, is how the intersection of class and race can become a delicate matter for critical theory. How do community organizers deal with a situation in which, for example, the majority of home-owners belong to one ethnic community while most renters belong to another? I do not know the answer to this question, but I do know that it is a question to which a properly political analysis of what happened in Granby *requires*. The danger of pursuing this line of questioning does, of course, pose real dangers. The potential for class struggle to turn into or be interpreted as racist is dangerously likely in such neighbourhoods. Because Merrifield does not explore this tension in any detail, it is impossible to determine the extent to which this adversarial relationship contributed to the failure of the redevelopment scheme; for the purposes of my analysis, it is also irrelevant. The fact that he does not explore the tension, but instead implies that property-owners and renters are part of the same community and have shared interests by virtue of their poverty, signifies something about Merrifield's approach to politics. He is either unwilling to acknowledge or he disavows the need to identify antagonisms internal to communities in order to develop a progressive political movement aimed at improving the lives of the most marginalized groups in urban neighbourhoods. In the absence of such a willingness to think in a properly political register, Merrifield can only resort to his "negative dialectical" ontology of urban political action. In material terms, this never-ending dialectic can only be conceptualized as a process of constant dialogue and stakeholders meeting in a search for internal community consensus. However, the very concept of negative dialectics, as theorized by Adorno, mitigates against ever finding a consensus in its normal operation. In this respect, one can see that Adorno was not a post-political thinker in the same vein as his student, Habermas. However, he also was not a properly political theorist either, as he rejected the legitimacy of, more or less, all the leftist political movements of his time in favour of thinking of modernist art as the site of politics. Adorno was a Messianic thinker who could not imagine social relations redeemed in such a way, because late modern relations of domination did not provide the conditions of possibility for such a redemptive outcome. Adorno's position was more one of "wait and hope." This is a secularized religious position, not a properly political one.[32]

After saying all this, it would be disingenuous if I did not mention that, in the conclusion of his book, Merrifield provides a thoughtful statement meant to sum up his position on urban political action that, indeed, appears to include some properly political analysis. He states:

> It's tricky as well because leftists now have to proceed carefully through questions of openness and closure in the city, about an urbanism that's fair yet free, that's just but imperfect, a space where invisible contradictions aren't fetishized and where visible conflicts are confronted without repression. We may never get that far, of course, may never know how far we can get in advance … Still, what's crucial here is to express our dissatisfaction collectively, to channel it rationally, to direct it against a common enemy, to utilize it creatively and relentlessly, forever pushing forth with it.[33]

The references to closure, justice, common enemies, and collectivity, all hint at a properly political understanding of conflict in the city. However, in his description of the Granby case, at least, such categories remain unspecified, as if he is reluctant to actually identify a legitimate example of closure, to name specific enemies and, therefore, how exactly collective dissatisfaction should be channelled. In fact, in the above quotation Merrifield comes closest to channelling the Messianic critical theory of Adorno: we can only hope that our spirited efforts will lead to a better future, but there are no guarantees and no real plan to achieve it. By being unwilling to take a particular place – the Granby neighbourhood – as a site of genuine political antagonism, Merrifield is unwilling to engage with uncomfortable power dynamics. Similarly, by stressing the importance of searching for overlapping consensus (at the expense of antagonism), he is unwilling to recognize the anti-democratic element of democracy constitutive of the political that, in specifically urban terms, I earlier designated as "place."

Notes

1 Blomley, *Unsettling the City*, 58.
2 Jean Swanson and Wendy Pedersen, "The Woodward's Redevelopment," Carnegie Community Action Project (2010), http://dtesnh.wordpress.com/about-2/housing/ccap/woodwards-a-symbol-of-exclusion-and-gentrification/
3 Karen Ward, "In the DTES, Social Mix is Exclusion," last updated January 16, 2013, https://dnchome.wordpress.com/2013/01/16/exclusion/
4 Jean Swanson works for "The Carnegie Community Action Project," and I took this quote from the podcast: "Cost of Poverty // Future of Social Housing," *The City*, CITR Radio, June 20, 2012.
5 Blomley, *Unsettling the City*, 99–101.
6 Lees et al., *Gentrification*, 264.
7 Engin Isin, "Introduction: Democracy, Citizenship, and the City," in *Democracy, Citizenship, and the Global City*, ed. Engin Isin (New York: Routledge, 2002), 5.
8 Blomley, "Enclosure," 316.
9 Ibid., 320.
10 Kohn, *Brave New Neighborhoods*, 10.
11 Staeheli and Mitchell, *The People's Property*, xx.
12 Ibid., 30.
13 Kennedy, *The Garden*
14 Ibid., 105.
15 Ibid., 131.
16 Ibid., 107.
17 Ibid., 108.
18 Ibid., 109.

19 Ibid., 110.
20 Ibid., 130.
21 Ibid., 92
22 Ibid., xiii–xiv.
23 Merrifield, *Politics of the Encounter*, xv.
24 Ibid., xviii.
25 Andy Merrifield, *Dialectical Urbanism: Social Struggles in the Capitalist City* (New York: Monthly Review Press, 2002), 170.
26 Ibid., 56.
27 CPOs operate serve the same function as "eminent domain" in the United States, and "expropriation" in Canada.
28 Merrifield, *Dialectical Urbanism*, 61.
29 Ibid., 62.
30 Ibid., 62.
31 Ibid., 67,
32 For more on the secular Jewish position of Adorno, see my article: Dan Webb, "'If Adorno Isn't the Devil, it's Because He's a Jew': Lyotard's Misreading of Adorno through Thomas Mann's *Dr. Faustus*," *Philosophy & Social Criticism* 35(5) (2009).
33 Merrifield, *Dialectical Urbanism*, 171.

Conclusion

As both a method and sentiment, interdisciplinarity is a requisite component of any critical theorist's approach to social scientific research. While it is now a commonly invoked truistic platitude, intellectual inquiry (as opposed to political positioning) should know no boundaries and, in the absence of such limitations, our knowledge of human phenomena can be greatly enriched. But broadening one's intellectual horizons and, in the process, realizing the limitations of staying within one's disciplinary borders, is the most obvious advantage of interdisciplinarity, there exists also a second, much more counter-intuitive benefit. Sometimes, interdisciplinary research leads not only to learning new things, but also to realizing the extent to which diverse fields of research have converged in their methods and normative commitments (a product, ironically enough, of interdisciplinarity). This is something I came to realize in the course of writing this book. When I began to explore the critical urban theory produced in (primarily) sociology and geography, I found myself reflecting upon the way in which concepts indigenous to my discipline – "politics" and "the political" – were being employed outside of political science. What often passed as politics in the critical-theoretical circles of these fields was not what I would consider political, at least in any strong sense, but instead I immediately intuited their use of politics as something I would call "ethics" or the "ethical." To say that I was dissatisfied with what I perceived to be a widespread substitution of politics for some form of inclusionary moral cosmopolitanism, would be an understatement. However, it is not entirely accurate to say that I did not *recognize* what passed for politics in sociology and geography; perhaps my experience is better described as more of an immediately "uncanny" reaction. While I did not *know* the specific way politics was being invoked, I nonetheless felt it to be somehow indeterminately *familiar*. This revelation led me to revaluate the status of politics and the political in my own disciplinary tradition of (critical) political theory. It became quite clear, rather quickly, that post-political thinking is not a phenomenon limited to the critical urbanism of sociology and geography, but indeed a core feature of contemporary critical theory across the liberal arts, including political science. Reviewing much of the literature, book after book, article after article, and blog post after blog post, reiterated the same basic message: to remedy inequality and injustice, political processes need to be rendered more inclusionary, transparent, and structurally less hierarchical. In other words, the essential normative thrust of so much ostensibly critical theory is (even when disavowed as such) that in order to address unequal power relations, one must seek out and reject all manifestations of *power*, as such. If the discipline devoted to the formal study of politics was now, in all but name, rejecting core components of the political and conflating politics and ethics, surely, I mused, this is symptomatic of a sea change in our normative and theoretical orientation toward power. This, I believe, should be regarded as a disconcerting development. More precisely, drawing on the lessons of Chantal Mouffe, this movement away from a willingness to engage with and exert power in the service of political ends can be considered a "post-political" or "ethical" understanding of politics; an approach that, I argue, needs to be de-fetishized, if not outright rejected.

While it would have been easy to write yet another moralizing manifesto ascribing the neoliberalization of progressive thought to the postmodern turn, this would have been as uninteresting as it would be redundant. Instead of simply following other theorists' political economy-informed (Fordism to post-Fordism) or deconstructionist (opposition to the hegemony of binary logic and grand narratives) explanations for the rise of post-political thinking, I wanted to think about the post-politicization of critical theory at the ontological level of subjectivity and desire. As I have argued throughout this book, the critical-theoretical tradition that provides the greatest explanatory power for understanding our current aversion to theorizing a normative relation to properly political action is Lacanian psychoanalysis, especially as developed by Slavoj Žižek. This means placing the category of enjoyment at the centre of one's political analysis: how is enjoyment produced in varying historical and cultural contexts and how is it distributed? How does enjoyment lead us to desire certain things, and disavow that we truly enjoy what we desire? Using numerous theorists, such as Wendy Brown, Jodi Dean, and Žižek, I showed that, in a nutshell, much of the academic Left have come to *enjoy* the futile desire to bring an end to power relations, the failure of the Left to achieve power, and the resentment of those with power; which is another way of saying that the Left has come to enjoy its powerlessness. But, again consistent with Lacanian psychoanalysis, this particular type of enjoyment is by and large *disavowed* on the Left, and therefore requires a type of textual psychoanalytic therapy to illustrate it, for which I have employed the technique of "immanent critique." By using such a method, disavowed desires – manifest in textual contradictions and inconsonant language use – can be found in all kinds of critical theory, from left-liberalism to radical post-structuralism. Once established as a broad methodological framework, one can apply this psychoanalytic critique to any subset of critical theory with which one might be interested. In my case, the object of analysis is critical urban theory, and I have found it to be particularly fertile ground for such critique.

If the crux of Lacanian psychoanalysis is that humans are animated by a desire for an unattainable enjoyment, and real worldly things often become fetishized as the object of this impossible desire, then for critical urbanism the object of desire is most certainly the "open" city – the city that operates outside of power relations and promises freedom for its inhabitants. It is this theoretical construction of the city and urban space, so consistent with its neoliberal variation, which I have argued against in this book. The open city is a distinctly post-political city; it is imagined as a democratic space governed by consensus, a place without antagonisms, without class conflict, and without hierarchy. But, as Mouffe warns us, there is no political consensus absent constitutive exclusions. Just as any political space, therefore, the city is and always will be a site of antagonism, and ownership/non-ownership of property is the schism that defines, arguably, the principal urban antagonism. In this respect, the contemporary city is saturated by overlapping property regimes. But as I have shown (as have many before me), property is always contestable; it is open to discursive, legal, and direct action challenges by organized political actors. In particular, from a leftist perspective, the category of common property is useful for imagining a more equal and socially just city. But common property, as a collective form of ownership always attached to a discrete community, is explicitly premised on a willingness to *exclude* non-owners from its use. This, I argue, requires a fundamental reorientation of the (at least, academic) Left's relationship to power because exclusions are an inconvenient reality of properly political action, despite being disavowed in much of the critical theory scholarship. The shibboleth of conflating exclusions with non-democratic practices needs to be de-mystified if common property is to be used effectively as a tool against gentrification and other manifestations of urban inequality.

It is worth reiterating that this book has primarily been oriented toward scholarly work in the field of critical urbanism. It was in no way intended to render judgment on or disparage the hard-working and committed activists organizing on the ground in cities around the world. Perhaps most inner-city activists already are well aware of the basic points I make here, perhaps they would consider them to be "no-brainers"; or perhaps they would tell me I'm way off in my analysis. This is a topic fit for another book. All I have done in this current volume is contributed to an existing scholarly debate within academia, and hopefully stimulated some reflection on the state of the field, as it were, with the aim of unsettling some prevalent assumptions regarding politics and the political in critical urbanism. If some of my ideas trickle down to street-level political organizing, then so much the better. I do know, however, that our collective future is inextricably tied to the fate of our cities. It would be nice, therefore, to conclude this book by saying that the more we place cities at the centre of our political theorizing, the more opportunities we will have for a better future. But this is not precisely true because we have at least an equal opportunity for failure the more we theorize the city as a site of politics as we have for success. That is just the nature of the *political*. Increasing *discussion* does not in itself lead to better outcomes, as a deliberative democrat might believe, especially if the discussion is informed by false premises. In the realm of the political there can be no assurances of success. The question is not, then, should we give greater consideration to the city as a site of politics? That question is more or less answered with a resounding "Yes!" The real line of inquiry is this: considering the increasing importance of cities to our shared political futures, what are the differing critical-theoretical registers in which “politics” and “the political” are given meaning, and what are the consequence of choosing one over another? Once a particular register is decided on, how can we understand urban life and urban social relations within that analytic framework? These, I believe, should be treated as the central questions of critical urban studies today.

References

Ahmed, Sara, *The Promise of Happiness* (London: Duke University Press, 2010).

Amin, Ash, "A Manifesto for a New Europe," last updated July 14, 2010, accessed March 16, 2014, www.theguardian.com/commentisfree/2010/jul/14/manifesto-new-europe-politics-hope.

Amin, Ash and Nigel Thrift, *Cities: Reimagining the Urban* (Malden, MA: Polity Press, 2002).

Amin, Ash and Nigel Thrift, "The 'Emancipatory' City?" in *The Emancipatory City: Paradoxes and Possibilities*, ed. Loretta Lees (London: SAGE Publications, 2004), 231–235.

Anderson, Benedict, *Imagined Communities: Reflections on the Origin and Spread of Nationalism*, new edition (New York: Verso, 2006).

Arendt, Hannah, *The Human Condition*, 2nd edition (Chicago: University of Chicago Press, 1998).

Aristotle, *Politics*, trans. Benjamin Jowett (Kitchener: Batoche Books, 1999).

Aristotle, *Nichomachean Ethics*, Book VIII, Chapter 3, trans. W.D. Ross (University of Adelaide, 2014), retrieved February 9, 2014, http://ebooks.adelaide.edu.au/a/aristotle/nicomachean/contents.html.

Aronowitz, Stanley, *Left Turn: Forging a New Political Future* (Boulder: Paradigm Press, 2006).

Attoh, Kafui A., "What *Kind* of Right is the Right to the City?" *Progress in Human Geography* 35(5) (2011): 669–685.

Austen, Ian, "Lululemon Athletica Combines Ayn Rand and Yoga," *New York Times*, last updated November 27, 2011, accessed February 7, 2014, www.nytimes/com/2011/11/28/business/media/combines-ayn-rand-and-yoga.html.

Bailey, Ian (interview with Chris Haddock), "Da Vinci Creator Floats Idea of Vancouver as a City State," *Globe and Mail*, last updated November 21, 2010, accessed March 21, 2014, www.theglobeandmail.com/news/british-columbia/da-vinci-creator-floats-idea-of-vancouver-as-a-city-state/article1314958/.

Barber, Benjamin R., *If Mayors Ruled the World: Dysfunctional Nations, Rising Cities* (New Haven: Yale University Press, 2013).

Baudrillard, Jean, *Forget Foucault*, trans. Phil Beitchman, Nicole Dufresne, Lee Hildreth, and Mark Polizzotti (New York: Semiotext(e), 2007).

Benjamin, Walter, "Theses on the Philosophy of History," in *Illuminations*, ed. Hannah Arendt (New York: Harcourt, 1968), 253–264.

Benjamin, Walter, *The Origin of German Tragic Drama*, trans. John Osborne (London: NLB, 1977).

Berlin, Isaiah, *Two Concepts of Liberty: An Inaugural Lecture Delivered Before the University of Oxford on 31 October 1958* (London: Clarendon, 1959).

Blomley, Nicholas, *Unsettling the City: Urban Land and the Politics of Property* (New York: Routledge, 2004).

Blomley, Nicholas, "Enclosure, Common Right and the Property of the Poor," *Social Legal Studies* 17 (2008): 311–332.

Braidotti, Rosi, *Nomadic Subjects: Embodiment and Sexual Difference in Contemporary Feminist Theory* (New York: Columbia University Press, 1994).

Braidotti, Rosi (interview with Kathleen O'Grady), "A Conversation with Rosi Braidotti," last updated August, 1995, accessed February 3, 2014, http://bailiwick.lib.uiowa.edu/wstudies/Braidotti/Braidotti2.html.

Broadbent, Alan, *Urban Nation: Why We Need to Give Power Back to the Cities to Make Canada Strong* (Toronto: HarperCollins, 2009).

Brown, Chris, "'Turtles All the Way Down': Anti-Foundationalism, Critical Theory and International Relations," *Millennium-Journal of International Studies* 23(2) (1994): 213–236.

Brown, Peter, "The Rise and Function of the Holy Man in Late Antiquity," *The Journal of Roman Studies* 61 (1971): 80–101.

Brown, Wendy, "Moralism as Anti-Politics," in Wendy Brown, *Politics Out of History* (Princeton: Princeton University Press, 2001), 18–44.

Brown, Wendy, "Democracy Against Itself: Nietzsche's Challenge," in Wendy Brown, *Politics Out of History* (Princeton: Princeton University Press, 2001), 121–137.

Brown-Sarcino, Japonica (ed.), *The Gentrification Debates* (New York: Routledge, 2013).

Buse, Peter, Ken Hirschkop, Scott McCracken, and Bertrand Taithe, *Benjamin's Arcades: An Unguided Tour* (Manchester: Manchester University Press, 2006).

Calhoun, Craig, "Class Consciousness of Frequent Travellers," in *Conceiving Cosmopolitanism: Theory, Context, and Practice*, ed. Steven Vertovec and Robin Cohen (Oxford: Oxford University Press, 2002), 86–109.

Call, Lewis, *Postmodern Anarchism* (Lanham: Lexington Books, 2002).

Castells, Manuel, *The Rise of the Network Society: The Information Age: Economy, Society, and Culture*, Vol. I, 2nd edition (Malden, MA: Wiley-Blackwell, 2010).

Caulfield, Jon, "'Gentrification' and Desire," in *The Gentrification Reader*, ed. Loretta Loretta Lees, Tom Slater, and Elvin Wyly (New York: Routledge, 2010), 161–170.

Curtis, Adam, *Century of the Self*, documentary film (London: BBC 4, 2002).

Dagger, Richard, "Metropolis, Memory and Citizenship," in *Democracy, Citizenship, and the Global City*, ed. Engin Isin (New York: Routledge 2002), 25–47.

Davis, Mike, *Planet of Slums* (New York: Verso, 2006).

Day, Richard, *Gramsci is Dead: Anarchist Currents in the Newest Social Movements* (London: Pluto Press, 2005).

Dean, Jodi, "Reiteration Again," *I Cite*, last updated March 9, 2006, retrieved February 10, 2013, http://jdeanicite.typepad.com/i_cite/2006/03/reiteration_aga.html.

Dean, Jodi, "The Democratic Deadlock," *Theory and Event* 10(4) (2007): no page numbers given.

Dean, Jodi, "Enjoying Neoliberalism," *Cultural Politics* 4(1) (2008): 47–72.

Dean, Jodi, *Democracy and Other Neoliberal Fantasies* (Durham, NC: Duke University Press, 2009).

Dean, Jodi, "Inept or Unwilling?" *I Cite*, last updated November 20, 2010, accessed December 10, 2013, http://jdeanicite.typepad.com/i_cite/2010/11/inept-or-unwilling.html.

Dean, Jodi, *The Communist Horizon* (New York: Verso, 2012).

Dean, Jodi, "Does the Lost Parallax Need Defending?" *I Cite*, last updated June 4, 2008, accessed February 10, 2013, http://jdeanicite.typepad.com/i_cite/2008/06/does-the-lost-p.html.

Dear, Michael, "Postmodernism and Planning," *Environment and Planning D: Society and Space* 4 (1986): 367–384.

Dear, Michael, *The Postmodern Urban Condition* (Malden, MA: Blackwell, 2000).

Dear, Michael, "The Postmodern Turn," in *Postmodern Geography: Theory and Praxis*, ed. Claudio Minca (Malden, MA: Blackwell, 2001), 1–36.

Dear, Michael, *Why Walls Don't Work: Repairing the US–Mexico Divide* (London: Oxford University Press, 2013).

DeFillipis, James, *Unmaking Goliath: Community Control in the Face of Global Capital* (New York: Routledge, 2003).

Deleuze, Gilles, "Nomad Art: Space," in *The Deleuze Reader*, ed. Constantin V. Boundas (New York: Columbia University Press, 1993), 165–172.

Deleuze, Gilles and Félix Guattari, *A Thousand Plateaus: Capitalism and Schizophrenia*, ed. and trans. Brian Massumi (Minneapolis: University of Minnesota Press, 2004).

Demographia, "World Urban Areas", 9th annual edition, published March 2013, retrieved May 16, 2014, http://demographia.com/db-worldua.pdf.

Dikeç, Mustafa, "Space, Politics, and the Political," *Environment and Planning D: Society and Space* 23 (2005): 171–188.

Eco, Umberto, *Baudolino*, trans. William Weaver (New York: Harcourt, 2000).

Elden, Stuart, *Understanding Henri Lefebvre: Theory and the Possible* (London: Continuum, 2004).

Ellickson, Robert, *Order Without Law: How Neighbors Settle Disputes* (Boston: Harvard University Press, 1994).

Ellickson, Robert, "*Controlling Chronic Misconduct in City Spaces:* Of Panhandlers, Skid Rows, and Public-Space Zoning," *Yale Law Journal* 105 (March 1996): 1165–1248.

Engels, Friedrich, "Draft of a Communist Confession of Faith," *Marx/Engels Selected Works*, Vol. 1 (Moscow: Progress Publishers, 1969), 47.

Engels, Friedrich, *The Condition of the Working Class in England in 1844* (London: Oxford University Press, 2009).

Fainstein, Susan, "Planning Theory and the City," *Journal of Planning Education and Research* 25(2) (2005): 121–130.

Farber, Henry S., "Job Loss and the Decline in Job Security in the United States," *CEPS Working Papers* 171 (Princeton University: Industrial Relations Section, 2008).

Florida, Richard, *Cities and the Creative Class* (New York: Routledge, 2004).

Garber, Judith, "The City as a Heroic Public Sphere," in *Democracy, Citizenship, and the Global City*, ed. Engin Isin (New York: Routledge, 2002), 257–274.

Glaeser, Edward, *Triumph of the City: How Our Greatest Invention Makes Us Richer, Smarter, Greener, Healthier, and Happier* (New York: The Penguin Press, 2011).

Gottfried, Paul, *Carl Schmitt: Politics and Theory* (Westport, CT: Greenwood Press, 1990).

Hardt, Michael and Antonio Negri, *Commonwealth* (Cambridge, MA: Harvard University Press, 2011).

Harvey, David, *Social Justice and the City* (Oxford: Blackwell, 1988).

Harvey, David, *The Condition of Postmodernity: An Enquiry into the Origins of Cultural Change* (Cambridge, MA: Basil Blackwell, 1989).

Harvey, David, *Justice, Nature and the Geography of Difference* (Cambridge, MA: Blackwell, 1996).

Harvey, David, *Spaces of Hope* (Berkeley: University of California Press, 2000).

Harvey, David, "Globalization and the 'Spatial Fix'," *Geographische Revue* 2 (2001): 23–30.

Harvey, David, "The Right to the City," *New Left Review* 53 (September–October 2008): 23–40.

Harvey, David, *Rebel Cities: From the Right to the City to the Urban Revolution* (New York: Verso, 2012).

Heidegger, Martin, "The Question Concerning Technology," in *The Question Concerning Technology and Other Essays*, trans. William Lovitt (New York: HarperCollins, 1977), 3–35.

Hern, Matt, *Common Ground in a Liquid City: Essays in Defense of an Urban Future* (Edinburgh: AK Press, 2010).

Horkheimer, Max, *Eclipse of Reason* (London: Continuum Press, 2004).

Huffington Post Canada, "Temporary Foreign Workers: 18 of 50 Largest Canadian Employers Using Them," last updated April 12, 2013, accessed January 15, 2014, www.huffingtonpost.ca/2013/04/12/temporary-foreign-workers_n_3064389.html.

Imbroscio, David, "Beyond Mobility: The Limits of Liberal Urban Policy," *Journal of Urban Affairs* 34(1) (2012): 1–20.

Imbroscio, David, "From Redistribution to Ownership: Toward an Alternative Urban Policy for America's Cities," *Urban Affairs Review* 49(6) (2013): 787–820.

The Invisible Committee, *The Coming Insurrection* (Los Angeles: Semiotext(e), 2008).

Isin, Engin, "Introduction: Democracy, Citizenship, and the City," in *Democracy, Citizenship, and the Global City*, ed. Engin Isin (New York: Routledge, 2002), 1–22.

Jacobs, Jane, *The Death and Life of Great American Cities* (New York: Vintage Books, 1961).

Jones, Richard Wyn (ed.), *Critical Theory and World Politics* (New York: Lynne Rienner Publishers, 2001).

Kaika, Maria, "Whither Urban Studies" (paper presented at "Whither Urban Studies" at the University of Manchester, Manchester, UK, November 16, 2012), retrieved November 16, 2014, http://progressivegeographies.com/2012/12/01/10340/.

Kennedy, Scott Hamilton (dir.), *The Garden* (Black Valley Films, 2008).

Kohn, Margaret, *Radical Space: Building the House of the People* (New York: Cornell University Press, 2003).

Kohn, Margaret, *Brave New Neighborhoods: The Privatization of Public Space* (New York: Routledge, 2004).

Lacan, Jacques, "The Mirror Stage as Formative of the *I* Function as Revealed in Psychoanalytic Experience," *Écrits: A Selection*, trans. Bruce Fink (New York: Norton, 1999), 75–81.

Lefebvre, Henri, *The Production of Space*, trans. Donald Nicholson-Smith (Malden, MA: Blackwell, 1974).

Lefebvre, Henri, "The Right to the City," in *Writings on Cities*, ed. and trans. Eleonore Kofman and Elizabeth Lebas (Malden, MA: Blackwell, 2000), 147–159.

Lees, Loretta, "A Reappraisal of Gentrification: Towards a 'Geography of Gentrification'," *Progress in Human Geography* 24(3) (2000): 389–409.

Lees, Loretta and Tom Slater (eds.), *The Gentrification Reader* (New York: Routledge, 2010).

Lees, Loretta, Tom Slater, and Elvin Wyly (eds.), *Gentrification* (New York: Routledge, 2013).

Lewchuk, Wayne, Michelynn Lafleche, Diane Dyson, Luin Goldring, Alan Meisner, Stephanie Procyk, Dan Rosen, John Shields, Peter Viducis, and Sam Vrankulj,

"It's More Than Poverty: Employment Precarity and Household Well-Being" (PEPSO, McMaster University Social Sciences, and the United Way Toronto, February, 2013).

Ley, David, "Gentrification and the Politics of the New Middle Class," in *The Gentrification Reader*, ed. Loretta Lees, Tom Slater, and Elvin Wyly (New York: Routledge, 2010), 134–152.

Logan, John and Harvey Molotch, *Urban Fortunes: The Political Economy of Place* (Los Angeles: University of California Press, 1987).

Madden, David J., "City Becoming World: Nancy, Lefebvre, and the Global–Urban Imagination," *Environment and Planning D: Society and Space* 30(5) (2012): 772–787.

Magnusson, Warren, *The Search for Political Space* (Toronto: University of Toronto Press, 1996).

Magnusson, Warren, "Politicizing the Global City," in *Democracy, Citizenship, and the Global City*, ed. Engin Isin (New York: Routledge 2002), 289–306.

Magnusson, Warren, *The Politics of Urbanism: Seeing Like a City* (New York: Routledge, 2011).

Marcuse, Herbert, *An Essay on Liberation* (Boston: Beacon Press, 1969).

Marcuse, Peter, "De-Spatialization and Dilution in the Ghetto: Current Trends in the United States," in *The Ghetto: Contemporary Global Issues and Controversies*, ed. Ray Hutchison and Bruce D. Haynes (Boulder: Westview Press, 2012), 33–66.

Martin, Lauren, "Staying is Settling: Why You Need to Move at Least 5 Times in Your Life," *Elite Daily*, September 11, 2014, accessed November 3, 2014, http://elitedaily.com/life/staying-settling-need-move-5-times-life/751829/.

Marx, Karl, "First Draft of Letter to Vera Zasulich," *MECW*, Vol. 24, 346, June 1989, accessed January 24, 2014, www.marxists.org/archive/marx/works/1881/03/zasulich1.htm.

Massey, Doreen, *For Space* (London: SAGE Publications, 2005).

May, Todd, *The Political Philosophy of Poststructuralist Anarchism* (University Park, PA: Penn State Press, 2005).

McGowan, Todd, *Enjoying What We Don't Have: The Political Project of Psychoanalysis* (Lincoln: University of Nebraska Press, 2013).

Medvetz, Thomas, "The Strength of Weekly Ties: Relations of Material and Symbolic Exchange in the Conservative Movement," *Politics & Society* 34(3) (2006): 343–368.

Merrifield, Andy, *Dialectical Urbanism: Social Struggles in the Capitalist City* (New York: Monthly Review Press, 2002).

Merrifield, Andy, *Metromarxism: A Marxist Tale of the City* (New York: Routledge, 2002).

Merrifield, Andy, *The Politics of the Encounter: Urban Theory and Protest Under Planetary Urbanization* (Athens: University of Georgia Press, 2013).

Merrill, Thomas W., "Property and the Right to Exclude," *Nebraska Law Review* 77(4) (1998): 730–755.

Mitchell, Don, "Postmodern Geographical Praxis? The Postmodern Impulse and the War Against Homeless People in the 'Post-Justice City'," in *Postmodern Geography*, ed. Claudio Minca (Malden, MA: Blackwell Publishers, 2001), 57–92.

Mitchell, Don, *The Right to the City: Social Justice and the Fight for Public Space* (New York: The Gilford Press, 2003).

Molotch, Harvey, "The City as a Growth Machine: Towards a Political Economy of Place," in *City Reader*, 5th edition, ed. Richard T. Legates and Frederic Stout (New York: Routledge, 2011), 251–262.

Mouffe, Chantal, *The Return of the Political* (New York: Verso, 1993).

Mouffe, Chantal, *The Democratic Paradox* (New York: Verso, 2000).

Mouffe, Chantal, *On the Political* (New York: Routledge, 2005).

Mouffe, Chantal, "Politics and the Limits of Liberalism," in *Hegemony, Radical Democracy, and the Political*, ed. James Martin (New York: Routledge, 2013), 115–131.

Newman, Saul, *From Bakunin to Lacan: Anti-Authoritarianism and Dislocation of Power* (Lanham: Lexington Books, 2001).

Nietzsche, Friedrich, *On the Genealogy of Morality*, trans. Carol Diethe (New York: Cambridge University Press, 2007).

Norris, Pippa, "Global Governance and Cosmopolitan Citizens," in *Governance in a Globalizing World*, ed. Joseph Nye and John D. Donahue (Washington, DC: The Brookings Institute, 2000), 155–177.

Ollman, Bertell, "Marx's Use of 'Class'," *The American Journal of Sociology* 3(5) (1968): 573–580.

Parker, Simon, *Urban Theory and the Urban Experience: Encountering the City* (New York: Routledge, 2003).

Peñalver, Eduardo M. and Sonia K. Katyal, *Property Outlaws: How Squatters, Pirates, and Protesters Improve the Law of Ownership* (New Haven: Yale University Press, 2010).

Plato, *Laws*, Book V, trans. Benjamin Jowett, digireads.com (2009).

Plato, *Republic*, Book IV, ed. Max Bollinger (London: The Big Nest, 2012).

Popper, Karl, *The Open Society and Its Enemies* (New York: Routledge, 2002).

Purcell, Mark, "Excavating Lefebvre: The Right to the City and Its Urban Politics of the Inhabitant," *GeoJournal* 58 (2002): 99–108.

Purcell, Mark, "Rancière and Revolution," *Space and Polity* 18(2) (2015): 168–181.

Rancière, Jacques, *Dis-agreement*, trans. J. Rose (Minneapolis: University of Minnesota Press, 1995).

Roberts, Hannah, "Venice Votes to Split from Italy as 89% of the City's Residents Opt to Form a New Independent State," *Daily Mail*, last updated March 22, 2014, accessed April 4, 2014, www.dailymail.co.uk/news/article-2586531/Venice-votes-split-Italy-89-citys-residents-opt-form-new-independent-state.html.

Rofe, Matthew W., " 'I Want to be Global': Theorising the Gentrifying Class as an Emergent Elite Global Community," in *The Gentrification Reader*, ed. Loretta Lees, Tom Slater, and Elvin Wyly (New York: Routledge, 2010), 411–423.

Rosenau, Pauline, *Post-Modernism and the Social Sciences: Insights, Inroads, and Intrusions* (Princeton: Princeton University Press, 1991).

Rousseau, Jean-Jacques, *On the Social Contract* (New York: Dover, 2003).

Rummens, Stefan, "Democracy as a Non-Hegemonic Struggle? Disambiguating Chantal Mouffe's Agonistic Model of Politics," *Constellations* 16(3) (2009): 377–391.

Sanbonmatsu, John, *The Postmodern Prince: Critical Theory, Left Strategy, and the Making of a New Political Subject* (New York: Monthly Review Press, 2003).

Schmid, Christian, "Henri Lefebvre's Theory of the Production of Space: Towards a Three-Dimensional Dialectic," in *Space, Difference, Everyday Life: Reading Henri Lefebvre*, ed. Kanishka Goonewardena, Sefan Kipfer, Richared Milgrom, and Christian Schmid (New York: Routledge, 2008), 27–45.

Schmitt, Carl, *The Concept of the Political*, trans. George Schwab (Chicago: University of Chicago Press, 2007).

Sennett, Richard, *Flesh and Stone: The Body and the City in Western Civilization* (New York: W.W. Norton, 1994).

Shapiro, Michael, *The Time of the City: Politics, Philosophy and Genre* (London: Routledge, 2010).

Sharma, Rajendra K., *Demography and Population Problems* (New Delhi: Atlantic Books, 2000).

Shaw, Kate, "A Response to the 'Eviction of Critical Perspectives from Gentrification Research'," *International Journal of Urban and Regional Research* 32(1) (2008): 192–194.

Silver, Jim, "Gentrification in West Broadway? Contested Space in a Winnipeg Inner City Neighbourhood" (Winnipeg: Canadian Centre for Policy Alternatives Manitoba, May 2006).

Slater, Tom, "The Eviction of Critical Perspectives from Gentrification Research," *International Journal of Urban and Regional Research* 30(4) (December 2006): 737–757.

Slater, Tom, "Unravelling False Choice Urbanism," *The City at a Time of Crisis*, April 11 (2014), retrieved March 5, 2015, http://crisis-scape.net/conference/item/180-unravelling-false-choice-urbanism.

Smith, Neil, *Uneven Development: Nature, Capital, and the Production of Space* (New York: Basil Blackwell, 1984).

Smith, Neil, "Commentary: Gentrification and the Rent Gap," *Annals of the Association of American Geographers* 77(3) (1987): 462–478.

Smith, Neil, "What's Left? Neo-Critical Geography, Or, The Flat Pluralist World of Business Class," *Antipode* 37(5) (2005): 887–899.

Smith, Neil, "On 'The Eviction of Critical Perspectives'," *International Journal of Urban and Regional Research* 32(1) (March 2008): 195–197.

Smith, Neil, "Toward a Theory of Gentrification: A Back to the City Movement by Capital, not People," *Journal of the American Planning Association* 45(4) (2008): 538–548.

Soja, Edward, "Taking Los Angeles Apart: Some Fragments of a Critical Human Geography," *Environment and Planning D: Society and Space* 4 (1986): 255–272.

Soja, Edward, *Postmodern Geographies: The Reassertion of Space in Critical Social Theory* (New York: Verso, 1989).

Soja, Edward, *Thirdspace: Journeys to Los Angeles and Other Real-and-Imagined Places* (Oxford: Blackwell, 1996).

Soja, Edward, *Seeking Spatial Justice* (Minneapolis: University of Minnesota Press, 2010).

Soja, Edward, Marco Cenzatti, and Allan David Heskin, *Los Angeles Through the Kaleidoscope of Urban Restructuring* (UCLA, Graduate School of Architecture and Urban Planning, 1985).

Sontag, Susan, *On Photography* (New York: Macmillan, 1977).

Springer, Mike, "Slavoj Žižek Responds to Noam Chomsky: 'I Don't Know a Guy Who Was So Often Empirically Wrong'," *Open Culture*, last updated July 17, 2013, accessed October 21, 2013, www.openculture.com/2013/07/slavoj-zizek-responds-to-noam-chomsky.html.

Staeheli, Lynn A. and Don Mitchell, *The People's Property: Power, Politics, and the Public* (New York: Routledge, 2008).

Stavrakakis, Yannis, *The Lacanian Left: Psychoanalysis, Theory, Politics* (Edinburgh: Edinburgh University Press, 2007).

Swanson, Jean (interview with), "The Carnegie Community Action Project," quote from the podcast: "Cost of Poverty // Future of Social Housing." *The City*, CITR Radio, June 20, 2012.

Swanson, Jean and Wendy Pedersen, "The Woodward's Redevelopment," Carnegie Community Action Project (2010), retrieved June 17, 2014, http://dtesnh.wordpress.com/about-2/housing/ccap/woodwards-a-symbol-of-exclusion-and-gentrification/.

Swyngedouw, Erik, "Designing the Post-Political City and the Insurgent Polis," *Civic City Cahier* 5 (London: Bedford Press, 2011).

Thaler, Mathias, "The Illusion of Purity: Chantal Mouffe's Realist Critique of Cosmopolitanism," *Philosophy and Social Criticism* 36(7) (2010): 785–800.

Thrift, Nigel, *Non-Representational Theory: Space, Politics, Affect* (New York: Routledge, 2008).

Thrift, Nigel, "If Britain Withdraws from the EU Education Would Suffer," *The Chronicle of Higher Education*, last updated December 20, 2012, accessed March 16, 2014, http://chronicle.com/blogs/worldwise/if-britain-withdraws-from-the-e-u-higher-education-would-suffer/31237.

Thrift, Nigel, "A Growing Global Appreciation for the Value of Compromise," *The Chronicle of Higher Education*, last updated July 9, 2013, accessed March 16, 2014, http://chronicle.com/blogs/worldwise/a-growing-global-appreciation-for-the-value-of-compromise/32369.

Turner, Bryan S., "Cosmopolitan Virtue: Loyalty and the City," in *Democracy, Citizenship, and the Global City*, ed. Engin Isin (New York: Routledge, 2002), 129–147.

United Nations, "UN Millennium Development Goals," 2011 Report. "UN Habitat State of the World's Cities," accessed March 10, 2014, http://unhabitat.org/.

Vigar, Geoff, Stephen Graham, and Patsy Healey, "In Search of the City in Spatial Strategies: Past Legacies, Future Imaginings," *Urban Studies* 42(8) (2005): 1391–1410.

Virilio, Paul, "Architecture Principe," *AA Documents 3: The Function of the Oblique* (London: AA Publications, 1996).

Virilio, Paul, *Speed and Politics*, trans. Mark Polizotti (Los Angeles: Semiotext(e), 2006).

Virilio, Paul (interview with Caroline Dumoucel), "Paul Virilio," *Vice*, last updated September 2, 2010, accessed December 4, 2013, www.vice.com/read/paul-virilio-506-v17n9.

Waldron, Jeremy, *The Right to Private Property* (New York: Oxford University Press, 1990).

Walker, Rob, *After the Globe, before the World* (New York: Routledge, 2009).

Ward, Karen, "In the DTES, Social Mix is Exclusion," last updated January 16, 2013, retrieved January 21, 2014, https://dnchome.wordpress.com/2013/01/16/exclusion/.

Webb, Dan, "'If Adorno isn't the Devil, it's Because He's a Jew': Lyotard's Misreading of Adorno through Thomas Mann's *Dr. Faustus*," *Philosophy & Social Criticism* 35(5) (2009): 517–531.

Webb, Daniel, "The Unbearable Truth of the Image: Žižek's Re-Reading of Iconoclasm and Peter Brown's Holy Man," *International Journal of Žižek Studies* 4(4) (2010): 1–22.

Woodcock, George, *Anarchism: A History of Libertarian Ideas and Movements* (Toronto: University of Toronto Press, 2004).

World Bank, quoted on tradingeconomics.com, accessed May 11, 2015, www.tradingeconomics.com/egypt/rural-population-percent-of-total-population-wb-data.html.

Young, Iris Marion, "The Ideal of Community and the Politics of Difference," in *Feminism/Postmodernism*, ed. Linda J. Nicholson (New York: Routledge, 1990), 300–323.

Young, Iris Marion, *Justice and the Politics of Difference* (Princeton: Princeton University Press, 1990).

Žižek, Slavoj, *Tarrying with the Negative* (Durham, NC: Duke University Press, 1993).

Žižek, Slavoj, *Conversations With Žižek*, ed. Glyn Daly (New York: Polity, 2003).

Žižek, Slavoj, *For They Know Not What They Do: Enjoyment as a Political Factor* (New York: Verso, 2008).

Žižek, Slavoj, *Violence: Six Sideways Reflections* (New York: Picador, 2008).

Žižek, Slavoj, *In Defense of Lost Causes* (New York: Verso, 2009).

Žižek, Slavoj, *The Sublime Object of Ideology*, 2nd edition (New York: Verso, 2009).

Žižek, Slavoj, *Living in the End Times* (New York: Verso, 2011).

Žižek, Slavoj, *Less Than Nothing: Hegel and the Shadow of Dialectical Materialism* (New York: Verso, 2012).

Žižek, Slavoj, "Why Obama is More Than Bush With a Human Face," *Guardian*, last updated November 13, 2012, accessed January 25, 2014, www.theguardian.com/commentisfree/2012/nov/13/obama-ground-floor thinking.

Žižek, Slavoj, "A Cup of Decaf Reality," *lacan.com*, accessed January 24, 2014, www.lacan.com/zizekdecaf.htm.

Zukin, Sharon, *Landscapes of Power: From Detroit to Disney World* (Los Angeles: University of California Press, 1991).

Zukin, Sharon, "Gentrification as Market and Place," in *The Gentrification Debates*, ed. Japonica Brown-Sarcino (New York: Routledge, 2013), 37–44.

Index

For Product Safety Concerns and Information please contact our EU
representative GPSR@taylorandfrancis.com
Taylor & Francis Verlag GmbH, Kaufingerstraße 24, 80331 München, Germany

www.ingramcontent.com/pod-product-compliance
Ingram Content Group UK Ltd.
Pitfield, Milton Keynes, MK11 3LW, UK
UKHW021959180926
475701UK00003B/96
9780367371784